Advance Praise for *Face to Face!*

"Compelling. Comprehensive. Truth seeking. *Face to Face* is a must read for those who labor to develop racial and ethnic tolerance in America. Waller unmasks modern racism and provides seven principles for reconciliation. Educators and others who wish to develop intentional strategies leading to racial reconciliation have, in this book, a substantive tool to begin a dialogue about race in America."

—**Gwendolyn J. Cooke, Ph.D.,** Director, Urban Services Office, National Association of Secondary School Principals, Reston, Washington

"*Face to Face* is a powerful and eloquent examination of racism in America, crucial for our nation's evolving consciousness. The convergence of races and cultures is felt acutely in our public schools; this book, therefore, is critical reading for those who recognize the potential and responsibility of our schools in fostering racial reconciliation."

—**Jeffrey A. Frykholm, Ph.D.,** Department of Teaching and Learning, Virginia Polytechnic Institute and State University, Blacksburg, Virginia

"A rare treat! Waller portrays racism as an all-too-human phenomena that will not just fade away. *Face to Face* will empower readers who are troubled by the persistence of racism to do something about it."

—**Aubyn Fulton, Ph.D.,** Professor of Psychology, Pacific Union College, Angwin, California

"Waller's book comes at a critical time in our nation's dialogue on racism. *Face to Face* unflinchingly examines the dual myths that life is good for racial minorities and that racism is on the wane."

—**Karol Maybury, Ph.D.,** Assistant Professor, Department of Psychology, Whitworth College, Spokane, Washington

FACE *to* FACE

THE CHANGING STATE OF
RACISM ACROSS AMERICA

FACE *to* FACE

THE CHANGING STATE OF RACISM ACROSS AMERICA

JAMES WALLER

INSIGHT BOOKS

PLENUM PRESS • NEW YORK AND LONDON

Library of Congress Cataloging-in-Publication Data

On file

ISBN 0-306-45865-9

© 1998 James Waller
Insight Books is a Division of Plenum Publishing Corporation
233 Spring Street, New York, N.Y. 10013-1578

http://www.plenum.com

An Insight Book

Printed in the United States of America

To my family, who have been so patient throughout this process:

To Brennan, I owe hours of baseball and soccer,
To Hannah, "horsies" and wrestling,
To Noah, who came in the middle of it all, holds and tickles,
and to Patti, I owe it all.

Contents

Foreword *by David G. Myers, Ph.D.* xiii

Preface xvii

Acknowledgments xxi

**Chapter 1. Introduction: Waking Up to America's Dirty
Little Secret** 1

The Three Myths 2
  Myth That Life Is Good for Racial Minorities 2
  Myth That Racism Is Declining 4
  Myth That America Can Be a Color-Blind Society 9
Perspective of Book 11
Organization of Book 13
  Background of Research 13
  Structure of Book 16
Conclusion 19

**Chapter 2. The Foundations of "Isms": Stereotypes,
Prejudice, and Discrimination** 21

The Foundations of Racism 25
  Stereotypes 25
  Prejudice 32
  Discrimination 35
Relationship of Stereotypes, Prejudice, and Discrimination 37
  Is There a Relationship between Stereotypes and Prejudice? 38

Is There a Relationship between Stereotypes and
   Discrimination? 39
Is There a Relationship between Prejudice and
   Discrimination? 40
Conclusion 41

Chapter 3. Racism 101 43

What Is Race? 43
Definition of Racism 45
   Power and Racism 50
What's in a Name? 53
Conclusion 54

Chapter 4. The Myth: Life Is Good for Racial Minorities .. 55

True Confessions 56
Life Is Good for Racial Minorities in America 59
   Measures of Racist Stereotypes and Attitudes 59
   Media Depictions of Minorities 61
   Quality-of-Life Indicators for Minorities 62
   Status of Race Relations 66
Conclusion 67

**Chapter 5. The Reality: Life Isn't Good for Racial
   Minorities** 69

Measures of Racist Stereotypes and Attitudes 69
Media Depictions of Minorities 72
   Print Advertisements 72
   Television Advertisements 73
   Television Programming 73
   News Reporting 76
Quality-of-Life Indicators for Minorities 80
   Economic Indicators 80
   Educational Attainment 85
   General Social Well-Being 91
Status of Race Relations 92
   Mistrust 93

White Indifference 94
The Future 94
Neighborhoods 95
Schools 95
Hate Crimes and Groups 96
Conclusion 97

Chapter 6.   The Changing Face of Racism in America 99

What Is "Real" Racism? 100
The Distraction of Blatant Racism 102
Old-Fashioned Racism 105
Measuring Old-Fashioned Racism 106
The Decline of Old-Fashioned Racism? 107
The Decline in Old-Fashioned Racism Is Genuine 108
The Decline in Old-Fashioned Racism Is Genuine but
Limited 108
The Decline in Old-Fashioned Racism Is Not Genuine 110
Old-Fashioned Racism Has Mutated into a New Face of
Racism 115
Conclusion 116

Chapter 7.   Modern Racism Unmasked 119

Modern Racism 120
Measuring Modern Racism 121
Faces of Modern Racism 123
Aversive Racism 124
Symbolic Racism 126
The Tax of Modern Racism 135
The Range of Modern Racism 138
Conclusion 139

**Chapter 8.   The Costs of Modern Racism: What Are We
Losing?** 141

Costs of Modern Racism to the Victims 142
Psychological Costs of Modern Racism to the Victims 142

Material Costs of Modern Racism to the Victims   151
Costs of Modern Racism to Whites   161
Psychological Costs of Modern Racism to Whites   162
Material Costs of Modern Racism to Whites   167
Conclusion   169

Chapter 9.   Can America Become a Color-Blind Society?
The Cognitive Traps of Racism   171

The Trap of Social Categorization   174
Consequences of Social Categorization: Who's In and
Who's Out?   176
Summary   181
The Trap of Automatic Cognitive Processing   181
The Trap of Explanation   183
Conclusion   188

Chapter 10.   Racial Reconciliation in America: How Do We
Find Unity in Diversity?   191

Be a Good Reconciler: Nurture Skills of Listening and
Disagreeing   192
The Art of Listening   193
The Art of Disagreeing   184
Teach Yourself to Think: Control Cognitive Processing of
Stereotypes   196
To Thine Own Self Be Known: Become More Self-Aware   199
Personal Racial, Ethnic, or Religious Stories   199
Personal Stereotypes, Prejudices, and Discriminatory
Behaviors   202
Open Your Mind: Appreciate the Panorama of the Borderland   203
Get in Touch: Engage in Personal Interaction with Racial
Diversity   207
Can We Make the World a Better Place?   212
The Power of Many: Draw on the Strength of Community   213
Invest in Our Future: Teach Antiracism Early   215
Conclusion   220

Appendix 221

Notes 227

Bibliography 253

Index 259

Foreword

To a microbiologist, skin color is trivial—a minuscule genetic variation that determines the shade of frosting on the physiological cake. We in the human family share not only a common biological heritage—cut us and we bleed—but also common behavioral tendencies. We are the slightly varied leaves of one tree. We sense the world, develop language, and feel hunger through identical mechanisms. Coming from opposite sides of the globe, we know how to read one another's smiles and frowns. Whether we live in the Arctic or in the tropics, we prefer sweet tastes to sour, we divide the color spectrum into similar colors, and we feel drawn to behaviors that produce and protect offspring. As members of one species, we affiliate, conform, reciprocate favors, punish offenses, organize hierarchies of status and grieve a child's death. A visitor from outer space could drop in anywhere and find humans playing sports and games, dancing and feasting, singing and worshiping, laughing and crying, living in families, and forming groups. To be human is to be more alike than different.

But what a difference the frosting makes, as this book convincingly explains. Although racial groupings have little biological reality— nature does not cluster humans into neat, nonoverlapping categories— race assuredly has social reality. Much as we organize what is actually a color continuum into what we perceive as distinct colors, so we cannot resist categorizing people into groups, and then associating ourselves with "us," and contrasting ourselves with "them." We label people of widely varying ancestry as "black" or "white," as if such categories were black-and-white.

Is the potency of race in America nevertheless waning? Increasing numbers of us do not fit neatly into established racial or ethnic categories. Witness Tiger Woods calling himself "Cablinasian," describing his Caucasian, black, Indian, and Asian ancestry. And compare Tiger's reception into the previously white-dominated sport of golf—accompanied by multimillion-dollar endorsements and hordes of adoring fans—with Jackie Robinson's epithet-laden reception into the previously white-dominated sport of baseball. If you or I were to repeat *Black Like Me* author John Howard Griffin's experiment in changing skin color, we would surely experience a kinder, gentler America. Much less often would we sit without service at a lunch counter. Rarely would we be called "nigger." Never would we see separate drinking fountains for "colored" and "white."

As recently as 1942, most Americans agreed that "there should be separate sections for Negroes on streetcars and buses." Today, the question would seem bizarre. In 1942, fewer than a third of all whites (only 1 in 50 in the South) supported school integration; by 1980, support for it was 90 percent. Considering what a thin slice of history is covered by the years since 1942, or even since slavery was practiced, the changes are dramatic. Old-fashioned racism is now gauche.

Yet beneath this nicer veneer, notes social psychologist James Waller in this well-argued book, racism—"modern racism"—lurks. It is subtler, yet, like arsenic in wine, still potent. Those of us in the economically dominant majority can perhaps identify the phenomenon from times that someone has been superficially nice to us, while forcing an appropriate smile, before snubbing us or taking offense over a slight. Now that blatant bigotry is boorish, we treat one another with greater civility. And yet …

- In one survey of students at 390 colleges and universities, 53 percent of African-American students felt excluded from social activities.
- When white students indicate racial attitudes while hooked up to a supposed lie detector, they admit to prejudice that they deny when answering standard surveys.
- A videotaped shove that looks "playful" to most white people when done by a white man much more often looks "violent" when done by a black man.
- Although we condemn racial bias, we often prefer what is familiar, similar, and comfortable.

- When "primed" with briefly flashed images associated with African-Americans, people who espouse little or no prejudice often react with increased hostility to an experimenter's annoying request. Such is the knee-jerk "prejudice habit' that often hijacks our emotions.

And such is the changing state of racism across America that Waller and his students encounter face to face on their cross-country travels as they seek out African-American urban pastors and residents, Hispanic-Americans, Native Americans, and Asian immigrants. With deep empathy, Waller gives voice to their experiences of 1990s-style racism.

Yet to those who say, "Show me the data!," Waller, the social scientist, offers more than true stories. He also offers the truth of new experiments, of Census facts, and of sensitive national surveys. His bottom-line message is that we have hardly reached the end of racism. Rather, as one of his students summarized, "life still sucks for minorities and racism is a supervirus that persists by mutating." But Waller does not leave us despairing. With his "seven principles for racial reconciliation" he points the way to "finding unity in diversity."

The appearance of this book just months after President Clinton beckoned Americans to a "great and unprecedented conversation about race" could hardly be more timely. As racial diversity continues to increase in the decades to come—the Census Bureau projects that non-Hispanic whites will decline from 69 to 62 percent of the population between 1995 and 2025—the need for such a conversation will not diminish. Kudos to James Waller for this fresh, passionate, and informed analysis of America's new racism, and how to combat it.

DAVID G. MYERS, PH.D.

Hope College
Holland, Michigan

Preface

In a 1979 paper, cleverly titled "Does the Flap of a Butterfly's Wings in Brazil Set Off a Tornado in Texas?", American meteorologist E. N. Lorenz suggested that a single flutter of a butterfly's wings can result in a drastic change in global weather patterns.[1] The notion that a small event in one place can amplify into a large effect elsewhere is not limited to weather prediction. The smallest events in one's life often leave the most dramatic and lasting impact.

When I was eight years old, my family and I lived in Petersburg, Virginia. My elementary school, like many others, had a one-person janitorial staff. The staff's name was John. John was an elderly and, we thought, ancient African-American. His stark differences in age, gait, mannerisms, and—most noticeably—skin color made him a source of constant intrigue to us. I remember one particular day, however, when the intrigue played itself out in ignorance. John was heading to the playground, for the umpteenth time, to remind us to stay away from some new shrubs he had planted. At the time he arrived, one of my classmates was just finishing a well-known refrain: "Eeny, meeny, minny, moe, catch a nigger by his toe, if he hollers, let him go, eeny, meeny, minny, moe." We looked up to see John's face. It is a sad comment that, had he not reacted, we would not have thought twice about what had just been said. John did react, however. His is the only face that I've ever actually seen "break" into tears.

John had lived through the Old South and surely had heard worse than this racist refrain. His life was a legacy of forbidden opportunities, unfulfilled dreams, and broken promises. Only in the past few years had he received the right to be served at the downtown lunch counter, sit in any seat he wanted on the city buses, drink from a fountain that actually offered cold water, see his grandchildren receive an education at schools where, for decades, the only faces of color had pushed brooms, emptied trash, and served meals. There was something, however, about this particular experience that assulted his spirit. Of course, I never had the chance to talk with him about it. I suspect, however, that the mindless play of a group of second-graders reminded John of how deeply ingrained racism is in American society. His heart recognized what his mind wanted to resist. The battle for racial equality and dignity was not—and perhaps never would be—over.

Today, nearly 30 years later, I hold a Ph.D. in social psychology—a field that explores how our thoughts, feelings, and behaviors are influenced by the presence of other people. I teach at a respected liberal arts institution that sits on the edge of a city (Spokane), that sits on the edge of a state (Washington), that sits on the edge of the country. I have three children of my own, one of whom will soon be entering second grade. I invest my teaching and research life in understanding how we "misrelate" to each other. Specifically, I study the psychological dynamics of why we hate and exclude others simply because of what they look like, where they come from, or what they believe. I have witnessed, and read about, far too many incidents of racial stereotyping and discrimination. I have probably forgotten more of them that I remember. I cannot, however, forget John's face from that day. That scene from an elementary school playground in Virginia is my earliest recollection of the personal pain caused by racism. It has, like the butterfly's wings, reverberated in my life, and it began a series of personal and scholarly reflections that ultimately brought me to write this book.

Race is and always has been our most divisive issue. It is the fault line running beneath our nation's landscape. Race is the only problem that ever sent us to war against ourselves, the only one that periodically requires troops to be stationed on the streets of our cities. It is the most frightening tear in our social fabric, the most important domestic dilemma we face. In his 1997 State of the Union Address, President Clinton reaffirmed its significance for Americans: "We still see evidence of abiding bigotry and intolerance, in ugly words and awful violence, in burned churches and bombed buildings. We must fight against this, in our country and in our hearts."[2] On that same exceptional evening, thousands of miles away in Santa Monica, California, issues of race in America were played out in an equally well-publicized event. A civil jury unanimously held Orenthal James Simpson responsible for the deaths of his ex-wife, Nicole Brown Simpson, and Ronald Goldman. This decision did not spark the rampant racial conflict that followed the 1992 verdict in which four white Los Angeles police officers were found not guilty—by a jury that included no blacks—of brutality against Rodney King. Despite the apparent calm, however, many Americans could not help but notice that Simpson was judged by a mostly white jury for a crime of which he had already been acquitted by a mostly black jury.

Issues of race in this country are intensified by the rapidly changing face of Americans. An April 1997 Census Bureau report found that nearly one in 10 of those living in the United States is foreign-born, our highest percentage of immigrants since the great migration of the 1930s. The report also offers vivid evidence of the changing origins of the most recent immigration wave. Twenty-seven percent were born in Mexico. Twelve percent came from Central or South America, and 27 percent from Asia. In stark contrast, as recently as the 1950s, over three-fourths of the immigrants came from Europe and Canada. Currently, one-third of the American people do not trace their origins to Europe.[3] Minorities already predominate in major cities across the country—New York, Chicago, Atlanta, Detroit, Philadelphia, San Francisco, and Los Angeles. Journalist William Henry maintains that by 2056, most Americans will trace their descent to "Africa, Asia, the Hispanic world, the Pacific Islands, Arabia—most anywhere but white Europe."[4]

As a society, how prepared are we to exist in a country in which the racial status quo of white majority–nonwhite minority will be reversed? How will whites handle the psychological transition from their dominant status? How will minorities reconcile the fact of their increasing numbers with the continuing existence of broad racial inequities? The results of a July 1993 Gallup Poll do not bode well. When asked about the effect of the increasing diversity in America, 55 percent of Americans said that diversity "mostly threatens" American culture; only 35 percent opted for "mostly improves" it.[5] A recent *USA Today* poll found that nearly one in two Americans believes that racial conflict is a major threat to the nation's future well-being. The threat of racial conflict will be multiplied if, as some economists predict, our nation falls into a time of economic recession and high unemployment. The urgency of *this* question for *this* country at *this* time is why I have chosen to focus *this* book on racism in America. This focus is not meant to minimize issues of intolerance related to ethnicity, religion, gender, or sexual orientation. Rather, I simply mean to center the discussion on the most potentially divisive form of prejudice facing America as we approach the twenty-first century—racism.

As everyone keeps reminding me, there is a plethora of books and articles written on racism each year. There is by now an impressive house of information that is part of a collective enterprise to understand, and improve, race relations in America. This book is a new and unique addition to that house. It will challenge the way you think about a fundamental issue in American life.

Acknowledgments

I am indebted to many people who have been influential in the development of this book. My colleagues in the Psychology Department at Whitworth College—William Johnson, Noel Wescombe, Karol Maybury, and Adrian Teo—have been a wonderful oasis of support, encouragement, and collegiality. Noel Wescombe was the first to suggest that I write this book, and I am especially appreciative of his enthusiasm during the early days when I wondered if the manuscript would ever see the light of day.

Several people read an early draft of the manuscript and offered outstanding direction. Among these were Carl and Judy Pearson, the 21 students of my 1998 study tour, David Myers, and Karol Maybury. I am particularly appreciative of Karol Maybury for her wonderful service as my primary reader and of David Myers for his encouragement to "reveal myself as an author" and his kindness in writing the foreword to this book.

Along the way, several colleagues have taken their time to offer general advice on publishing or resources for specific sections of the book. Thanks here go to Forrest Baird, Bob Clark, Aubyn Fulton, Gordon Jackson, Lois Kieffaber, Doris Liebert, Linda Hunt, Bill Robinson, Richard Schatz, and Gerald Sittser. To Jim Singleton, thanks for the friendship and the examples—it's nice to be on the other side for a change! To the CORE 150 team, thanks for picking up some of my classroom responsibilities during the final push of writing. Over the past several years, I also have had the privilege of having both my mind and heart nurtured by a wonderful group of friends—Forrest Baird (again), Terry McGonigal, Dick Mandeville, Ron Pyle, Gerald Sittser (again), and Dale Soden.

Whitworth College deserves a great deal of credit for supporting and encouraging me in the development of the study tour. In addition, a large portion of this book was completed during my Spring 1997 sabbatical. Thanks again to the institution for providing that window of opportunity. I also am indebted to Nicole Earin, Monica Parmley, and Nicole Polen for last-minute help on typing and tracking down needed library materials.

I especially want to acknowledge the students of the 1996 and 1998 study tours, as well as the students in my on-campus courses, who have taught me as well as—if not better than—I have taught them. Over the past two years, I also enjoyed the privilege of serving on the Inquiring Minds Speakers Bureau of the Washington Commission for the Humanities. The opportunity to present my developing thoughts to audiences across the state as I was writing this book was invaluable.

A few quotes in this book are composites of different interviews from the tour. Some details (e.g., gender, age, location) were changed to protect people's privacy. To everyone who welcomed us on these tours, as well as those who called or wrote to express their support, a very big "Thank you!"

Finally, I am indebted to my editor, Frank K. Darmstadt, and his assistant, Charlie Cates, for seeing early promise in an original manuscript and, most important, for helping me to see it as well. Author and writing-to-learn guru William Zinsser once told me: "I don't like to write. I like to have written." Amen and amen.

JAMES WALLER

Spokane, Washington

1

Introduction

Waking Up to America's Dirty Little Secret

Somebody's got to hit the whites with a two-by-four to wake them up.... They see no crisis, yet there is a crisis.

—Louis Harris[1]

After a recent lecture in Florida, a white woman told me of a particularly hateful example of racism directed at a Hispanic in that town. She went on to roundly condemn the action, express sincere sympathy for the victim, and confess personal shame that such an event could happen in that community. Refusing to be deflated by reality, however, she concluded by expressing an optimistic analysis: "At least these things don't happen as much as they used to. Minorities really have it pretty well off now. I know a lot of minorities who live in better houses than I do! I really think racism is a thing of the past. My grandchildren won't have to worry about these problems in the future."

On one hand, she was right. Sensational, headline-grabbing examples of racism are seen less frequently than they were in the past several decades. When they do occur, we typically associate them with extremist hate groups—not mainstream Americans. From a distance, there seem to be reasons for optimism. Racist stereotypes and attitudes appear to have decreased; media depictions of racial minorities seem more favorable; in absolute terms, quality-of-life indicators for minorities have improved and, to judge by the relative absence of open bigotry and hostility, race relations seem less strained.

1

On the other hand, however, her buoyant optimism betrayed three myths that are common to white Americans. These include the mistaken beliefs that (1) life is good for racial minorities, (2) racism is declining, and (3) America can be a color-blind society. These myths are no longer the sole intellectual property of uneducated, narrow-minded bigots. They are now included in the beliefs and attitudes of well-educated, supposedly open-minded persons. These related myths share one common purpose—to soothe white guilt about white racism.

The small-minded deliberations of race in America by some intellectuals, media commentators, jurists, academics, and politicians lend pseudolegitimacy to these myths. They foster what sociologists Joe Feagin and Hernan Vera call "sincere fictions."[2] Sincere fictions, usually unfeigned and genuine, are personal myths that allow whites to define themselves as "not racist," as "good people," even as they think, feel, and act in ways that are racist. Unfortunately, these myths, however "sincere," greatly distort the public conversation surrounding race in America. Most dangerously, these myths allow racism to become even more entrenched, because they remove any compelling reasons to deal with its causes and consequences. For America to continue the long process of racial reconciliation, these three myths must be challenged— that is the central purpose of this book.

THE THREE MYTHS

Myth That Life Is Good for Racial Minorities

The first myth is that life is good for racial minorities. This myth rests on the assumptions that (1) America provides racial minorities with all the opportunities they need and (2) being a racial minority in America today confers a wealth of significant legal, educational, and financial advantages over whites. These comments from a white professional reflect these assumptions: "They [blacks and whites] are equal; they do not need to become equal. In my mind, they are. Progress has been made in the laws and in jobs. And there are thousands and thousands of blacks who are making twice as much money as I am making and have better jobs than I have."[3]

Nathan Glazer, in his influential 1975 book *Affirmative Discrimina-*

tion, was one of the first intellectuals to broadly articulate the myth that life is good for racial minorities. He argues that America is winning the battle against racism, that no one is now excluded from the broadest access to the American mainstream.[4] A few conservative black intellectuals also have contributed to this myth. University of Chicago sociologist William J. Wilson's controversial 1978 book, *The Declining Significance of Race*, argued that "talented and educated blacks are experiencing unprecedented job opportunities in the growing government and corporate sectors, opportunities that are *at least* comparable to those of whites with equivalent qualification."[5] More recently, Shelby Steele, an English professor at San Jose State University, and Stephen Carter, a Yale law professor, have argued that racism is no longer the roadblock it once was, and that blacks are as free as they want to be.[6] Political scientist James L. Robinson contends that blacks' negative attitudes and a lack of self-esteem are as accountable as discrimination and racism for the plight of the black underclass.[7] In a 1997 book, Stephan and Abigail Thernstrom maintain that African-Americans should rejoice in the progress they have made since the 1960s and stop playing the "race card."[8] According to these thinkers, educational, legal, and social policymakers have done their jobs well—life can be good for racial minorities if they will only take advantage of the opportunities and promises available for all Americans.

Unfortunately, empirical evidence stands in stark contrast to these optimistic assertions of equality of opportunity and promise. The current existence of profound racial inequities in economic strength, educational attainment, and general quality of life (reviewed in Chapter 5) betrays an America in which race, and its real-life consequences, remains a critical national issue. Relative to whites, racial minorities continue to experience significant deprivation—across occupation, class, and educational level. The demolition of *de jure* (legal) segregation has not yet resulted in *de facto* (real-life) equality or justice.

The strain of *de facto* inequality is reflected in the increasingly tense relations between whites and minorities in America. In Chapter 5, I review data revealing that race relations in America are even more strained today than they were during the civil rights era! Most disconcertingly, whites seem relatively oblivious to the dissatisfaction so apparent among racial minorities. In 1994, Louis Harris, in reviewing recent polling responses, stated,

> Back in the sixties and seventies, whites recognized that there was
> a widespread discrimination that hadn't been attended to. Now ...
> an ominous number of whites have a view that somehow race
> relations are behind us, somehow whatever [needed to be done] has
> been done and it's probably worked.... What you get is a complete
> insensitivity on the part of a majority of whites as to what minorities
> think of them and what the problems confronting minorities ... are.[9]

To accept the myth that life is good for racial minorities in America
is to ignore a wealth of empirical evidence suggesting otherwise. Life
isn't good for minorities. The hope of the civil rights era has been only
partially fulfilled. It would be so comfortable to believe that whatever
needed to be done has been done. The reality, however, is that the great
promises of America remain unattainable for a significant—and disproportionate—portion of the racial minority population.

Myth That Racism Is Declining

The second myth, that racism in America is declining, builds directly on the first. If life is so good for minorities, then racism must have
declined to the point of near-disappearance. This myth has been fueled
by a growing conservative backlash attacking cultural diversity, multiculturalism, and race identity. In 1987 bestsellers, Allan Bloom and E. D.
Hirsch both argued that an "overemphasis" on race and ethnicity in
human experience is divisive.[10] More recently, author Jim Sleeper casti-
gated liberals for making race and ethnicity the central organizing
principles of public life.[11] Shouldn't we, these critics contend, move
"beyond race and ethnicity" to forge a more cohesive culture and
homogeneous America? This question has gathered increasing attention in the national debate surrounding affirmative action. In 1996, the
U.S. Fifth Circuit Court of Appeals, in ruling against an affirmative
action program at the University of Texas School of Law, declared that
the school could not use race as even one of the many factors considered
for admission. Judge Jerry Smith asserted that the promotion of racial
diversity "fosters, rather than minimizes, the use of race" and, as such,
promotes racial stereotypes and could fuel hostility.

Can Americans be sold on the idea that the promotion of diversity
is divisive? Can we believe that we have become too race-conscious and
have no special obligations to racial minorities? If so, we can also sell

ourselves on the corresponding idea that the burdens of race for minorities are not really that heavy. If we can believe that race has been overemphasized in opportunities, then we can believe it has been overemphasized in explanation for the inequities as well. This is exactly what Dinesh D'Souza, a well-known critic of both multiculturalism and affirmative action, argues in his provocatively titled book *The End of Racism*.[12] D'Souza, an East Indian immigrant, contends that racism in America has largely disappeared. His dismissal of the existence of racism is the logical end of the denial of race and ethnicity as a vital part of human experience. If the goal is to "move beyond race and ethnicity," then conversations that emphasize the continuing destructive impact of racial stereotypes and discrimination only work against that goal.

As I listen to my students, and to hundreds of other people in audiences across the country, I realize that many white Americans believe that prejudice, especially racial prejudice, is fast becoming a distant footnote of American history. In their view, racism is no longer a serious problem or, at least, it no longer adversely affects nonwhites' prospects in life. They explain away the meager remnants of continuing racism as the fault of a few isolated individuals or the result of the oversensitivity of racial minorities. These views rest on the assumption that racism has one, and only one, face—that of blatant hostility and overt discrimination. As journalist Ellis Cose writes,

> Racism, in many minds, is equated with lynchings, beating blacks with hoses, and refusing black people service at lunch counters. It is about separate drinking fountains for blacks and whites, restrictive covenants, and openly calling black people "niggers." It is the systematic and brutal denial of basic human rights and dignity that characterized Jim Crow and whose very memory distresses many Americans who lived through it.[13]

The danger in confining our understanding of racism to this face is the corresponding assumption that, if this one face of racism is disappearing, then racism itself is on the decline in America.

As a social psychologist, I am aware that research counters this argument by contending that racism has some new "modern" forms that vary significantly from our general recognition of "old-fashioned" racism (Chapters 6 and 7 will explore these distinctions in greater depth). As an individual, my conversations and experiences with African-Americans, Asian-Americans, Hispanic-Americans, and Native Americans further confirm that racism is not declining but, rather, has taken on new, and perhaps more debilitating, forms. Like a clever virus, old-fashioned racism responded to the escalation of tolerant social and legal reforms by mutating into more subtle, covert, and socially acceptable modern forms of racism. These modern forms of racism are unlikely to be the target of public service announcements, doubtful to make bold headlines in newspapers, improbable to stir community task forces, remotely likely to appear as a segment on *60 Minutes*.

Minorities know this new face of racism well. They recognize it when they are tailed by a clerk in a music store, when they see the subtle stereotypes still perpetrated by mass media and television, in the un-thinking slurs of co-workers, or when they encounter inferior service in restaurants. Such is the daily awareness of being a minority in a white-dominated society. Even minorities who have "made it" testify to the continuing burden of modern racism. A few months before he died of AIDS in 1993, tennis legend Arthur Ashe was asked if that deadly disease had been the most difficult challenge he had faced in his life. Surprisingly, Ashe, one of the most well-respected and best-loved sports figures of his time, replied, "Being black is. No question about it. Even now it continues to feel like an extra weight tied around me."[14] That statement seems perfectly appropriate for the segregated Virginia of Ashe's childhood. But "even now," in 1993, to bear the "extra weight" of racism?

How Can Whites Understand?

How do whites begin to grapple with an understanding of modern racism? How can whites identify with the daily struggles of living as a racial minority in America? Texan John Howard Griffin had one answer. In the fall of 1959, Griffin, a white "specialist" in race issues, used accelerated treatments of medication and a sunlamp to darken his skin. By shaving his head, he was able to complete a physical transformation that allowed him to pass as an elderly African-American man. For a month, he hitchhiked, walked, and rode the buses through Mississippi, Alabama, Louisiana, and Georgia. He learned what it was like to travel as "an aging, bald Negro—through a land hostile to my color, hostile to my skin."[15] For a brief time, he could see with the other's eyes. It was a dangerous, insightful, and often humiliating experience. By the end of the trip, he ached with hurt and humiliation. The adventure had turned into an ordeal. His account of the four weeks, published as the book *Black Like Me*, has sold more than 12 million copies and been translated into 14 languages.

I don't have the time or, to be honest, the courage to replicate Griffin's journey. As a college teacher, however, I do have the obligation to assist my students—most of whom come from white, middle-class backgrounds—to see with the other's eyes. This is a "rubber meets the road" issue. How does one go about "translating" the experiences of racial minorities in America to students who, similar to me, are not regularly victimized by prejudice or discrimination? Somehow, I must complement the intellectual understanding of racism with a deeper empathy for its victims. Unfortunately, most of the psychological research tends to ignore the voices of the victims even while dissecting the thoughts, feelings, and behaviors of the perpetrators. How could I reverse the tide and emphasize the issues from the perspectives of the victims?

In my teaching, I became much more intentional in exposing students to primary source testimonies, novels, documentaries, and guest speakers that could detail the legacy of pain and suffering caused by hatred in this country—both historically and in contemporary times. This approach, while a clear improvement, still allowed students the luxury of retreating to their dormitories and comfortable relationships, and remaining at a safe distance from this pain and suffering. Consistent with the nature of higher education, the students and I live our lives in an intellectual environment that is wonderfully nurturant, but also perilously enclosed.

Then, in late 1994, I read Douglas Brinkley's *The Majic Bus: An American Odyssey*.[16] Brinkley, a historian, provides an engaging account of a six-week cross-country bus tour in which 17 Hofstra University students explored American history. The tour represents the best of what higher education has to offer—innovative, stimulating, and life-changing instruction. I was inspired by Brinkley's unique commitment to enlivening the educational experience. I began to plan a similar tour, focusing on the history of prejudice and discrimination in America. I envisioned this tour as a unique opportunity to move students from the sheltered environment of higher education and closer to the daily realities faced by victims of hatred in America.

By the fall of 1995, I had planned, and received approval for, a month-long cross-country study tour that would immerse students in the experiences of racial, ethnic, and religious minorities in America. In January 1996, 16 Whitworth College students and I met in San Francisco and traveled by rail to Los Angeles, Denver, Chicago, Memphis, New Orleans, Atlanta, and Washington, D.C. At each stop along the way, we heard first hand from members of various minority groups regarding their history, culture, celebrations, and personal experiences as victims of prejudice and discrimination. I lectured very little on the tour. The focus was on the excluded rather than the excluders. The direct testimonies of the people with whom we interacted—unfiltered by my experiences, thoughts, and biases—were the keynotes of the course.

The tour drew national media attention from CNN, news wire services, and *The Chronicle of Higher Education*. In each city we visited, we were featured on local television and radio news reports. Our trip spawned similar tours in colleges and universities across the country. In January 1998, I again led 21 students on a second tour, with stops in Los Angeles, San Francisco, Chicago, Memphis, New Orleans, Birmingham, Atlanta, and Washington D.C. In the pages that follow, portions of the exciting potential, and intriguing realities, of those tours will be encountered. Outside of the classroom, in the concrete truth of America's inner cities, there was no comfort zone or escape hatch. The students and I were directly confronted by the voices of the victims. For 90 minutes, we looked squarely into the eyes of an African-American in Chicago whose legacy of pain and suffering was so great that he had no desire for racial reconciliation. On a beautiful southern California day, we wept as an Asian-American recounted his internment in World War II, his subsequent work as a civil servant in state government, and his abiding bitterness and resentment at the legacy of discrimination he had suffered. We could not escape the pain of a young Hispanic-American woman in Denver who described her struggle with questions of assimilation. How much should her heritage be part of her daily life in a world that often penalizes those who do not fully assimilate to the dominant cultural blueprints?

These real, and often very painful, testimonies put a new vibrancy on the intellectual ideas, definitions, and theories from my classroom. The students, rapt with attention, finally were able to complement their intellectual understanding with the authentic legacy of prejudice and discrimination. They came to the stark realization that racism, though in a new guise, is alive and well in America. While the face of hatred is changing, the inheritance remains the same—forbidden opportunities, unfulfilled dreams, inner guilt, tension and fear, societal strife, and diminished productivity.

To accept the myth that racism is declining is to ignore the new face of racism in America. The biannual study tours will remain an important point of contact for my students in understanding this new face of racism. This book is meant to provide a similar point of contact for a much broader audience.

Myth That America Can Be a Color-Blind Society

The final myth, resting on the previous myths that life is good for minorities and racism has largely disappeared, states that American society can become color-blind, race-neutral, or nonracial. The pretext of this myth lies in Justice John Marshall Harlan's dissenting opinion in the 1896 *Plessy v. Ferguson* Supreme Court decision. That decision, commonly known as the "separate but equal" ruling, held as constitutional the practice of segregated, but supposedly equal, public accommodations. Harlan, however, could not reconcile the constitutionality of public accommodations segregated by race with his perception of the color blindness of the U.S. Constitution. He wrote: "Our constitution is color-blind, and neither knows nor tolerates classes among citizens."[17] While he did not convince his fellow judges that the Constitution was color-blind, Harlan's endorsement of color blindness did set up a prescriptive ideal. A century later, today's Supreme Court is enamored with the constitutional ideal of color blindness. White society has extended this constitutional ideal and transformed it into an imagined societal reality. "Our Constitution is color-blind" has become "we are a color-blind society."

What is the motivation for this myth? Much of it is the misapplication of an ideal. It is wishful thinking. We want to believe in our boundless capacity for enlightenment. After a recent presentation in central Washington, most of the questions and comments from the audience centered on my pessimism regarding the future of racism in America. I had argued that the tendency toward prejudicial thinking is inherent in each of us and that socially responsible plans to address racism in America must recognize the realistic limitations of our humanity. To say that some members of the audience did not agree is to say that the eruption of Mt. St. Helens was a light spring rain. They were livid that I did not recognize the perfectibility of human nature. Why couldn't I see, they argued, that the sure and certain progress of human evolution would inevitably lead to a prejudice-free society?

I would agree with them if they were right. They are, however, wrong. I contend that, while color blindness should be retained as an ideal, we must recognize that America *can never* be a color-blind society simply because of the mechanisms of our individual minds. Ellis Cose writes in *Color-Blind: Seeing beyond Race in a Race-Obsessed World*: "I would not be so foolish or so pessimistic as to proclaim that the race-related problems the United States faces today will always be with us."[18] I *am* that pessimistic—though, I hope, not so foolish.

I am not the first to advance a pessimistic view. Derrick Bell, a prominent constitutional scholar, believes that racism is so fundamental to this nation that racial minorities will never gain equality with white Americans.[19] Andrew Hacker, a political scientist at Queens College in New York City, argues that "racial tensions serve too many important purposes to be easily ameliorated, let alone eliminated or replaced.... In short, our time is not one receptive to racial remedies."[20] Richard Delgado, presently a law professor at the University of Colorado, posits a Law of Racial Thermodynamics in which racism is never destroyed but always comes back in new forms.[21] Sociologists Joe Feagin and Hernan Vera offer the bleak recognition that at "some time in the not-too-distant future a racial war between the haves and the have-nots in the United States is not inconceivable. The hour is already late to take action to prevent such a racial war."[22] Finally, journalist Carl T. Rowan has recently argued that the "so-called American melting pot has become a tinderbox that seems ready to explode. Before the end of the century, this country seems destined to look more like the South Africa of a decade ago than any dream of racial and ethnic tranquility."[23]

Why such pessimism? Bell, Hacker, Delgado, Feagin, Vera, and Rowan focus on the larger societal, cultural, and procedural barriers to a race-neutral state. My analysis, however, is at the individual level. I contend that, despite all of the societal, educational, legislative, and spiritual changes that we may bring to bear, we still remain—because of how our minds work—prone to thinking in rigid, stereotypical categories. These limitations of our thinking render prejudice an eternal problem for human society. As long as we differ in skin, eye, or hair color, height or weight, religion, gender, physical attractiveness, and so on, we will have the social categories necessary for our minds to deal in stereotypes and prejudices. The specific content of these categories may vary from individual to individual. How I, for instance, stereotype Californians may be very different from the characteristics you would ascribe to them. Regardless of the specific content, however, a basic rule of human nature is that we all rely on social categories and stereotypes to deal with the complexity of our world.

To accept the myth that America can be a color-blind society is to ignore the massive body of information we have about how our minds work. This book provides a sweeping psychological analysis of how we categorize, stereotype, and discriminate against others. Though I believe the problem to be perpetual, I don't fall into the trap of assuming that nothing can be done to alleviate the evils of racism. I conclude the book with seven principles for racial reconciliation that offer sensible— if unromantic—hope for the future of race relations in America.

PERSPECTIVE OF BOOK

Racism in America is a critical topic deserving national conversation. In a June 14, 1997, commencement address at the University of California, San Diego, President Clinton vowed "to lead the United States into a great and unprecedented conversation about race."[24] Love him or hate him, President Clinton stands as the first president since Lyndon Johnson to make race relations a cornerstone of his administration. To further the national discussion, he has appointed a seven-member board to advise him on potential policy changes and pledged to lead four town-hall meetings to help the country confront issues of racism and race relations. The board, led by Duke University historian John Hope Franklin, includes William Winter, Linda Chavez Thompson, Robert Thomas, Angela Oh, the Reverend Susan Johnson Cook, and Thomas Kean. To this point the work of the advisory board is floundering. Like similar groups charged with the task of racial reconciliation, no one seems quite sure what to say or do.

History will judge the success of President Clinton's initiative. Regardless, any dialogue about racism in America must not be reduced to a conversation by anecdote. Academic research and opinion must have a prominent place at the table of public debate. Social scientists have occasionally been criticized for discussing important and valuable information among themselves without communicating that material to the general public. As Patrick DeLeon, from the office of Senator Daniel K. Inouye (D–Hawaii), recently said: "Psychology has a tremendous amount to offer, but it talks a lot to itself, offers very little and society keeps moving on anyhow."[25]

The critique is as true as it is painful. Scientific writing is at its best when it informs a broad audience. The articulate works of Harvard paleontologist Stephen Jay Gould and biologist Lewis Thomas, for example, have been vital in enhancing general cultural knowledge by communicating important natural scientific information. Such writing, however poorly mirrored, is the inspiration for this book. It is important that white social scientists, like myself, speak publicly and authoritatively about racism in America. This book is not "pop" psychology. It does not retreat from scientific respectability. As an "intellectual water carrier," I simply channel the latest scholarship in social psychology and fill in the abstractions of that scholarship with good, concrete, sensory reporting.

I am an academic and a teacher. It is in my nature to dispense information. This book has a lot of information. I don't apologize for this. A lack of information leads to distorted chatter and unproductive prattle. Good information is necessary if we are to engage in meaningful dialogue about race in America. I have learned, however, that even the best information can go unheard if it is not embedded in a framework that draws—and keeps—attention. Thus, the information in this book is anchored in the compelling and painful voices of victims of racism in America.

Each of these voices vibrantly re-creates moments, capturing the complexities of human thoughts, feelings, and behaviors. They provide authentic and vivid examples of the dynamics and impact of racism in America. This book is an attempt to put a "heart" back into the "mind" of our understanding of racism in America. I want to place our psychological understanding in a more inclusive human context of the voices of the victims of racism in America. This approach, coupled with an understanding and widened heart by all Americans, is necessary if we are to continue the process of racial reconciliation in America.

This book is clearly needed for white America's awareness. I write as a white American to other white Americans about the beast of racism in our country. Racial justice and reconciliation will not occur until white Americans fully recognize that the legal successes of the civil rights movements were not the death knell of racism in America. Rather, they simply spurred the beast of racism to take on a new, more easily veiled, face.

Racial minorities who read this book, however, also will benefit on two levels. First, they will be able to connect themselves to a larger narrative by recognizing the similarities and differences inherent in the experiences of other minority groups. Though still an underresearched area, the existence of racial tensions *between* minorities is extensively documented. One of the legacies, for instance, of the 1992 racial explosion in Los Angeles was the painful recognition of racial tensions between minorities—most notably, the hostility between Korean- and African-Americans. Out of the Los Angeles conflict came a sense that the old vocabulary of race relations in America—"black" and "white"—no longer resonated with reality. It was a multiracial riot that revealed the latent enmity not only between whites and several racial minorities but also between racial minorities themselves. A healing of the tension between racial minorities can begin with a reconnection to the collective narrative of the minority experience in America.

Second, racial minorities who read this book will benefit from a clearer realization of the authentic possibilities for racial reconciliation in America. Often, the utopian ideals of both whites and minorities prevent us from delving into the nuts and bolts of how we will find unity in our diversity. This book lays out the realistic limits of that possibility and is forthright about recognizing that the work of racial reconciliation is not easy.

ORGANIZATION OF BOOK

Background of Research

Though the book includes voices from the African-American, Asian-American, Hispanic-American, and Native American communities, much of the cited psychological research specifically addresses dynamics of black–white interactions. There are three significant reasons why this particular form of race relations has traditionally dominated psychological research. First, the relationship between blacks and whites has been a defining issue in our development as a nation. The glaring existence of black–white inequality, Jim Crow segregation, and pervasive discrimination ultimately forced America to look at itself in the mirror and ask: "Are we *really* a land of great, and equal, opportunity?"

Second, perhaps because of the historical prominence of black–white relations in America, racial stereotypes and attitudes appear to be particularly strong and self-relevant in this area. In other words, whites think and feel about blacks in ways that are more vivid and literal—and, thus, more easily measurable—than the ways in which they think and feel about other racial minorities.

Third, it can be argued that black–white relations are *the* crucial paradigmatic case of racism historically and in the present. As a result, racism against other minorities cannot be adequately addressed until the character and history of racism against African-Americans is clearly understood.[26] This recently was implied in comments by John Hope Franklin, chair of the presidential task force on race relations: "This country cut its eyeteeth on racism with Black–White relations.... They [whites] learned to do this [racism] to other people at other times because they'd already become experts [on blacks]."[27] Unfortunately, Franklin's view has led to a public and embarrassing debate among the board that he chairs. The debate over how the race question in America should be framed and addressed threatens to undo the board's work even before it begins.

One can take issue with any of these reasons. I, for instance, am not particularly convinced that a complete understanding of black–white relations is a prerequisite for addressing racism against other minorities. Regardless, it remains true that studies of whites' racial stereotypes and attitudes toward African-Americans provide the largest database in psychological research.

Since the mid-1970s, considerably more attention has been devoted to the effects of racism on Asian-Americans, Hispanic-Americans, and Native Americans. Much of this newer research has drawn from the earlier findings about racism toward African-Americans. This extension can be justified on the basis that all minorities share the (1) mainstream experience of being citizens in America and (2) common experience of being a minority in America.

Obviously, all of us share in the mainstream experience of being citizens in America. There are commonalities in that experience that shape our understanding of each other. But how much common experience is found in being a minority in America? Does a Native American have significantly different life experiences than an Asian-American in this country? There is reason to suspect some general commonalities in living as a minority. A colleague of mine recently pointed out that there are some peculiar cases in America where whites are the minority and report feelings that are in common with the general experiences of racial minorities. The National Basketball Association, for instance, offers one of the most unusual circumstances in the American workforce: whites as minorities in a high-paying industry closely scrutinized by the public. On NBA basketball teams, 81 percent of the 1995 active players and all of the top-20 scorers were black. In 1997, 80 percent of the 361 active players were black, and no whites finished the regular season among the top-15 scorers or 10 leading rebounders.

In a *New York Times Magazine* article, Bruce Schoenfeld reported that most white players in this unique, reverse-image experience, where they found themselves a pronounced minority, reported feelings of loneliness and disrespect that were similar to those reported by racial minorities in predominately white settings.[28] We shouldn't stretch this comparison too far. After all, away from the basketball court, whites in the NBA return to a white-dominated society. Any lingering feelings of loneliness or disrespect can be quickly alleviated by turning on the television, reading the newspaper, hailing a taxi cab—all reminders of the "privilege" of being white in America. The on-the-job feelings of whites in the NBA do remind us, however, that there are *general* commonalities in living as a minority that may not be unique to any one racial group.

What may be dangerous about extending from these general principles, however, is neglecting the fact that minority groups do have *specific* experiences that are peculiar to being African-American, Asian-American, Hispanic-American, or Native American in this country. Thus, the question of how much similarity exists between the experiences of African-Americans and other minority groups remains controversial.

On one side of the debate, there is no doubt that scholarship on the African-American experience in America has enriched our understanding of the experiences of other racial groups. Many of the underlying mechanisms of prejudice and discrimination discovered in that research are applicable to all oppressed racial minority groups.

On the other side of the debate, however, some have argued that the experiences of Asian-Americans, Hispanic-Americans, and Native Americans cannot be *fully* understood through the psychological perspectives developed on black–white relations. As author Paul Kivel argues: "Using the African-American experience as the model for all communities of color in the United States distorts the history of the African-American struggle for justice and full participation and renders invisible the identities and issues of other communities."[29] Educational psychologist Don Nakanishi of the University of California–Los Angeles contends that the Asian-American experience must be analyzed in a broader international framework than the largely domestic focus of most research on African-Americans.[30] Similarly, psychologist Albert Ramirez of the University of Colorado urges a heightened awareness of the unique circumstances surrounding the Hispanic-American experience as victims of prejudice and discrimination.[31] Joseph Trimble, a psychologist at Western Washington University, also argues that it is an oversimplification to claim that Native Americans and African-Americans share similar problems simply because they both have suffered at the hands of whites.[32] As one example, the historical subtext of Native American persecution, similar to that of Hispanic-Americans, includes resistance to colonization rather than enforced slavery. Such historical contrasts may form the background for differing contemporary issues among the four major racial minority groups. Recognizing this controversy, I have carefully tried to acknowledge the potential limitations in generalizing conclusions from studies of black–white relations to other intergroup relations. It is clear that generalizability is a significant issue for the present and future development of scholarship and public policies dealing with race relations in America.

Structure of Book

Chapter 2 lays the necessary groundwork for our discussion by considering the definitional background of concepts related to racism—stereotypes, prejudice, and discrimination. For most of us, defining terms is not the most exciting part of a discussion. It is, however, the most important step in structuring a clear and meaningful dialogue. In addition to defining these often-misunderstood terms, the interrelationships among them are examined. Chapter 3 follows with a working definition of racism as well as distinctions between individual, institutionalized, and cultural racism.

Following the definitional context of Chapters 2 and 3, I've structured this book around the dismantling of the three myths that (1) life is good for racial minorities, (2) racism is declining, and (3) America can be a color-blind society.

Chapters 4 and 5 confront the myth that life is good for racial minorities. Chapter 4 begins with a discussion of the dilemma of reconciling the American ideals of equality and justice with the reality of individual, institutionalized, and cultural racism. Does the evidence suggest that there remains a striking contradiction between America's promises and the daily realities of American minorities? Is life good for racial minorities in America? The survey and demographic data reviewed in these chapters clearly indicate the continued, and pronounced, existence of racial inequities in America. While, in some cases, racial minorities are better off in absolute terms now that they have been in previous years, I argue in Chapter 5 that racial inequities still exist relative to other groups—especially relative to whites. The playing field is far from level.

The "footprints" of the racial inequities documented in Chapter 5 reveal the continued presence of an intruder—racism. In earlier decades, this intruder was overt, conspicuous, and flagrant. Today's intruder is more covert, stealthy, and pernicious. Because the intruder has adopted a new strategy, however, does not mean that the consequences of the intrusion are any less severe or less crippling. This more subtle form of racism, while not sensational and headline-grabbing, grinds exceedingly small on minorities and shatters the myth that life is good for racial minorities in America.

Chapters 6 and 7 dispel the myth that racism is declining by distinguishing between what psychologists have termed "old-fashioned" and "modern" racism. Chapter 8 continues to dismantle the myth that racism is declining by highlighting the continuing and, in some cases, escalating costs of modern racism to the victim and the perpetrator. Clearly, the costs are far greater for the victim of racism. Costs to the victim include weighty psychological, physical, and financial losses.

These costs are direct, heavy, and immediately painful. Costs to the perpetrator are more indirect and less easily recognized. We must acknowledge, however, the heavy price that all Americans pay for the persistence of racism. Racism deprives us of valuable human talent and energy, and many social, economic, and political resources.

Chapter 9 attacks the myth that America can be a color-blind society. While acknowledging the existence of motivational and sociocultural factors, my attention in Chapter 9 is focused on the cognitive bases of racism. Human brains are finely tuned decision-making machines designed to make quick judgments about a wide variety of confusing events. While such processing is essential for survival, it also traps each of us into the inevitable use of stereotypes—racial or otherwise. The specific content of those stereotypes may vary by personal experience, culture, time in history, and so forth.

For example, what is your stereotype of the group that dominates American basketball? You didn't have to think long, did you? Contrast your response with that of a 1937 sportswriter, Paul Gallico, who wrote about the group who dominated American basketball at that time in history:

> Curiously, it [basketball] is a game that above all others seems to appeal to the temperament of Jews, and for the past years Jewish players on the college teams around New York have had the game all to themselves.... Jews flock to basketball by the thousands.... It appeals to the Hebrew with his Oriental background.... The game places a premium on an alert, scheming mind and flashy trickiness, artful dodging, and general smart-aleckness.[33]

While the specific content may vary, the general use of stereotypes remains part and parcel of human nature. As author Daniela Gioseffi writes,

> It's clear, as psychology explains, that none of us can be perfectly free of social prejudices, those subtle stereotypical reactions to surnames or cultural backgrounds or skin tones or eye slant or nose width and breadth or sexual orientation that are jumbled in the haunted attic of our psyches, causing us to prejudge people before any evidence is in.[34]

The limits of our cognitive capacities, or "haunted attics," must be recognized as we begin our discussion of the possibilities for racial reconciliation in America.

Chapter 10 begins with a reminder that just as we cannot be comfortable in pretending that racism is dead and gone, we must not fall into the trap of believing that it is intractable and insoluble. To be sure, the work of racial reconciliation is long and difficult. Racism's persistence throughout American history can lead to the weariness of "problem fatigue." Even many of the well intentioned ultimately lapse into inaction and resign themselves to a belief that racism is an inevitable condition of human life. Short-term enthusiasms will not win the day in America's struggle for racial reconciliation.

Recognizing, however, that we can never be a color-blind society, how do we learn to live with each other? Chapter 10 concludes with a presentation of seven principles for racial reconciliation in America. Communities, organizations, schools, and families who wish to develop intentional strategies leading to racial reconciliation will find principles outlined in the concluding chapter very beneficial.

For those wanting to follow up on specific statements or issues raised in the book, detailed chapter notes provide the least intrusive— and most accurate—way of referring readers to extensive documentation or additional information. Finally, I conclude with (1) an appendix of addresses (ground and electronic) and phone numbers of organizations concerned with the issues discussed in this book, and (2) a detailed bibliography for additional recommended readings.

CONCLUSION

On the last Sunday of our 1996 study tour, we attended a morning worship served at Mt. Zion United Methodist Church, a predominately African-American church in Georgetown, just outside of Washington, D.C. Mt. Zion has a rich heritage reaching back to its pre–Civil War days as a stop on Harriet Tubman's underground railroad. Following the service, an elderly African-American woman pulled me aside. She asked if I had enjoyed the service. I responded positively, expressing my deep appreciation for the congregation's warmth and hospitality. Still clutching my arm, she looked searchingly into my face and said, "I hope you felt the pain. I really hope you felt the pain." She was communicating a central truth about racial reconciliation in America. This truth is that until we can understand the pain inflicted on individuals because of hatred and exclusion, we will never fully understand why racial reconciliation is so essential to the future of America. It is my hope that you begin to feel, and understand, their pain as you read this book. The pain is not meant to be a destination in and of itself; rather, it is a crucial step in the long journey of racial reconciliation in America.

2

The Foundations of "Isms"

Stereotypes, Prejudice, and Discrimination

Arnold Toynbee has said that some twenty-six civilizations have risen from the face of the earth. Almost all of them have descended into the junk heaps of destruction. The decline and fall of these civilizations, according to Toynbee, was not caused by external invasions but by internal decay. They failed to respond creatively to the challenges impinging upon them. If Western civilization does not respond constructively to the challenge to banish racism, some future historian will have to say that a great civilization died because it lacked the soul and commitment to make justice a reality for all.
—MARTIN LUTHER KING, JR.[1]

"Isms"—sexism, ageism, anti-Semitism, racism, and so forth—represent one of the most destructive aspects of human social behavior. They are an internal rot that can imperil the health of even the strongest societies. American history is littered with violent examples of "isms" directed against groups of people simply for who they are, what they look like, what they believed, or where they come from. This book focuses on racism—the exclusion, persecution, and marginalization of blacks, Asian-Americans, Hispanics, and Native Americans.

When the Declaration of Independence was proclaimed in 1776, slavery of minorities had existed in the Western Hemisphere for nearly two centuries. Blacks have a 378-year history on this continent—245 involving slavery, 100 involving legalized discrimination, and only 33 years involving anything else. The first Africans were brought to what is now the United States in 1619. Whereas these first 20 likely came as indentured servants, Africans were eventually shackled into complete slavery. The U.S. Constitution, with its Bill of Rights, legitimized the enslavement of African-Americans in three of its provisions. By the time slavery was officially abolished by the Thirteenth Amendment in 1865, 10–15 million Africans had been brought to America; another 30–35 million died in transport! Following the abolition of slavery, economic and cultural exploitation, political disenfranchisement, legal segregation, and frequent violent attacks against blacks continued throughout the country.

The civil rights movement of the 1960s centered the country's attention on the discrepancy between the promises of America and the reality of everyday life for blacks in this country. Today, the legal successes of the civil rights movement have been countered by the ingeniousness of white society to develop new social and economic systems to continue the legacy of racial exploitation. The *de jure* residential and educational segregation of pre-1960s America still remains as *de facto* segregation. According to the 1990 census, there are approximately 30 million African-Americans in the United States, accounting for about 12 percent of the population. As the largest minority group in American society, blacks continue to be at the cutting edge of the struggle for racial equality and liberty.

Asian-Americans have immigrated from more than 20 countries and have been here for over 150 years. Following the abolition of slavery, large numbers of Chinese were recruited by American businesses to come and work in this country. Shortly after, however, their presence became highly contested. They were often persecuted, not for their vices, but for their virtues. In 1882, the Chinese Exclusion Act became the first law to prohibit the entry of immigrants on the basis of nationality. Until the 1965 Immigration Act, Asian immigration remained either illegal or so sharply limited as to be virtually nonexistent. In the late 1800s and early 1900s, more than 600 pieces of anti-Asian legislation limiting or excluding persons of Asian ancestry from citizenship were passed. In 1942, in what the American Civil Liberties Union (ACLU) has called the worst single, wholesale violation of civil rights of American citizens in our history, the U.S. government sent 120,000 Japanese-Americans to internment camps for the duration of World War II. It was not until 1952 that the last barriers to Asians becoming citizens were removed.

Today, the 1990 census counted 7.5 million Asian-Americans living in the United States, comprising about 3 percent of the population. They represent the fastest-growing minority group and are expected to make up 4.5 percent of the population by the year 2000 and 10.7 percent by 2050. The economic and educational achievements of this "model minority" are seen as representative of what America can offer to minorities who claim their given birthright. Such a label disparages those minorities who still suffer significant economic and educational deprivation. It distorts the reality of the Asian-American experience by exaggerating their "success." Economic indicators, for example, neglect the fact that most Asian-Americans reside in states with higher costs of living than the national average (e.g., California, New York). Higher family incomes often only reveal the presence of more workers in each family rather than higher individual incomes. In addition, the "model minority" status has obscured the psychological and social needs of Asian-Americans to the point that some are now calling this population the "invisible minority." In an era anxious about the growing minority underclass, the Asian-American "model minority" is a helpful fiction.

The historical legacy of Hispanic-Americans is not one of abduction or slavery, nor of recruitment for labor. Rather, many were victims of colonization by American forces seeking new territories to provide markets for American goods. Hispanics were initially enclosed by America's expanding border following the 1846–1848 war against Mexico, in which Mexico ceded all of California, New Mexico, Nevada, and parts of Colorado, Arizona, and Utah—a total of over one million square miles. Since that time, groups of Hispanics have been uprooted, exiled, or forced to migrate. Others have come to America seeking asylum and economic opportunity. Between 1942 and 1964, the Bracero program brought more than five million Mexican workers to America as cheap agricultural labor.

The Hispanic population numbered 22.8 million in 1993, comprising about 9 percent of the U.S. population. Due to younger ages, high birthrates, and increasing immigration, the Hispanic population is growing rapidly. According to U.S. Census projections, by the year 2010, Hispanics will surpass African-Americans as the largest racial minority group in this country. By the year 2050, 22.7 percent of the U.S. population is projected to be Hispanic, with disproportionate concentrations in California, Texas, and New York.[2] They continue to struggle against social exclusion, persecution, and extensive employment discrimination— a struggle not always recognized by society. In the 1992 Los Angeles uprising, for example, Latinos suffered the greatest number of people killed and had the greatest amount of property damage—facts lost in much of the reporting and conversation.

Native Americans did not share in the immigrant experience. Their resident status did not, however, prevent them from becoming aliens in their native land. The fact that our frontier was another's homeland was conveniently overlooked. The Naturalization Act of 1790 excluded Native Americans from citizenship. They were regarded as domestic subjects—analogous to children of foreign diplomats born here. Ultimately, however, they were not accorded the courtesies typically given domestic subjects. The fulfillment of our "manifest destiny" by westward expansion and government removal efforts in the 1800s made clear the Native Americans' true standing—"savage dogs." They were thought so little of that American soldiers made bridle reins from strips of skin taken from their corpses, and tobacco pouches from their severed testicles.[3] In 1891, the Census Bureau proclaimed that the frontier was closed. In the following decades, extermination policies became peace policies. Physical genocide became cultural genocide, with the mandated assimilation of Native Americans and the consequent denial of tribal identity and authority.

Today, Native Americans still survive, though in drastically fewer numbers. At the time that Columbus arrived in the West Indies, there were about 15 million indigenous people in North America. In 1990, the census counted only about 2.1 million Native Americans living in all 50 states, only 0.8 percent of the total U.S. population. Today's Native Americans represent more than 500 tribes, each with unique cultural, genetic, and sociodemographic characteristics. The states with the largest Native American populations are California, Oklahoma, Arizona, New Mexico, and North Carolina. Native Americans remain the poorest and most disadvantaged of all racial groups. Their national identities are threatened as their lands are being mined, logged, used for hunting, used for toxic waste dumping, and developed without permission or fair compensation. They are the only major racial group not to be represented on President Clinton's advisory board on race relations. We have constructed a mythologized, "New Age" image of Native Americans that requires them to be increasingly vigilant in their quest to protect their racial identity.

The specific histories of these four major racial groups vary. Some were brought here for indentured servitude and, ultimately, slavery; others were enlisted and exploited for cheap labor; still others came of their own free will to seek the American dream. Some were victims of colonization; others simply were "in the way" of America's lust for additional living space. Perhaps, in part, because of their historical contrasts, the contemporary struggles of these groups are different as well. There is, however, one common thread underlying all of their experiences. In both past and present, these people have been treated differently—as inferiors—simply because of the color of their skin. In other words, they have all been, and continue to be, victims of racism. What is the nature of this beast called racism?

THE FOUNDATIONS OF RACISM

To develop an analysis of racism, we must initially create a clear definition. The work of creating clear definitions is hard and exacting. While rarely exciting, it is absolutely necessary for productive dialogue. The background for our definition of racism rests on clarifying three related terms—stereotypes, prejudice, and discrimination. These terms, though often used as synonyms, are, in fact, very different concepts. While not quite rivaling the mystery of the Holy Trinity for theologians, these three concepts have been remarkably difficult for psychologists to isolate and define. The traditional understanding tied them together as examples of thoughts (stereotypes), attitudes (prejudice), and behaviors (discrimination). As we will see, however, contemporary investigation reveals that these simple contrasts mask some underlying associations. Let's begin our discussion by examining the concept drawing the most current attention from psychologists—stereotypes.

Stereotypes

It is an undeniable fact of human existence that people are organized into groups. We are all members of many different types of groups. These groups range from small, intimate collections of family and friends to large social categories such as gender, religion, and nationality. Consider our four major racial minority groups—African-Americans, Asian-Americans, Hispanic-Americans, and Native Americans. Suppose you were asked to list the traits perceived to be most characteristic of each group. Would you find this to be a difficult task? Probably not. You likely would be able to quickly construct a fairly detailed list for each group. You could probably construct such a list even for other groups with whom you have had limited or no contact. In some surveys, for instance, respondents have constructed very detailed lists of characteristics for a group called the "Whisnits." You haven't heard of the Whisnits? It's because they don't exist—they are a fictional group. Still, respondents were able to rank them on the basis of their intelligence, morality, social skills, athleticism, and so forth. Why? The reason involves the existence and operation of stereotypes.

History of Research in Stereotyping

When the word was coined in 1798, a *stereotype* referred to an aspect of the printing process in which a mold is made so as to duplicate patterns or pictures onto a page. In 1922, Walter Lippmann, a famous American editorialist and political journalist, borrowed the term to represent the typical picture that comes to mind when thinking about a particular social group:

> Stereotypes are loaded with preference, suffused with affection or dislike, attached to fears, lusts, strong wishes, pride, hope. Whatever invokes the stereotype is judged with the appropriate sentiment. Except where we deliberately keep prejudice in suspense, we do not study a man and judge him to be bad. We see a bad man. We see a dewy morn, a blushing maiden, a sainted priest, a humorless Englishman, a dangerous Red, a carefree bohemian, a lazy Hindu, a wily Oriental, a dreaming Slav, a volatile Irishman, a greedy Jew, a 100 percent American.[4]

Lippmann theorized that these pictures help us to manage the complexity of our environment by simplifying the social world.

In the next several decades, two major lines of empirical research shaped how we thought about stereotypes. In 1933, the seminal work of Princeton psychologists Daniel Katz and Kenneth Braly defined stereotypes as beliefs shared by a large number of people within a *culture*.[5] In an elegantly simple procedure, Katz and Braly listed 84 character traits (e.g., ignorant, musical, progressive, artistic, etc.) and had 100 male American undergraduates select those traits they believed most characteristic of various racial and ethnic groups. The responses revealed an incredibly high rate of agreement regarding the traits believed most characteristic of a specific group. Negroes, for instance, emerged as superstitious, lazy, happy-go-lucky, ignorant, and musical. Jews were seen as shrewd, mercenary, industrious, grasping, and intelligent. Americans were depicted as intelligent, materialistic, ambitious, and progressive.

For Katz and Braly, the high degree of agreement in stereotyping among the students reflected common cultural forces that molded familiar stereotypes. Such stereotypes served the function of helping people fit in and identify with their own social group. For this perspective, negative stereotypes were seen as shared products of our worst cultural tendencies.

Following World War II, a second major line of empirical research came from the work of a team of German-Jewish refugees from the Frankfurt (Germany) Institute for Social Research and their American colleagues at the University of California at Berkeley. In their book *The Authoritarian Personality*, these investigators shifted the research and definitional emphasis away from cultural stereotypes to the investigation of *individual* stereotypes held by highly prejudiced people.[6] They concluded that certain personality types are predisposed, because of child-rearing practices and family dynamics, to stereotypical thinking. Authoritarian personalities admire power, are rigid, conventional, aggressive, stereotyping and superstitious, cynical, and have problematic—usually puritanical—attitudes toward sex. They are drawn to conservative, fascistic, or rightist ideologies.

For these troubled minds, stereotypes serve to protect the ego. They make persons feel better about themselves and less threatened by other groups of people. The focus shifted from negative stereotypes as the *shared* products of our worst cultural tendencies to negative stereotypes as the *individual* products of disturbed minds that did not process information correctly.

Until the 1970s, these two contrasting perspectives dominated the majority of stereotyping research. By the mid-1970s, however, increasing interest in *social cognition* stimulated renewed interest on research in stereotyping. Social cognition focuses on the thinking processes involved in understanding, and in guiding, social behavior. A significant component of this area involved examining people's perceptions and judgments of others. This new social cognitive perspective argued that stereotypes are simply beliefs we have about people in groups. These beliefs, rather than resulting from common cultural forces or troubled minds, are derived from the general cognitive processes we all share. In the words of psychologist David Schneider, stereotypes are "for better or worse, the products of everyone's minds."[7] Psychologists Richard Ashmore and Frances Del Boca concur that stereotypes are "nothing special ... not essentially different from other cognitive structures and processes."[8] Today, a substantial amount of empirical interest in stereotyping, primarily based in the social cognitive perspective, continues unabated. More than 1,500 scholarly articles on stereotyping appeared in print from 1983 to 1992 alone.

Definition of Stereotypes

Contemporary definitions of stereotypes are almost as numerous and diverse as the authors who formulate them. Generally, however, we may define a stereotype as a *cognitive shortcut that contains beliefs about the attributes of an individual because of his or her membership in a specific group*. The process of applying the beliefs contained in a stereotype is called *stereotyping*.

The beliefs contained in a stereotype involve generalizations suggesting that *all* members of some certain group share particular traits, characteristics, or opinions, at least to a degree. At various times throughout the twentieth century, for example, Native Americans have been stereotyped as silent, passive, drunken, lazy, and immoral. Responses to national surveys still reveal strong negative stereotypes of African- and Hispanic-Americans and relatively positive stereotypes of Asian-Americans.

Most people believe that stereotypes are negative, invariably inaccurate, and inevitably harmful. In truth, however, stereotypes may be positive or negative, accurate or inaccurate, helpful or harmful. Stereotypes are probabilistic rules of thumb that do accurately depict *some* members of a group. When accurate, they help us make quick and often difficult decisions in a world of overwhelming information. They are, however, clearly overgeneralized—and potentially dangerous—when they are applied to *all* members of a group. When inaccurate, they compromise the individuality of a specific person by assuming certain characteristics simply on the basis of membership in a specific group.

Most early researchers agreed that the tenacity with which we hold specific stereotypes is striking. Today, while recognizing the capacity for change, we are still struck by the awareness that stereotypes are more rigidly held than many other generalizations. Two factors reinforce this tenacity. First, some stereotypes contain what psychologist Gordon Allport termed a *kernel of truth*.[9] In other words, some stereotypes are grounded in reality, even if they constitute an exaggeration of reality or were outdated by the reality that contributed to their expression. Regardless, the broad application of stereotypes—even when based on some "kernel of truth"—involves inappropriate overgeneralizations about many quite different individuals. Stereotypes become particularly destructive when they are applied to many group members for whom they do not fit at all, or as they foster a perception that *only* members of this particular group evidence a specific stereotypical behavior. As psychologist David Myers points out,

> Someone who stereotypes African-Americans as more likely than European-Americans to bear babies outside of marriage or to be on welfare would be correct. But to presume that most nonmarital births or most welfare clients are African-American is to overgeneralize because it just isn't so.[10]

The tenacity of our stereotypes is reinforced by a second factor. Quite simply, we have a distinct tendency to attend to, and remember, information that is consistent with our stereotypes. Conversely, when we encounter information inconsistent with a stereotype, we actively refute or even deny it. In other words, under the influence of a stereotype, we tend to see what the stereotype primes us to see. For example, each semiliterate Hispanic migrant farmworker we see solidifies our perception that most Hispanics are uneducated and employed in menial labor. When faced with the reality of a Hispanic businessperson, professor, politician, or skilled professional, we dismiss his or her appearance as an anomaly, an exception that proves the rule that most Hispanics are uneducated and work in menial labor. As a result, the stereotypes become, to a large degree, self-confirming and relatively resistant to new information.

At times, the self-confirming and resistant nature of stereotypes defies logic. Consider this exchange reported by psychologist Gordon Allport:

> Mr. X: The trouble with Jews is that they only take care of their own group.
>
> Mr. Y: But the record of the Community Chest campaign shows that they gave more generously, in proportion to their numbers, to the general charities of the community than did non-Jews.
>
> Mr. X: That shows they are always trying to buy favor and intrude into Christian affairs. They think of nothing but money; that is why there are so many Jewish bankers.
>
> Mr. Y: But a recent study shows that the percentage of Jews in the banking business is negligible, far smaller than the percentage of non-Jews.
>
> Mr. X: That's just it; they don't go in for respectable business; they are only in the movie business or run night clubs.[11]

Judging one person by a stereotype of the many seems grossly unfair. Why, then, do we rely so heavily on stereotypes? It is important to recognize that stereotyping is not, in and of itself, pathological. As a matter of fact, stereotyping is as natural to our mind as breathing is to our lungs. We are very miserly when it comes to our mental effort. We embrace any opportunity to employ cognitive shortcuts to process information about things, events, places, and people. These shortcuts, known as cognitive schemas, are indispensable labor-saving devices for making sense out of a very complex social world. Cognitive schemas, of which stereotypes are one example, assist us in organizing, interpreting, and remembering information. In other words, they give meaning to information and promote parsimonious and effective processing of that information.

When my daughter was two years old, for example, she used one cognitive schema (i.e., "bird") to describe any flying object (planes, helicopters, butterflies, her older brother, etc.). It was a schema that, while inaccurate, simplified an incredibly complex world for her imma-ture and evolving mind. It gave meaning to the vast amount of new information that she encountered every day. For a two-year-old, it is an adorable trait. If she still uses this specific schema as a high school senior, we will be concerned. We hope—and expect—that she will "grow out" of this and continue to mature cognitively. In truth, though increasing in sophistication, she—like each of us—will always process information about her world on the basis of cognitive schemas.

As cognitive schemas go, stereotyping can't be beat. It is efficient, saves a lot of mental effort, and gives us a convenient way to deal with the thousands of people with whom we interact in our lifetimes. Though stereotyping may serve a social (e.g., Katz and Braly) or ego-protective (e.g., *The Authoritarian Personality*) function, its primary purpose is that of cognitive economy. The simple frugality of stereotyping ensures its continued and persistent application.

In addition, recent research by psychologists Steven Fein of Williams College (MA) and Steven Spencer of the University of Waterloo suggests that the negative character of many stereotypes may actually help restore the self-image of the person holding the stereotype. Their study found that people whose self-image had recently been bolstered were less likely to evaluate another person stereotypically than were people whose self-image had recently been threatened. This secondary purpose of stereotyping, that negative stereotypes of others makes us feel better about ourselves, only serves to boost our reliance upon the stereotyping process.[12]

Individual and Cultural Stereotypes

As we have seen, the modern social cognitive perspective focuses on stereotypes as the products of *individual* experiences. As Katz and Braly originally suggested, however, stereotypes may also be thought of as the products of *cultures*—acquired in the same ways we acquire any other culturally ingrained idea. These levels of analysis present us with two distinct forms of stereotypes—individual and cultural.

Individual stereotypes are represented within the mind of a particular person. The preceding discussion has focused on the defining features of individual stereotypes. As we have seen, such stereotypes serve a function to the individual by systematizing and simplifying information. Cultural stereotypes, however, are a much larger part of the social fabric of a society, shared by the people within that culture. The transmission of cultural stereotypes comes from language, the media, and social roles. Cultural stereotypes serve a society by offering culturally acceptable explanations for events, by justifying group action

or inaction, and by providing a way for groups to differentiate themselves positively from other groups. When negative cultural stereotypes
are consensually shared within a society, their consequences become
much more damaging, because they affect entire groups of people in a
common way. As psychologist Robert Gardner expressed, a racial
group member "may be somewhat chagrined to find that a few individuals in the larger community have beliefs about the characteristics of the
group of which he is a member, but it has major implications ... when
such beliefs are relatively widespread in the community."[13]

Claude Steele is a psychologist who has demonstrated the major
implications of cultural stereotypes in influencing individual behavior.[14] Steele argues that there is a powerful cultural stereotype that
African-Americans do poorly on academic tasks. African-Americans
are aware of this stereotype and recognize that failure in academic tasks
will perpetuate this collective belief. As a result, they experience extra
pressure, called "stereotype threat," to defy the stereotype by succeeding at academic tasks. Ironically, however, the extra pressure itself may
be so great as to sabotage their academic performance. The debilitating
results of these cultural stereotypes are seen in the fact that 70 percent of
all African-American college students drop out at some point in their
academic careers—as compared with 45 percent of whites. The influence of cultural stereotypes on dropout rates cannot be explained away
by deficits in skill or preparation that blacks might suffer because of
background disadvantages. Even at the highest levels of preparation
(combined SATs of 1,400), 18–33 percent of blacks dropped out, compared to only 2–11 percent of whites.[15]

In the final analysis, individual and cultural stereotypes are inherently intertwined. It is impossible to separate cultural and individual
experiences, because they shape one another. Culturally shared stereotypes are meaningless if not for the fact that individuals translate those
beliefs into specific actions.

Prejudice

Recall our previous discussion, when I asked you to list some of
your beliefs about African-Americans, Asian-Americans, Hispanic-
Americans, and Native Americans. Those descriptions were defined as
stereotypes (i.e., cognitive shortcuts containing beliefs about the attrib-

utes of individuals because of their membership in a specific group). Whenever we describe some of our beliefs about a group of people, it is natural to have a corresponding evaluation of those beliefs. Our evaluation, favorable or unfavorable, of our beliefs about people (or things or places) is called an *attitude*. Some attitudes are positive; others are negative. Occasionally, our negative attitudes may be strong enough to evoke a pronounced visceral, gut-level revulsion to the stimulus. Louis Agassiz, a nineteenth-century Swiss naturalist, wrote the following to his mother following his first contact with an African-American.

> In seeing their black faces with their thick lips and grimacing teeth, the wool on their head, their bent knees, their elongated hands, their large curved nails, and especially the livid color of the palm of their hands, I could not take my eyes off their face in order to tell them to stay far away. And when they advanced that hideous hand towards my plate in order to serve me, I wished I were able to depart in order to eat a piece of bread elsewhere, rather than dine with such service.[16]

Agassiz's revulsion reveals the degree to which our descriptive beliefs about a group of other people can contain intense evaluative and emotional components.

Definition of Prejudice

The term *prejudice* is derived from the Latin *praejudicium*, from *prae*, meaning before, and *judicium*, meaning judgment. As used in psychology, the term is in some ways broader and in some ways narrower than its definition in Webster as a "preconceived judgment or opinion ... to anything without just grounds or before sufficient knowledge."[17] Prejudice is broader in psychological usage, because it includes not only preconceived judgments or opinions but also their evaluative and emotional correlates. It is narrower for two reasons. First, the term is generally applied only to people's view about social groups and their members rather than more generally to "anything." Second, in practice, the term has been mainly restricted to *negative* preconceptions about groups other than one's own.

Generally, we can define prejudice as *a positive or negative attitude toward an individual because of his or her membership in a specific group*. Prejudice implies the underlying operation of stereotypes as prejudgments; our prejudice is based solely on our identification of a person with a particular group (e.g., race, gender, age, ethnicity, religious preference, disability, weight, sexual orientation, etc.). In addition, prejudice adds the affective component of evaluative and emotional responses (i.e., attitude).

It is important to note that we can be biased toward a person and not necessarily prejudiced—as long as that bias is based on his or her individual characteristics and not simply membership in a specific group. Several years ago, I was lecturing on prejudice and racism at a small college in Kentucky. One afternoon, a white student came by my office for a chat. I had gotten to know this particular student very well through his enrollment in this course and a couple of other courses I had taught at the college. He was a bright and inquisitive young man. He was also an openly vocal bigot. Our conversation began with his saying, "You know, you lecture an awful lot about the evils of prejudice and I know that you think I'm a racist. But you are just as prejudiced as I am!" He had caught my attention, if not my anger, and I asked him to continue. "Suppose I came to your door to take your daughter out on a date," he continued. "You wouldn't let me, would you?"

It took a moment for me to catch my breath. The thought of him dating my daughter kept my wife and me childless for the next several years. I had to admit that he was a few fries short of a Happy Meal if he thought I would—if it was in my power—let him anywhere near my yet-to-be-born daughter. I am a man betrayed by my expressions—he saw all of these thoughts race across my face. "That's it!" he screamed. "You're as prejudiced as I am!"

As delicately as possible, I tried to explain to him that my negative feelings about him would only be considered a form of prejudice if they were based on his membership in a specific group—for example, age, race, gender, or major. In reality, though, my dislike for him was very individual. I knew him well enough as a person to know that his individual values, beliefs, and ideals were very discrepant from what I saw as mature, enlightened, and socially desirable—certainly far from what I would envision in an ideal son-in-law. It is, of course, not very admirable to dislike someone like that. I should have made a greater effort to find parts of him that I could appreciate. Regardless, my dislike for him as an individual did not classify as an accurate example of prejudice.

Prejudice is most often represented as an *individual* attitude. Similar to our discussion on stereotypes, however, we also can conceptualize prejudice in terms of *cultural* attitudes peculiar to particular communities or regions. Thus, prejudice—in addition to its expression in individual, interpersonal relationships—also can be manifest in cultural attitudes toward individuals because of their membership in a specific group.

Our working definition of prejudice has two notable distinctions that render it a bit less restrictive than most other psychological definitions. First, many psychologists have emphasized *only* the negative attitude in their attempts to define prejudice. Our definition reflects the fact, however, that prejudice can have positive forms. As a person born and raised in the South, who now teaches in the far reaches of the Pacific Northwest, I must admit to a strong positive prejudice for students from my "home." When I discover a student with any connection to the South, it activates an entire list of positive traits in my mind—warm, good sense of humor, kind, gregarious, and so forth. These traits all carry a very positive evaluation that may result in some distinctly favorable treatment. Though positive prejudices can be problematic, especially when paired with corresponding negative prejudices, they scarcely constitute the major social problem represented by many negative prejudices—especially racism. Thus, while this definition allows for both positive and negative prejudices, this book will focus exclusively on the negative prejudices associated with racism.

Second, many psychologists have emphasized the "illogicality," "incorrectness," "inaccuracy," or "unjustifiability" of the attitudes expressed in prejudice.[18] Similar to our previous discussion of stereotypes, however, I do not believe it is necessary to imply that the holding of various prejudices *always* indicates a faulty generalization or irrational process. Similar to the development of stereotypes, some prejudices are built on Allport's "kernel of truth"—even if they are grossly overextended. As social psychologist Rupert Brown suggests, to think of prejudice as having no rational function is to fail to do justice to the variety and complexity of the forms it can take.[19]

Discrimination

In the criminal justice system, African-Americans are more likely than whites to be excluded from juries (especially in cases involving

African-American defendants), to receive harsher sentencing, to serve longer in prison, and to be sentenced to death (especially for violence against whites). These biases hold up even when such factors as severity and frequency of offense are held constant. Clearly, our most significant social problems occur when our stereotypical beliefs and prejudicial attitudes are translated into behavior.

Definition of Discrimination

Compared to the complex interconnections between stereotypes and prejudice, discrimination is relatively straightforward to define. Discrimination is prejudice in action. A 1949 official memorandum of the United Nations defined discrimination as including "any conduct based on a distinction made on grounds of natural or social categories, which have no relation either to individual capacities or merits, or to the concrete behavior of the individual person."[20] More specifically, we may define discrimination as *positive or negative behaviors toward an individual because of his or her membership in a specific group.*

This definition is consistent with most in psychological literature in connecting discrimination as the behavioral manifestation of stereotypical beliefs and prejudicial attitudes. It is broader, however, in recognizing that positive forms of discrimination may exist as well. Following my description of a personal, positive prejudice toward students from the South, positive forms of discrimination occur when I ask those students to join my family for dinner or go sledding with my kids and me at a local ski lodge. These students probably receive, intentionally or unintentionally, some particularly favorable treatment in the classroom as well.

Continuing our analysis at the *individual* and *cultural* levels, we should also note that discrimination, though practiced by individuals, is often reinforced by the well-established rules, policies, and practices of organizations. Such organizational discrimination may include actions that are often regarded simply as part of the organization's way of doing business but which—in reality—have an adverse effect on minorities and women. This may include, for example, height and weight requirements that are *unnecessarily* geared to the physical proportions of white males and therefore, exclude females and some minorities from certain jobs. Though not all discriminatory organizational actions are intentional, the common denominator of many are unequal results on a very large scale.

RELATIONSHIP OF STEREOTYPES, PREJUDICE, AND DISCRIMINATION

The traditional distinction of stereotypes as a set of cognitive associations, prejudice as an attitude, and discrimination as behavior has been replaced by more complex views. Many researchers argue that the terms are not particularly clear, and all three areas should be reconceptualized within a single paradigm. Given the continuing debate, what can we summarize—at this point in our inquiry—about the interrelationships among these three concepts?

Clarifying the interrelationships among stereotypes, prejudice, and discrimination is more than an intellectual exercise. I'll draw from a recent news story to illustrate my point. On a stunning April weekend in 1997, 21-year-old Eldrick "Tiger" Woods astonished the sports world by overwhelming the field to win the prestigious Master's golf tournament by 12 strokes. It was the most dominant performance in a major golf tournament this century. He became the first golfer of color, the son of an African-American father and an Asian-American mother, to win this—or any other—major golf event.

The days surrounding Woods's victory were filled with newspaper columnists, television analysts, and radio talk-show hosts discussing the racial significance of his breakthrough. In the midst of that celebration, however, age-old stereotypes reared their ugly head. Fuzzy Zoeller, in a taped interview with CNN, called his fellow golfer "a little boy." He said he hoped Woods wouldn't request fried chicken and collard greens on the menu at next year's Champions Dinner. Zoeller's comments raised a furor. At least one of his lucrative endorsement contracts was withdrawn, and some called for his immediate removal from the P.G.A. Tour. Others cited his "jokester" reputation as a way of contextualizing the inappropriate remarks. "It was just Fuzzy being funny," his defenders argued. "He doesn't hate blacks or any other groups." Others saw the mean-spiritedness of a racial stereotype that wouldn't die. Some argued that a person holding such a stereotype is very likely to hold related prejudicial attitudes and engage in related discriminatory behaviors.

At the heart of this controversy is the question of the interrelationship among stereotypes, prejudice, and discrimination. Did Zoeller's comments "merely" reflect an overgeneralized stereotype and nothing more? Or did his comments betray a deeper prejudice against African-Americans? If so, is he—if given the opportunity—likely to act on that prejudice and behave in a discriminatory manner? These questions are impossible to answer unless we analyze how stereotypes, prejudice, and discrimination relate to each other.

Is There a Relationship between Stereotypes and Prejudice?

Today, a growing number of psychologists are investigating the possibility that stereotypes are more than simply cognitive beliefs. Recent evidence suggests that stereotypes also have an emotional component or, at least, are influenced by emotional states to an important extent. Most psychologists now assert that the traditional conception of stereotypes as cognitive representations and prejudice as emotional reactions is misleading. It has become clear that both stereotypes and prejudice reflect a mixture of cognition and affect. In addition, they are inextricably intertwined, because our emotional reaction toward a group strongly influences whether we accept positive or negative stereotypes about that group.

Can the strength of our stereotypical beliefs predict the corresponding strength of our prejudicial attitudes? Does a stereotype necessarily translate into a corresponding prejudice? A review of the relevant literature makes a clear statement regarding the relationship between racial stereotypes and racial prejudice: Stereotypes and prejudice are positively associated. In other words, as the strength of our stereotypical beliefs increases, or decreases, so does the strength of our prejudicial attitudes.

Contemporary research has now moved beyond this question to address issues of *how* we explain this relationship. Even the clearest demonstration of the stereotype–prejudice relationship does not imply a causal relationship between the two. On one hand, stereotypes may form the cognitive basis for prejudice. One could also argue, however, that prejudice tends to generate stereotypes. In other words, stereotypes perform a function for prejudiced people by allowing them to rationalize their preexisting hostility and negative feelings toward a particular group. Psychologist G. Haddock and colleagues, for instance, have demonstrated that simply knowing someone is gay leads to a strong emotional reaction that makes one adopt the appropriate negative stereotypes.[21]

Is There a Relationship between Stereotypes and Discrimination?

Do our stereotypes make us more likely to discriminate against racial minorities? Contrary to the clear relationship between stereotypes and prejudice, the findings of the very few studies to examine stereotypes and discrimination are mixed and inconclusive.

There are, however, some theoretical reasons to expect a positive relationship between stereotypes and discrimination. One option is that stereotypes may directly influence behavior by impacting the way we perceive, process, store, and retrieve information. A stereotypical belief that crime is associated with African-Americans may lead one to process information differently about the actions of those group members and behave accordingly. As we discussed previously, any information supporting that stereotypical belief will be attended to and used to solidify that belief. Information challenging that stereotypical belief, however, is often ignored or explained away as an "exception that proves the rule." It seems reasonable to assume that the different means of processing this information would affect subsequent behaviors.

Alternatively, stereotypes may serve to justify discrimination. From this perspective, stereotypical beliefs may be a consequence, rather than a cause, of discriminatory behaviors. For instance, we may legitimize existing social inequities by constructing stereotypical beliefs to explain those inequities. The beliefs, rather than being the foundation for behaviors, become a justification for discriminatory behaviors.

Is There a Relationship between Prejudice and Discrimination?

The relationship between stereotypes and discrimination is difficult to demonstrate. The gap between belief and action seems wide. What about the gap between attitude and action? Might we find a clearer relationship between prejudice and discrimination?

The traditional assumption has been that prejudicial attitudes are strong and accurate predictors of behavioral discrimination. If I know someone holds a negative prejudice against Hispanics, I believe I can safely predict that he or she will behave in a discriminatory manner against Hispanics if given the opportunity. This assumption of consistency has focused much of our racial reconciliation efforts on encouraging more tolerant and liberal attitudes. By changing those attitudes, we have thought, appropriate changes in behavior will automatically follow. In fact, however, the intuitive connection between prejudicial attitudes and discriminatory behavior is not nearly that certain. Indeed, the issue of attitude–behavior *in*consistency is a recurring theme in the specific analysis of prejudice and discrimination, and in the general study of social psychology.

Can prejudicial attitudes be present without the corresponding existence of clear and objective marks of discrimination? This is difficult to answer because of the external pressures that may occasionally prohibit even the most prejudiced person from acting in a discriminatory manner. Laws, moral prohibitions, social pressure, fear of retaliation, economic motives—all may serve to deter people from putting their prejudicial attitudes into open practice. Our earliest empirical evidence suggesting that prejudicial attitudes may not always be manifested in discriminatory behaviors came from a 1934 study by sociologist Richard LaPiere.[22] LaPiere, a white professor, traveled the western region of the United States with a young Chinese-American couple. They stopped at 66 hotels and motels and ate at 184 restaurants. Contrary to the prevailing anti-Asian sentiment and behavior at that time, all but one of the hotels and motels gave them space, and they were never refused service at a restaurant.

Six months later, LaPiere sent a letter to these same establishments asking whether they would accept Chinese as guests. The responses were directly contrary to their previous experiences. Of the 128 establishments replying, 92 percent said they would not accept Chinese-Americans as guests. LaPiere's work was the first of many similar studies to suggest that prejudicial attitudes are not always expressed in discriminatory behaviors. In 1952, for instance, psychologists B. Kutner and colleagues conducted a parallel study with African-Americans and found comparable results.[23] Today, this kind of prejudice–discrimination inconsistency is quite common because of the many laws that forbid discrimination based on race, gender, and national origin.

The prejudice–discrimination inconsistency cuts the other way as well. Can a person engage in discriminatory behaviors that are not necessarily connected to any underlying prejudicial attitudes? In other words, must discriminatory behavior *always* have its source in prejudicial attitudes? The answer is clearly no. There are forms of discrimination against a group or its individual members that are not necessarily associated with prejudice. For example, some people may propose restrictions on immigration without necessarily harboring hostile attitudes toward the groups upon whom they wish to impose the limitations.

So there appears to be a general inconsistency between prejudicial attitudes and discriminatory behaviors. We must also note, however, that such inconsistencies are difficult to sustain over a period of time. Leon Festinger was the first of many psychologists to propose that people find inconsistency aversive.[24] We feel uncomfortable when there is an inconsistency between our attitudes and our actions. As a result, prejudicial attitudes that are forced to survive without a clear means of expression may either weaken or—most likely—find alternative forms of expression. Likewise, discrimination against certain groups, which may start from an absence of hostility, often ends up as discrimination accompanied by prejudice. Perhaps because of these prods to consistency, psychologist John Dovidio and his colleagues state that an extensive review of literature reveals that white prejudice systematically predicts discrimination against African-Americans.[25] We see a real-life confirmation of this in a study reporting that when Jesse Jackson first ran for the presidency in 1984, the most prejudiced whites were the most likely to vote against him.[26]

CONCLUSION

Understanding how stereotypes, prejudice, and discrimination relate to one another may seem like an esoteric exercise. In truth, however, such an understanding is essential if we are to increase our understanding of the dynamics of intergroup relations. I use the Woods–Zoeller incident only as a timely illustration. Each of us recognizes that Fuzzy Zoeller's remarks are no different from thousands of other comments uttered across this country every day. Should such insensitive comments be dismissed because they are "only" humorous stereotypes? Or should we recognize in those stereotypes the potential for related prejudicial attitudes and discriminatory behaviors? The research suggests the latter. Stereotypes, however "innocently" expressed, bear a significant connection to related prejudicial attitudes and discriminatory behaviors. Ongoing research on attitude–behavior relationships is very important to this area.

3

Racism 101

With this foundation laid, we finally can approach a definition of racism. The term *racism* is frequently used without definition. The term has such widespread usage that most people believe they are aware of what is meant. Closer examination reveals, however, that a common meaning for the term *racism* is more assumed than actual.

WHAT IS RACE?

A significant difficulty in defining *racism* is the prior complication of defining *race*. Race is generally defined in terms of physical characteristics (e.g., skin color, facial features, hair type and color, eye color, head shape and size, etc.) that are common to an inbred, geographically isolated population. Racial groups are simply people with common geographic origins, who, to European taxonomists, looked somewhat alike. From 1950 to 1967, international scholars and experts drafted four statements used by the United Nations to dispel fictions associated with *race*. In their third statement, written in 1964, the scholars asserted: "There is great genetic diversity within all human populations. Pure races—in the sense of genetically homogeneous populations—do not exist in the human species."[1] In other words, none of us is genetically pure. Pure human races are imaginary constructs. As author Shirlee Taylor Haizlip states, we all "have roots in many gardens."[2]

Classification of people in one of the three broad, old-fashioned racial groups (Caucasoid, Negroid, and Mongoloid) is arbitrary and depends primarily on legal, social, or cultural definitions. Prior to the Civil War in America, for instance, anyone with any black ancestry was defined by law of southern states as black. In South Carolina, anyone with ⅟₃₂nd degree of black "blood" (one ancestor, five generations back) was defined as black, regardless of his or her physical appearance. Conversely, in Brazil, anyone with any degree of Caucasian appearance is regarded as white. In 1860, Louisiana's census classified Chinese as whites; in 1870, they were listed as Chinese. In 1880, children of Chinese men and non-Chinese women were classified as Chinese, but in 1900, all of these children were reclassified as blacks or whites, and only those born in China or with two Chinese parents were listed as Chinese!

America's struggle with racial classification continued into the twentieth century. In the early 1900s, the struggle was amplified by a growing obsession with the genetic "integrity" of the white race. For decades, American society had explicitly asserted the superiority of white genetic stock by classifying children of interracial lineage on the basis of their lowest-status background. This rule of "hypodescent" was articulated in a popular 1916 book, *The Passing of the Great Race*, written by Madison Grant. In Grant's words, "The cross between a white man and an Indian is an Indian; the cross between a white man and a Negro is a Negro; the cross between a white man and a Hindu is a Hindu; and the cross between any of the three European races and a Jew is a Jew."[3] Grant's work was racist, reactionary, and inflammatory. It also was, however, well received in the American (and English) social climate in the early part of the twentieth century. Thus, the complexity of racial classification was compounded by a decidedly racist agenda to save the "true American" genetic pool from contamination. This obsession with genetic integrity found its most widespread, and ultimately horrific, acceptance in Nazi Germany. It was the Nazi's unprecedented application of genetic social theory, combined with the dawn of modern genetics, that finally led to the rejection of "genetic integrity" movements in American conversation.

Today, however, racial minorities—especially blacks—generally continue to be defined by hypodescent. The absurdity of such classification is revealed in a story related by Ellis Cose. Lisa Page's father is black, and her mother is white. Before her birth in 1956, her mother was situated in the white section of a Chicago hospital, but Page's arrival ridiculously forced their removal to the "colored" section![4] How logical is it to say that a white woman can give birth to a black baby, but a black woman can't give birth to a white baby? As Marvin Harris wrote in 1964, "That a half-white should be a Negro rather than a white cannot be explained by rational argument.... The rule of hypo-descent is, therefore, an invention which we in the United States have made in order to keep biological facts from intruding into our collective racist fantasies."[5] The racist principle of classifying all the offspring of one white parent and one black parent as "black," even though they have just as much "white" in their genetic mapping, illustrates that race is a distinction without a difference.

The scholarly doubt that the concept of race has much meaning is amplified by the growing movement of people who refuse to consider themselves members of any one racial category. These mixed-race Americans refer to themselves as "multiracialists." Though unsuccessful in their recent attempt to be included as a designated racial category on the 2000 census (seven states presently include this category), multiracialists have, with their life experience, made the same point raised by many scholars: Racial groups provide a distinction without a difference.

Our attempt to make concrete the abstract concept of race is futile. Race is simply a social construction, a myth, not an immutable biological given. As psychologist Jefferson Fish contends,

> There is no biological basis for classifying race according to skin color instead of body form—or according to any other variable for that matter. All that exists is variability in what people look like— and the arbitrary and culturally specific ways different societies classify that variability. There is nothing left over that can be called race. This is why race is a myth.[6]

Today, not a single anthropology textbook even gives the notion of "race" credence. The trend is toward making distinctions—if at all—at a regional level, sometimes referred to as "microraces," rather than trying to force all of our diversity into three broad categories.

In the final analysis, race is—in and of itself—a harmless notion. As Cose points out, however, "It is the attributes and meaning we ascribe to race that make it potentially pernicious."[7] It is to those attributes and meaning that we now turn.

DEFINITION OF RACISM

In the 1937 edition of Webster's unabridged dictionary, the term *racism* was not even included. By 1949, however, it had clearly entered into the national vocabulary, probably because of the increased sensitivity resulting from the racist philosophy and policies of Nazi Germany. Early definitions of racism emphasized an assumption of inherent or biologically based differences between racial groups. Even as recently as 1981, *Webster's Third New International Dictionary of the English Language, Unabridged* emphasized the role of biological race in determining racist assumptions. The terrible consequence of ascribing racial differences—such as in intelligence—to biology is, ultimately, the corresponding conclusion that the differences are inevitable and unalterable. Individuals who believe that racial differences are caused mainly by biological factors, as opposed to environmental influences, often overestimate the magnitude and inevitability of specific differences between racial groups.

Today, most psychologists contend that emphasizing underlying biological factors in racial differences, especially as a justification for discriminatory behavior, is becoming increasingly untenable. Though Richard Herrnstein and Charles Murray's 1994 book *The Bell Curve: The Reshaping of American Life by Difference in Intelligence* drew a massive amount of media and public attention, its excessive emphasis on biological influences on intelligence did not accurately reflect a social scientific consensus. Bernie Devlin, a professor of psychiatry at the University of Pittsburgh School of Medicine, and his colleagues, for instance, recently analyzed 212 studies and concluded that genes account for only 48 percent of the factors that determine intelligence. That figure, though substantial, is so much smaller than that cited by Herrnstein and Murray that it severely undercuts the main conclusions of *The Bell Curve*.[8]

Increasingly, social scientists see behavioral race differences as stemming from a complex interaction of biology with the environment. Psychologists Carol Lynn Martin and Sandra Parker offer empirical evidence suggesting that a skepticism regarding the role of biological factors in racial differences has filtered into the public consciousness as well. Their 1995 survey of 464 undergraduate students revealed a general agreement that biology does not solely or largely determine whether racial differences can be eliminated. Rather, environmental influences are perceived as the crucial factors in the development, and elimination, of racial differences.[9]

The prevalent and abiding reliance on the term *racism* can be traced to its use in the Report of the National Advisory Commission on Civil

Disorders (1968). In describing the basic causes of the wave of race riots that swept America in the summers of 1964–1967, the Commission, appointed by President Lyndon Johnson, made the following observation: "White racism is essentially responsible for the explosive mixture which has been cumulating in our cities since the end of World War II."[10] In the contemporary lexicon, *racism* began to replace *racial prejudice* as a more inclusive term that encompassed hatred, discrimination, segregation, overt hostility, and other negative actions directed toward a racial group.

I define racism as (1) *an individual's negative prejudicial attitude or discriminatory behavior toward people of a given race* or (2) *institutional personnel, policies, practices, and structures (even if not motivated by prejudice) that subordinate people of a given race.*

There are three features to note in this definition. First, this definition tries to capture the comprehensive, systematic nature of racism. It goes beyond prejudical attitudes to include the existence of discriminatory behavior toward people of a given race. As sociologist Joe Feagin notes, this discriminatory behavior can take at least four forms: (1) verbal or physical aggression; (2) exclusion and rejection, including social ostracism; (3) avoidance; and (4) dismissal of, or insensitivity to, cultural preferences, including values, dress, and groups.[11] Implicit in the prejudicial attitudes and discriminatory behavior are potent stereotypical beliefs based on the assumption that all members of a given race are alike.

Second, racism is explicitly defined as "*negative* prejudicial attitudes and discriminatory behavior." In this sense, the term *racism* is more pejorative than the related concepts of stereotypes, prejudice, and discrimination. The negativism of the stereotypical beliefs and prejudical attitudes often includes as much emphasis on the positive attributes of one's own race as on the negative attributes of the other.

Third, similar to the discussion in Chapter 2 of individual–cultural stereotypes and individual–organizational discrimination, our definition encompasses three different varieties of racism as outlined by psychologist James Jones.[12] The first, *individual racism*, is reflected in the phrase "(a) an individual's negative prejudicial attitude or discriminatory behavior toward people of a given race." Individual racism suggests a belief in the superiority of one's own race over another, and the behavioral enactments that maintain those superior and inferior positions. Chapters 6 and 7, in which I address the changing face of racism in contemporary America, discuss several forms of individual racism.

A second variety of racism, *institutional racism*, is reflected in the second component of our definition: "(b) institutional personnel, policies, practices and structures (even if not motivated by prejudice) that subordinate people of a given race." This recognizes that institutions often advance racist objectives, either intentionally (i.e., motivated by prejudice) or unintentionally (i.e., not motivated by prejudice). This form of racism is most similar to the Feagin and Vera definition of *white racism* as the "socially organized set of attitudes, ideas, and practices that deny African-Americans and other people of color the dignity, opportunities, freedoms, and rewards that this nation offers white Americans."[13]

The conscious manipulation of institutions to perpetrate racist policies was clearly seen in the 1896 Supreme Court ruling of *Plessy v. Ferguson* upholding the constitutionality of segregation, the poll taxes, and literacy requirements for suffrage levied against African-Americans and countless other "legalized" indignities. Such institutionalized segregation was the iron rule of Birmingham, Alabama, in the 1960s. City officials closed down the municipal parks and playgrounds rather than desegregate them. The city even banned a textbook because it had black and white rabbits in it!

Institutional racism involves the *intentional, de jure*, uses and manipulation of duly constituted institutions to enforce and maintain racist policies and practices. It was the fight against institutional racism that focused the energy of the civil rights movement. In the words of Julius Lester of the Student Nonviolent Coordinating Committee (SNCC),

> The social, political, cultural and economic institutions of white America are designed to tell whites that they are superior and to tell blacks that they are inferior. Either those institutions (and the attitudes which created them) must be changed or blacks must remove themselves from them and create their own social, political, cultural and economic institutions which will give them the opportunity to live their lives feeling that they are, indeed, "somebody."[14]

In addition, institutions may play a more subtle role in perpetrating racism—a role not necessarily motivated by prejudice. For instance, the heavy reliance on standardized test scores as criteria for admission to colleges and graduate schools often discriminates against racial minority groups who have inferior training in both test taking and the content of test materials. Insurance costs for black businesses are often higher than for their white counterparts because of the areas where they operate. Seniority laws tend to benefit whites more than blacks, because blacks have not been in well-paying jobs for very long. This form of institutional racism is a by-product of certain embedded practices that operate, *de facto*, to restrict the choices, rights, and mobility of persons on a racial basis. These *consequences*, while not necessarily malevolently intended, are still harshly debilitating.

Finally, *cultural racism* represents a blend of both individual and institutional racism. Cultural racism can be defined as "the individual and institutional expression of the superiority of one race's cultural heritage over that of another race."[15] Expressions of cultural racism, on both the individual and institutional level, are manifested in the twin beliefs that (1) white western-European religion, music, philosophy, law, politics, aesthetics, economics, values, science, and medicine are inherently superior; and (2) racial minority groups have contributed little or nothing to the American expression of these cultural forms. In other words, cultural racism entails a general devaluation of culturally different values and modes of behavior. In its 1981 publication, *Indian Tribes: A Continuing Quest for Survival*, the U.S. Commission on Civil Rights described the cultural racism directed at Native Americans:

> This racism has served to justify a view not repudiated, but which lingers in the public mind, that Indians are not entitled to the same legal rights as others in this country.... At one extreme the concept of inferior status of Indians was used to justify genocide; at the other, apparently benevolent side, the attempt was to assimilate them into the dominant society. Whatever the rationale or motive, whether rooted in voluntary efforts or coercion, the common denominator has been the *belief that Indian society is an inferior lifestyle* [italics mine].[16]

Cultural racism does not have to be as overt and intentional as that found in policies regarding Native Americans. Often, cultural racism is manifest in what we choose to conveniently forget, not mention, or fail to teach. E. D. Hirsch's *Cultural Literacy: What Every American Needs to Know*, for instance, offers a long list of terms that excludes much of the history of minority groups.

The House of Blues is a chain of multidimensional restaurants that combines Delta-inspired cuisine and live music. Part of founder Isaac Tigrett's vision was to use the House of Blues to promote racial harmony through cultural education and preservation. The House of Blues Schoolhouse Program in Los Angeles fulfills this vision by providing a unique opportunity for area grade-school children to learn about African-American history and contributions. In January 1996, our study tour sat in on one of these presentations. I'll be honest. I was worried that my college students would not be challenged or enriched enough by a program directed at grade-school children. I'd forgotten, however, that my college students were products of an educational system with a selective memory regarding the contributions of various racial and ethnic groups to American life. We sat enthralled for nearly two hours, listening to an incredible musical and spoken-word presentation of the many contributions made by African-Americans that our teachers and textbooks had neglected—their important roles in the creation or patent of the baby stroller, air conditioner, refrigerator, elevator, roller coaster, and so forth. It was a great reminder that cultural racism is not only a sin of commission, but it may also be a sin of omission.

These three forms of racism are intertwined in a self-perpetuating chain. The culture creates or determines the nature of its institutions; the institutions consistently socialize generation after generation of individuals, and individuals sustain the cultural character. Jones clearly views cultural racism as the background for the development of institutional racism and, subsequently, for the evolution of individual racism resulting from socialization to racist norms by racist institutions. Whereas institutional racism may be remedied by affirmative action programs (I discuss this in more detail in Chapter 7), Jones contends that cultural racism is the most intractable, subtle, and insidious form.[17] Psychologist Dalmas Taylor exemplifies the interconnectedness of these forms when he emphasizes the cumulative effects of individuals, institutions, and cultures on racism.[18]

Power and Racism

A key issue in defining racism relates to the role of *power*. Many definitions of racism exclude the existence of minority racism by restricting the phenomenon only to white Americans or those in power. Joseph Barndt, for instance, a pastor in the Bronx in New York City, argues: "Racism is the power to enforce one's prejudices. More simply stated, racism is prejudice plus power.... Racial prejudice is transformed into racism when one racial group becomes so powerful and dominant that it is able to control another group and to enforce the controlling group's biases."[19] Similarly, a reader edited by psychologist Paula Rothenberg supports a "whites-only racism theory" by contending that "racism requires something more than anger, hatred, or prejudice; at the very least, it requires prejudice plus power."[20] Rothenberg argues that minorities may be considered "prejudiced" against whites, but their attitudes and behaviors cannot be called "racist." For James Jones, the emphasis on power in the definition of racism resonates as well. He broadly defines racism as resulting "from the transformation of race prejudice and/or ethnocentrism through the exercise of power against a racial group defined as inferior, by individuals and institutions with the intentional or unintentional support of the entire culture."[21]

In a provocative essay entitled "Can a Black Be Racist?", George Yancey, a black sociologist at the University of Wisconsin at Whitewater, agrees that whites in this country possess power over the various racial minorities. He takes issue, however, with the "whites-only racism theory." Yancey argues that whites who subscribe to this theory are trying to make partial repayment to the minorities they have cheated by giving them the right to hate in ways that are morally wrong for whites. In addition, Yancey argues, minorities are quick to accept this right to hate, because it gives them a weapon that whites do not have. The theory that racism requires power and that only whites can be racists, ironically, Yancey argues, becomes a tool of power that minorities can use to justify their own racist attitudes and practices.[22]

So, what role does "power" play in our working definition of racism? Let's look first at our definition of racism as "(1) an *individual's* negative prejudical attitude or discriminatory behavior toward people of a given race." The role of power is noticeably absent in this definition of individual racism. I have intentionally excluded it for two reasons. First, I believe that all individuals have the power, however defined, to hold racist attitudes or practice racially discriminatory behaviors. Even for rare individuals who are utterly powerless to exhibit racist behaviors, individual racism can still exist in their holding of racist attitudes.

Second, though the focus of this book is on white racism in America, a responsible definition of individual racism must leave room to acknowledge the reality of minority racism. On an individual level, the negative attitudes and behaviors directed by minorities against other minorities can constitute examples of racism. Such examples, for instance, include African-American animosities toward Korean-Americans, or Asian-American antagonism toward Mexican-American farmworkers. I agree with Harvard Law Professor Alan Dershowitz's quote from 1991: "Nor have racial minorities been entirely innocent of all such bigotry. Blacks, Hispanics, Asians and others have discriminated against each other. There is more than enough prejudice in every corner of American life to allow anyone to feel superior."[23]

In addition, minorities—as individuals—may hold negative attitudes and engage in discriminatory behaviors aimed at the majority. In a radio interview a few years ago, noted author Alex Haley cited the unprecedented rise in black racism against whites as one of our emerging racial problems. Although this is far less frequent than white racism, minority racism does rear its head in specific situations. Nick Jans, a white journalist living in Ambler, Alaska, recently wrote of his experiences as a victim of racism in Alaska:

> I know it's not politically fashionable for a Caucasian to claim discrimination at the hand of any minority, but racism is racism, no matter who it's practiced against ... We're just *naluagmiu*, second-class citizens. There are jobs for which we can't apply, huge stretches of unposted land we're not supposed to travel, meetings at which we're not welcome.... In the end, I and my *naluagmiu* neighbors endure the face of racism the way we accept the face of 40 below zero. It's part of our environment. But its sting, unlike winter's, never goes away.[24]

Let's now turn to our definition of racism as "(2) institutional personnel, policies, practices, and structures (even if not motivated by prejudice) that subordinate people of a given race." The role of power is implicit, and important, in this definition of institutional racism. The capacity of one group of people to utilize institutional practices to subordinate people of a given race clearly assumes a differential level of power between those groups. Although individual racism may characterize any of us, institutional racism—at this point in history—is limited to white America. Though the balance may someday shift, none of the racial minority groups in America presently has the collective power to dominate society in a way that whites historically have dominated, and continue to dominate, most of American society.

WHAT'S IN A NAME?

It was Iago who said in Shakespeare's *Othello*: "Who steals my purse steals trash; 'tis something nothing; 'Twas mine, 'tis his, and has been slave to thousands; But he that filches from me my good name; Robs me of that which not enriches him; And makes me poor indeed." Similarly, Alice, in Lewis Carroll's *Through the Looking Glass*, worried about entering the woods where things were nameless: "I wonder what'll become of my name when I go in? I shouldn't like to lose it at all—because they'd have to give me another, and it would almost certain to be an ugly one."

Names and language have the power to define others. As such, names and language can perpetrate racism. The term *nonwhite*, for instance, sets white as the norm or standard from which everything else can only deviate. Similarly, *racial minority* can be misleading, because people of color are a majority of the world's population. The names by which we refer to various racial or ethnic groups must convey a sense of respect and dignity. At the time of this writing, the most common terms for the four major American racial minority groups are African-American, Asian-American, Hispanic-American, and Native American. I recognize that these terms are problematic for at least two reasons.

First, these terms are imprecise and mask some tremendous within-group diversity. For instance, unlike other countries and cultures, the United States rejects the idea of a graduated spectrum between black and white. The last use of an intermediate term (i.e., *mulattoes*) was in the 1910 census. Our grossly inadequate categories of "black" and "white" ignore the complex shades of reality. Similarly, the broad category of "Asian-Americans," including Chinese, Japanese, Filipinos, Koreans, Asian Indians, Vietnamese and the Hmong, among others, represents 24 ethnic populations who speak more than 30 major languages or dialects. The grouping of "Hispanic-Americans" includes Chicanos (or Mexican-Americans, the largest of the Hispanic groups in this country), Puerto Ricans, and Cuban-Americans. Finally, the wide stamp of "Native Americans" includes more than 500 distinct tribes, each with unique cultural, genetic, and sociodemographic characteristics. Clearly, there is enough diversity within each of the four major racial minority clusters to warrant separate examinations of the experiences of each of the various subgroups.

Second, given the constancy of change in the commonly accepted terms describing various racial groups in America, it is highly likely that these terms will be supplanted by new ones as they become misused and take on offensive or racist connotations. In the early part of this century, for instance, "Negroes" and "Coloreds" were largely accepted as social, scientific and political denotations. As the connotations of those terms became offensive, they were replaced by "blacks" and "African-Americans."

Today, psychological and survey research commonly refers to African-Americans as "black" and Hispanic-Americans as "Hispanic." Though some might consider the term *black* pejorative, Gallup Polls consistently show that for the vast majority of blacks, it is a nonissue. In an August 1995 poll, for instance, 58 percent of black respondents said they had no clear preference between "African-American" and "black." At most points in the book, I use the terms *African-American* and *Hispanic-American*. When discussing psychological and survey research, I use the terms *black* and *Hispanic*. Finally, though I have chosen to use the term *Native American* throughout the book, readers should recognize that there is an increasing preference among Native American communities for the term *American Indian*.

CONCLUSION

Given this background, we are now prepared to turn our attention to a most important question: What is the state of racism in contemporary America? Are racial inequities on the decline, or are they increasing? Is life good for racial minorities in America? As we will see in Chapters 4 and 5, the great promise of America remains unattainable for a significant—and disproportionate—portion of the racial minority population.

4

The Myth
Life Is Good for Racial Minorities

Racism is as American as apple pie.
—H. RAP BROWN, Civil rights activist[1]

From its inception, America has dealt with the dilemma of reconciling
the American ideals of equality and justice with the realism of individual, institutionalized, and cultural racism. In 1903, W. E. B. DuBois
confirmed that the American dilemma was still conspicuous when he
stated, "The problem of the twentieth century is the problem of the color
line."[2] In 1944, Swedish sociologist Gunnar Myrdal provided comprehensive documentation of the "problem" posed by DuBois 40 years
earlier. The theme of Myrdal's influential book, *An American Dilemma:
The Negro Problem and Modern Democracy,* was the contradiction of America's promises of liberty and freedom, and the denial of these rights to
specific racial minority groups—most notably, African-Americans. Two
decades later, the civil rights movement had as one of its key objectives
the highlighting of this very contradiction. Noting the enduring and
profound significance of this dilemma, Myrdal remarked that it "is a
problem in the heart of the American."[3]

Over two-thirds of our current population lived during a time
when segregation and discrimination were the law: Blacks had to sit in
the back of a bus, give up their seats to whites, use different restrooms
and water fountains, and eat at different restaurants. Though the civil
rights laws of the early 1960s prohibited such overt racial exclusion,
is the American dilemma still with us? Does there remain a striking
contradiction between America's promises and the daily realities of

55

American minorities? In Myrdal's words, is the dilemma still in our hearts?

Last week, my son and I were sitting in our den. On the wall is a framed copy of his certificate of live birth. He asked me what the certificate meant. I explained that it was the legal evidence that he was born live, that he had the given name Brennan Martin Waller, and that we were his parents. He looked confused. After a moment he said, "But, Dad, the best proof that I'm Brennan Martin Waller is me!" He is absolutely right. The daily reality of his seven-year-old life is the clearest and most incontrovertible verification of his existence. The fact that he lives, breathes, eats, sleeps, and torments his younger sister and brother tells the world that he *is*.

In a similar way, the best barometer of racism is the reality of its daily consequences. The footprints of individual, institutional, and cultural racism are seen in the history of racial inequities and disparities in America. Answering Myrdal's question depends, in part, on examining the continuing existence of those inequities and disparities. If the American dilemma is still with us, we can expect to find that fact manifested in the continuing presence of restricted opportunities and advancements for racial minorities. Are America's rich economic, educational, and social promises any more attainable for the youngest generation of racial minorities than they were for its ancestors? Is life good for racial minorities in America?

TRUE CONFESSIONS

There are three kinds of lies: lies, damned lies, and statistics.
—Disraeli[4]

This chapter, and the next, relies heavily on national survey and demographic data. It is tempting to say that I'm simply letting this data speak for itself in an objective, nonbiased way. Viewing scientists as automatic data collectors, however, is a thing of the past in the philosophy of science. In truth, any interpretation of data is at least somewhat tainted by the subjectivity of the interpreter.

In this chapter and the next, I aim to debunk the myth that life is good for racial minorities in America. I clearly have a point to prove. In this chapter, I present some contrary evidence suggesting that racial inequities are declining significantly, and that life may indeed be good for minorities. It's easiest for me, however, to find and emphasize the information that proves my point. So it's very important that your eyes not glaze over while you're reading these chapters. The information must not become mind numbing. Rather, it should serve as the essential litmus test for the hypothesis that life is good for racial minorities in America.

Review the information carefully and spend time examining the tables. I don't want to claim more than the evidence allows. Though it may seem tedious, it is necessary that you check my explication and see if the data imply a different interpretation to you. You have to make sure that I don't use the data the same way a drunk uses a light pole—for support instead of illumination.

To examine the contemporary state of racial inequities in America relative to past levels, it is important that *survey* data provide us with (1) early baselines and (2) a large number of related questions that have been asked at two or more different times. An earlier baseline, or date of original questioning, gives us a broader historical perspective. A large number of questions that have been asked at two or more different times allows us to analyze the trend (positive or negative) in responses to a specific question over a period of time.

Two nationally recognized organizations provide survey data, with early baselines, that are amenable to trend analysis. The first, a leading academic survey research organization, is the National Opinion Research Center (NORC) at the University of Chicago. From 1942 to 1972, NORC data on racial attitudes were collected as part of a variety of different surveys. Nearly every year since 1972, however, NORC's General Social Survey (GSS), utilizing a representative national sample of noninstitutionalized adults aged 18 years and older, has included a standard set of items related to racial attitudes.

The second source, the Gallup Poll, is the oldest continuous commercial survey organization producing trend data. The Gallup Poll gathers information both in personal interviews and in interviews conducted by telephone. The goal is to provide representative samples of adults living in the United States. The standard size for Gallup Polls is 1,000 interviews.

The primary source of *demographic* data in the following discussion is the United States Bureau of the Census. Though best known for its count of the population and housing every 10 years, the Census Bureau also regularly publishes information on the economy and the population. The Current Population Survey (CPS) is a monthly, nationwide survey of about 50,000 households. The CPS, conducted for more than 50 years, is a significant source of data on the labor-force characteristics of the U.S. population. Estimates obtained from the CPS include employment, unemployment, earnings, hours of work, and other economic indicators.

Finally, in Chapter 3, I stated that the concept of race is fraught with problems. Nowhere is this more evident than in the shifting classifications of race in survey and demographic data. For many years, for instance, NORC and Gallup surveys simply coded race as white, black, or other. Almost all Hispanics included in those samples were classified as white. Even when categories were expanded to include white, black, and Hispanic, it still meant that many people of other races were collapsed into the category of Hispanic.

The Census Bureau has had similar struggles. Following Statistical Policy Directive Number 15 of the U.S. Office of Management and Budget, the Census Bureau collects data under the four basic racial categories of American Indian or Alaska Native, Asian or Pacific Islander, black and white, and one distinct ethnic group, Hispanic. On one census question, respondents may fill in one of the four racial categories; in another place, they may also indicate that they are Hispanic. As a result, persons in categories labeled "Hispanic" in Census Bureau data actually may be of any race. In other words, there are Hispanics in every racial group. In 1990, for example, the census located 7,687,938 residents of California who selected the Hispanic designation. Within that group, 49.5 percent chose to say that they also had a race—black, white or, in a few cases, Asians or Native Americans. The remaining 50.5 percent, however, did not complete the race question. For them, to be Hispanic was, in Andrew Hacker's words, "a sole and sufficient identity."[5]

On July 8, 1997, a presidential task force rejected a campaign to add a "multiracial" classification to the year 2000 census. They recommended retaining the four basic racial categories but allowing individuals—for the first time—to claim membership in more than one racial group when responding to the Census and other federal data solicitations. So questions of precision remain. I have been as exact as the data will allow.

Where this has not been possible, the racial classifications used in the following data must be recognized for what they are—slippery, imprecise, and overly simplistic.

LIFE IS GOOD FOR RACIAL MINORITIES IN AMERICA

On the surface, there is some evidence to support the belief that life is good for racial minorities in America. Evidence that racial inequities have declined over the past three decades will be discussed in four sections: (1) measures of racist stereotypes and attitudes, (2) media depictions of minorities, (3) perceived quality of life for minorities, and (4) status of race relations.

Measures of Racist Stereotypes and Attitudes

Valid measures of racist stereotypes and attitudes are terribly difficult to construct. This is especially true in an era in which racist responses are not socially acceptable. Most of us go to great lengths to project ourselves as open-minded, tolerant, and nonracist. I am not interested in the appearances we project to each other. Rather, I am interested in the reality of our "true" stereotypes and attitudes. What do we really think and feel about racial minorities?

In 1971, psychologists Edward Jones and Harold Sigall developed a clever, yet deceitful, way to fool people into disclosing their "true" attitudes. Students were first told that a new machine could use their physiological responses (e.g., muscular twitches) to measure their personal beliefs and feelings. Once the students were convinced, the machine was hidden, and they were asked questions about their beliefs and feelings toward African-Americans. They were also asked to guess what the machine revealed, thus revealing their personal stereotypes and attitudes. Compared to other students who had responded to a standard survey, those responding to the machine admitted more negative beliefs and feelings.[6]

This technique for measuring attitudes, known as the "bogus pipeline," stirred debate about the ethics of experimentation with humans. As a result, though offering a promising way to measure socially undesirable attitudes, the bogus pipeline method is seldom used in contemporary research. We must settle for carefully constructed surveys and interviews.

Results of many surveys by social scientists imply that white Americans are apparently becoming more liberal and egalitarian in their attitude toward racial minorities. Seventy-five percent of whites opposed segregation in 1964, by 1978, 95 percent opposed segregation. In 1958, only 37 percent of whites reported they would vote for a well-qualified black person for president if nominated by their own party; by 1989, 81 percent reported they would vote in that situation. By 1997, 93 percent of whites said they would be willing to vote for a black person as president. In 1963, 52 percent of whites objected to a family member bringing home a black friend for dinner; by 1985, that figure had decreased to 20 percent.[7] In 1989, the National Research Council's Committee on the Status of Black Americans concluded that "whites attitudes concerning black–white relations have moved appreciably toward endorsement of principles of equal treatment."[8]

Tom Smith and Paul Sheatsley of the NORC also were struck by the steady, massive growth in racial tolerance.[9] They maintain that every *de jure* and many *de facto* manifestations of racism disappeared. For example, in 1942 only 30 percent of whites thought that blacks and whites should attend the same school. By 1984, a prointegration consensus of 90 percent had emerged. By 1985, that figure had risen to 93 percent. Similar gains were observed in acceptance of a black neighbor who has the same education and income, integrated public transportation, and equal opportunities, as all moved from less than 45 percent support in the early 1940s to well over 70 percent support by 1970. (Because approval had reached such a consistently high level by the late 1960s, these questions were discontinued from NORC surveys.) By the early 1990s, more than 80 percent of whites disagreed with the statement that whites have a right to keep blacks out of their neighborhoods; by 1996, that figure had risen to 85.6 percent. In summary, the NORC series indicates that a massive and wide-ranging liberalization of black–white attitudes has swept America in the past five decades.

Similarly, a 1990 Roper survey indicated a more positive view among Americans of the country's growing Hispanic population. In 1983, 66 percent of respondents felt that Hispanics added to the welfare rolls, the 1990 survey revealed that the figure had decreased to 50 percent. In 1983, 52 percent believed that Hispanics were taking jobs away from other Americans; in 1990, that had fallen to 29 percent. In 1983, only 9 percent agreed that Hispanics had given "a new vitality and energy to the communities they have settled in"; that figure had risen to 20 percent by 1990.[10]

Finally, we continue to see significant positive changes in white American stereotypes of racial minorities. Table 4.1, for instance, reveals some positive historical changes in white American stereotypes of blacks.

Media Depictions of Minorities

Since many whites have relatively little direct, face-to-face contact with racial minorities, the mass media's depiction of minorities is likely to influence white attitudes heavily. This assertion is consistent with a 1971 Educational Testing Service report that children who had watched the racially integrated *Sesame Street* had more favorable attitudes toward minorities than did nonwatchers.[11] Psychologist G. J. Gorn later confirmed this finding in an experimental setting. Gorn reported that white, preschool children who were shown television inserts of minority children were more likely to want to play with minority children when given the chance than were children in a control group.[12]

The positive changes in the stereotypical perception of African-Americans are consistent with the fact that mass media portrayals have become more frequent and increasingly positive. A series of studies on magazine advertisements, for example, revealed that in 1949 and 1950,

Table 4.1. Percent of Subjects
Selecting Negative Traits
to Describe Blacks

Negative trait	1933	1967	1990
Superstitious	84	13	3
Lazy	75	26	4
Ignorant	38	11	5
Stupid	22	4	3
Physically dirty	17	3	0
Unreliable	12	6	4

Source: Rupert Brown, *Prejudice: Its Social Psychology* (Oxford, UK: Blackwell, 1995), p. 209.

only 0.5 percent of advertisements showed African-Americans; by 1982, that figure had risen to 9 percent. Virtually all of the African-Americans appearing in magazine advertising in 1949 and 1950 were in low-skilled labor categories; in 1980, only 14 percent of African-Americans in advertisements held low-skilled labor jobs.[13]

Journalist John J. O'Connor of *The New York Times* contends that television "is one part of the American scene in which the black presence over the last decade has become dramatically less separate and more equal."[14] Psychologist Russell Weigel and his colleagues at Amherst College concurred that the black presence in prime-time programming had increased substantially from 1978 to 1989. As compared to 1978, the proportion of time that one or more black characters were on the television screen more than doubled by 1989. The frequency of cross-racial interactions more than tripled in the same time period.[15] Increasingly, more African-Americans are being cast as "regulators" of society in positions such as teachers or law enforcers.

Sociologists Joe Feagin and Hernan Vera report that many whites credit media images of racial minorities with increasing white sensitivity to racial issues. One interviewee reports a strong sense of positive change from the media:

> I think it's changing; and it has changed tremendously within the last five years. Previous to that I think it was not very good. I think it is changing more because we are being more sensitive to ... we are getting to view more of their culture through TV and sports. And the media have made these people who once were not considered to have feelings, were inferior, now we are seeing that they have just as much pain as anyone else. They have families, and they care like anybody else. I think it's come a long way.[16]

Quality-of-Life Indicators for Minorities

Overall, the quality of life in the United States has improved for both racial minorities and whites. Three significant factors related to the quality of life are economic indicators, educational attainment, and general social well-being.

Economic Indicators

J. A. Parker, president of the Lincoln Institute of Research and Education, contends that recent economic trends offer proof of a decline in economic racial disparities. Parker states that the *median income* in 1986 for all black families ($17,600) and for black married-couple families ($26,580) increased by about 14 percent from 1982. Black families with a female householder, no husband present, had a median income of $9,300, up 9.8 percent from 1982. In the same time period, the median incomes of all Hispanic-American families and married-couple families both increased by about 9 percent. Parker favorably contrasts these relative increases with those of whites (families increased by 10.2 percent; married-couple families by 11.3 percent). In addition, Parker cites work by economics writer Warren Brookes, noting that the median income for black families rose 4.4 percent in 1986 from a year earlier, and 12.7 percent since 1981. This growth rate was almost 46 percent higher than that of white families in the same time period.[17]

Asian-Americans, often portrayed as the "model minority," stand out most clearly in their recent economic attainments. A 1988 study by the Civil Rights Commission, for example, found that the *hourly wages* of most American-born Asian men exceed those of whites with comparable levels of education and experience.[18] Though their 1995 *poverty rate* remained higher than that of whites (14.6 percent compared to 11.2 percent), the 1995 median income of Asian-Americans ($40,614) was significantly greater than that of whites ($35,766).[19]

Additional economic evidence for the decline of racial economic disparities and, some contend, the effects of reverse discrimination, is revealed in an analysis of the *absolute numbers of poor persons* in America. A 1993 U.S. Bureau of the Census report indicated that, though the poverty rate for whites was lower than that for the other racial groups, the vast majority of poor persons in America were white (66.8 percent).[20]

Finally, a tremendous *growth in black-owned businesses* suggests an increasing strength in the black economic base. In 1970, there were only 45,000 black-owned businesses in the country. Today, 621,000 businesses are black-owned, an increase of 46 percent just since 1987. The top 100 black-owned businesses have annual sales of more than $12 billion.[21]

Educational Attainment

Educational attainment, primarily due to its link with economic advancement, stands as one of the most significant quality-of-life indicators. Fifteen years ago, the average college graduate earned 50 percent more than a worker with just a high school diploma. Now college graduates earn nearly 100 percent more.[22] A 1994 survey by the U.S. Census Bureau distinctly demonstrated a significant increase in yearly earnings with corresponding increases in educational attainment. Non–high school graduates earned an average of $13,697, high school graduates, $20,248; some college/associate degree, $22,226; bachelor's degree, $37,224; advanced degrees, $56,105.[23] *Career Opportunity News* cites data revealing the cumulative, lifelong impact of educational attainment on earnings:

- Workers who fail to graduate from high school will earn an average of $608,000 during their lifetimes.
- Workers who graduate from high school will earn an average of $802,000.
- Those who have some college experience will earn $922,890.
- Workers with an Associate (two-year) degree will earn $1,062,130.
- Those with Bachelor's degrees earn an average of $1,420,850.
- Those who have earned a master's degree will average $2,142,440.
- Those with professional degrees (law, medicine, etc.) will make an average of $3,012,350.[24]

The high school diploma has become a ticket to nowhere. It is no longer enough to ensure a good job with a wage to sustain a family. Increased levels of educational attainment clearly have become a passport to the American middle class.

Evidence of the equalization of educational attainment opportunities is seen in declining annual *high school dropout* rates. The annual high school dropout rate for blacks enrolled in grades 10–12 declined from 11 percent in 1970 to 6.2 percent in 1994. The corresponding dropout rates for whites changed slightly, from 5 percent in 1970 to 4.7 percent in 1994.[25] The differential between blacks' annual high school dropout rates and those of whites has clearly closed. Consistent with the lower dropout rates, blacks have continued to make significant gains in attaining high school and college degrees.

Historically, Hispanic-Americans have evidenced the highest proportion of population with very little formal education. That proportion, however, also continues to decrease. The proportion of Hispanics 25 years old and over with less than a fifth-grade education, for instance, decreased from 15.6 percent in 1983 to 11.8 percent in 1993.[26]

Similarly, the annual high school dropout rate for Hispanics decreased slightly, from 10 percent in 1973 to 9.2 percent in 1994 (although it was only 5.4 percent in 1993).[27]

Consistent with economic indicators, educational attainment for Asian-Americans stands in marked contrast to most of the patterns evidenced for African-Americans, Hispanic-Americans, and Native Americans. In 1994, the rate of people, 25 years old and over, in all races completing four or more years of *high school* was 80.9 percent; for whites 84.9 percent. The rate for Asian-Americans was nearly identical to that of whites—84.8 percent. This general rate for Asian-Americans masks some substantial variation between specific segments of that population. In 1990, for instance, only 31 percent of Hmongs had completed four or more years of high school, compared to 88 percent of Japanese-Americans. As a whole, however, educational attainment for Asian-Americans remains high. In 1994, nearly 9 out of 10 Asian-American males and 8 out of 10 Asian-American females had at least a high school diploma.[28]

An elevated rate of Asian-Americans completing four or more years of *college* paralleled the high rate of high school completion. The percent of persons, 25 years old and over, completing four or more years of college for all races in 1994 was 22.2 percent; for whites, 24.3 percent. For Asian-Americans, however, a whopping 41.2 percent of the population, 25 years old and over, completed four years of college or more.[29] At elite universities, Asian-Americans are disproportionately represented: In 1986, Asian-Americans made up 12 percent of the freshman class at Harvard, 22 percent at MIT, and 27 percent at the University of California at Berkeley.[30] Both male and female Asian-Americans were more than 1½ times likely to hold a bachelor's degree than whites.[31]

General Social Well-Being

A sense of general social well-being is impacted by our perception of social structures. Several surveys report an increasing level of minority satisfaction with social structures. In a 1990 Roper survey, for instance, fewer than one-third of African-Americans complained of juvenile delinquency in their neighborhoods, down from half in 1978. Only 28 percent cited a lack of good local housing, down 11 percent from 1978. Fewer than 20 percent criticized treatment by police, down 10 percent from 1978. When asked to consider a situation in which a black and white person of equal intelligence and ability applied for the same job, only one-third of the respondents thought the white person would have the better chance of being hired, down from half in 1978. Forty percent of the respondents said both candidates would have an equal chance. Finally, 50 percent of all respondents surveyed in 1990 called conditions for African-Americans excellent or good, up from only 39 percent in 1978.[32]

Some surveys also suggest that considerably less than a majority of Americans—black or white—actually encounter discrimination in their daily lives. An August 1991, Gallup Poll, for instance, found that only 36 percent of black Americans reported having at some time been the victim of discrimination in employment, jobs, housing, or promotion. By contrast, 21 percent of white Americans said they had been the victims of discrimination or reverse discrimination in these same areas.[33] A 1997 Gallup Poll reported that only 30 percent of blacks said they experienced discrimination when shopping within the past 30 days, 21 percent when dining out, 21 percent at work, 15 percent with police, and only 6 percent on public transportation.[34] It should be noted, however, that it is common for people to deny, or underestimate, the extent to which they experience personal discrimination. So even while we may be aware of racial discrimination against other people, we may lack the information with which to make adequate judgments about our own experiences.

Status of Race Relations

Burns W. Roper, chairman of the Roper Organization, Inc., a public opinion firm based in New York, contends that an increased sensitivity to racial discord, heightened by the news media, exaggerates the degree to which such discord actually exists in America.[35] Writer Philip Perlmutter agrees that our perception of race relations in America has been too selective—racial injustices are sensationally reported, and improvements are too easily ignored.[36] In other words, the media have a "bad news" bias that tends to ignore good news when it appears.

Dinesh D'Souza, a policy analyst in the Reagan White House, paints a similarly optimistic picture of the present state of race relations in America:

Surveys have shown that today's generation of young people has remarkably tolerant views, including widespread acceptance of interracial dating. Even though many whites may not have lived or studied with blacks, Hispanics, or other minorities in the past, they seem generally committed to equal rights and open to building friendships and associations with people whom they know have been wronged through history.[37]

Some people find evidence for optimism in the most curious places. Edgar Beckham, a program officer at the Ford Foundation, spins the current racial tension on college campuses into an assertion that race relations have actually improved since the desegregation era:

One has to remember that until the 1960s, Duke didn't have a racial problem ... because they didn't admit any blacks to Duke. So Duke has racial tension. Hallelujah! Our society is making progress and that racial tension proves it.... Imagine thirty years ago a debate, an acrimonious debate on the Chapel Hill campus, about where to locate a black cultural center. I mean, my goodness, how far we've come. I mean in those areas, how long has it been since they were lynching blacks?[38]

Following the odd logic that increased racial tensions demonstrate that race relations have improved, Walter Williams, in an editorial in *The Washington Times*, facetiously suggests that additional evidence for the drastic decline in racism can be seen in the new causes taken by civil rights leaders:

What makes us unique is not a history of racial intolerance, but a history of having done something about it. Our Constitution, which once provided little if any protection to blacks, proved to be the strongest weapon in the civil rights struggle. That struggle is now over.... The surest sign that the civil rights struggle is over lies in the new causes taken by civil rights "leaders" who don't want to be unemployed. Jesse Jackson goes around praising tyrants like Fidel Castro and Yassar Arafat, and trying to organize farmers.[39]

CONCLUSION

We have made some significant advances in race relations in America. It is no small achievement that people are actually less openly racist than they used to be. Racial minorities, as never before in history, are a significant presence in American public life. In numbers and influence, they cannot be easily disregarded. It would, however, be foolish to feel too satisfied about these changes. As Chapter 5 will demonstrate, opportunities flourish side by side with continued disparities and discrimination. As psychologists Robert Lauer and Warren Handel express, although racial minorities now have access to an outer circle "from which they had been previously excluded (such as eating at a public restaurant) they encounter inner circles from which they are still excluded (such as equal access to economic opportunities) and with an even greater hostility than that with which they were barred from the outer circles."[40]

5

The Reality

Life Isn't Good for Racial Minorities

"You know," he said, "I've always had a theory that you ain't really Indian unless, at some point in your life, you didn't want to be Indian."

—THOMAS BUILDS-THE-FIRE[1]

Though the differences have narrowed, I contend that the experiences of racial minorities in America are still worse than those of whites. Closer analysis reveals that in relative terms (i.e., relative to whites), racial inequities still persist and are even increasing in some respects. As in Chapter 4, evidence for the sustained, even increasing, existence of racial inequities will be presented in four sections: (1) measures of racist stereotypes and attitudes, (2) media depictions of minorities, (3) perceived quality of life for minorities, and (4) status of racial relations.

MEASURES OF RACIST STEREOTYPES AND ATTITUDES

Tom W. Smith, codirector of the GSS, suggests that, despite progress in race relations since the 1950s, negative stereotypes of blacks and other racial minorities continue to be pervasive. This assertion is supported by the results of the 1990 GSS, in which respondents were asked to rate their perceptions of various racial groups on six characteristics.[2] Table 5.1 reveals the wording of the questions.

To analyze the stereotypes, Smith took the ratings that people gave whites and subtracted from it the score they gave each of the other racial groups. For example, if a person rated whites as 3 on wealth and rated

Table 5.1. Perceptions of Various Racial Groups

Now I have some questions about different groups in our society. I'm going to show you a 7-point scale on which the characteristics of people in a group can be rated. In the first statement, a score of "1" means that you think almost all of the people in that group are "rich." A score of "7" means that you think almost all of the people in the group are "poor." A score of "4" means you think that the group is not toward one end or another, and, of course, you may choose any number in between that comes closest to where you think people in the group stand.

A.   1   2   3   4   5   6   7

                  Rich   Poor

    1. Where would you rate whites in general on this scale (Wealth)?
    2. Blacks?
    3. Asian-Americans?
    4. Hispanic-Americans?
B. The second set of characteristics asks if people in the group tend to be hardworking or if they tend to be lazy (Work ethic).
C. The next set asks if people in each group tend to be violence prone or if they tend not to be violence prone (Violence).
D. Do people in these groups tends to be unintelligent or tend to be intelligent (Intelligence)?
E. Do people in these groups tend to prefer to be self-supporting or do they tend to prefer to live off welfare (Dependency)?
F. Do people in these groups tend to be patriotic or do they tend to be unpatriotic (Patriotism)?

Source: Tom W. Smith, "Ethnic Images," *GSS Topical Report No. 19* (University of Chicago: National Opinion Research Center, 1990).

blacks as 5, he calculated a black wealth difference score of -2. Thus, scores could range from $+6$ to -6. A positive score meant that a group was rated closer to the positive image (rich, hardworking, not violence-prone, intelligent, self-supporting, and patriotic), a negative score was rated closer to the negative image (poor, lazy, violence-prone, unintelligent, living off welfare, and unpatriotic).

Results reveal that, in every case, blacks, Asian-Americans, and Hispanic-Americans are evaluated more negatively than whites (see Table 5.2). Though some differences appear small, it should be noted that (1) the range of the scale itself is relatively restricted (1 to 7), and (2) whites were usually rated near the middle of the scale, thus further restricting the possibility of maximum difference scores.

Table 5.2. Stereotypical Images
of Racial Groups Compared to Whites

Characteristic	Blacks	Asians	Hispanics
Rich/poor	−1.60	−0.77	−1.64
Hardworking/lazy	−1.24	−0.19	−0.99
Violence-prone/not	−1.00	−0.15	−0.75
Unintelligent/intelligent	−0.93	−0.36	−0.96
Self-supporting/welfare	−2.08	−0.75	−1.72
Unpatriotic/patriotic	−1.03	−1.16	−1.34

Source: Tom W. Smith, "Ethnic Images," *GSS Topical Report No. 19* (University of Chicago: National Opinion Research Center, 1990).

Summing up the difference scores on all items, except the more factually grounded wealth dimension, Asian-Americans rate immediately below whites (−2.65). Hispanic-Americans (−5.70) and African-Americans (−6.29) rate considerably lower. As Smith notes, the belief that Americans are approaching a color-blind society is easily disabused by the results of this survey.

In 1992, the Anti-Defamation League gave a sample of white respondents a list of eight blatantly negative stereotypes of black Americans. Seventy-six percent of whites agreed with one or more of the negative stereotypes; 55 percent agreed with two or more; 30 percent agreed with four or more.[3] Similarly, research by psychologist Patricia Devine found that the most common theme in white undergraduates' survey responses was that blacks are aggressive, hostile, or criminal-like.[4] These results provide additional evidence that antiblack stereotypes are not a thing of the past for many white Americans.

In summary, stereotypical racial images are still commonplace in American society. These images are neither benign nor trivial. Many Americans continue to view racial minority groups in a decidedly negative light on a number of important characteristics. To what degree do these stereotypes impact racial attitudes? Smith documents the fact that negative racial stereotypes are related to corresponding negative attitudes toward civil rights and racial integration policies, social distance, and ratings of countries.[5] Though not all race-related issues are necessarily driven by racial stereotypes, these stereotypes remain important determinants of many racial attitudes.

MEDIA DEPICTIONS OF MINORITIES

Images of African-Americans in the early years of the movie and advertising industry were unrestrainedly racist. Whether it was in the form of watermelon-eating Sambos or kerchief-wearing Mammies, these depictions drew substance from, and gave strength to, the grossest stereotypes. As political scientist Michael Parenti writes,

> Whether he was called Sambo or Rastus, whether played by Blacks or black-faced Whites, the cinematic African-American male was usually a simple-minded buffoon, quick to laugh, irresponsible, lazy, fearful, and rhythmic. His female counterpart was good-natured, motherly yet sometimes sassy, able to work but complaining about it, and employed as a cook, seamstress, or servant.... From the 1920s through World War II, grotesque black-faced caricatures with huge red lips and bulging eyes appeared as cannibals and dancing darkies in animated cartoons.[6]

Such blatantly racist depictions are now seldom seen. Previously, we reviewed data suggesting that mass media portrayals of blacks and other racial minorities have become more frequent and increasingly positive. Not everyone, however, is persuaded. Following a recent lecture in Tacoma, Washington, a young black man approached me to discuss some of the issues raised by the audience. Although many in the audience asserted that media depictions of minorities had made tremendous strides, he remained impressed by the inequities revealed in the *absence* of certain media depictions. In his words "I watch *Baywatch* and I KNOW that there are Black women who look great in bikinis—I just never see them on that show!" He may be somewhat encouraged by the 1997 selection of supermodel Tyra Banks as the first African-American to be featured on the cover of the *Sports Illustrated* swimsuit issue. He is not, however, alone in his perception that the media depiction—in print, television, and news reporting—of minorities remains skewed.

Print Advertisements

Over the past several decades, we have seen a significant increase in the number of racial minorities appearing in print advertisements. On closer inspection, however, the increase may only be cosmetic—literally. Movie studios have been accused, for instance, of "lightening" the facial or body images of black actors and actresses in movie posters! Following the release of posters for the recent film *Losing Isaiah*, for example, some alleged that the image of Halle Berry, a black costar, was artificially lightened.

In addition, the majority of the dramatic proportional increases of blacks appearing in print advertisements in the 1970s were token blacks appearing with 5 to 1,000 white people, or were children interacting with a white teacher, counselor, or superior. This trend continued throughout the 1980s, with white authority figures frequently depicted as helping poor blacks or supervising black children.

Television Advertisements

Similar tokenism is found in television advertising. I previously mentioned a 1995 paper by psychologist Russell Weigel and his colleagues at Amherst College. Their study, comparing 1978 and 1989 samples of television advertising, found that the frequency of black appearance in prime-time product commercials has remained remarkably stable. In both the 1978 and 1989 samples, blacks appeared in only 19 percent of the network product commercials broadcast during prime time. Inequities in "appearance" time were even more pronounced. In 1989, whites constituted 95 percent of the appearance time in product commercials versus 9 percent for blacks. Simultaneous appearances by black and white actors comprised only 4 percent of the appearance time in 1989 commercials, with less than 2 percent of that time actually involving cross-racial interactions. As Weigel and colleagues conclude, "The black presence in prime-time product commercials has remained virtually unchanged for more than a decade."[7]

Television Programming

But what about other television programming? For centuries, children have learned about life from stories told by parents and teachers, and in churches and schools. Now, television tells the stories. Do these stories include portrayals of racial minorities in prominent and significant roles? If so, what do the roles portray? Are viewers simply given a stereotypical picture of an incredibly diverse population group?

No one would deny, for instance, that Native Americans were the

first minority to receive significant roles in television programming
(and, earlier, in movies). But what is the legacy of those roles? As psychologist Joseph Trimble of Western Washington University points out,

> The Indian becomes the infamous "bad guy"—enemy and scourge
> of the cavalry and white settlers. An Indian portrayed as a "good
> guy" is usually a "scout," for the military, the "handmaiden" of a
> white trapper or settler, or the white hero's sidekick. In such exam-
> ples, the role is always *subordinate* [italics in original] to that of the
> hero; and the character is inevitably inferior to whites, but slightly
> more sophisticated than other Indians.[8]

Sherman Alexie, a Spokane/Coeur d'Alene Native American author, often reflects on the influence of television on Native Americans.
In his novel *Reservation Blues*, he writes,

> He [Thomas Builds-the-Fire] turned on his little black-and-white
> television to watch white people live. White people owned every-
> thing: food, houses, clothes, children. Television constantly re-
> minded Thomas of all he never owned. For hours, Thomas searched
> the television for evidence of Indians, clicked the remote control
> until his hands ached.[9]

Elsewhere, Alexie describes the influence of television on his self-
perception:

> I lusted after white girls and white women more than I lusted after
> Indian girls and Indian women. Television taught me to do this.
> Television taught me that the bodies of white women were more
> beautiful than the bodies of brown women. Television taught me
> that white skin was inherently good and pure, but that brown skin
> was inherently evil and dirty. On television, white men were heroes
> and Indian men were savages. On television, Indian women were
> primitive and ugly, while white women were primitive and gor-
> geous. I learned to hate my brown skin....[10]

Surely, though, the legacy of other roles is more favorable. The
1980s ratings success of Dr. and Mrs. Heathcliff and Clair Huxtable in
The Cosby Show must have ushered in a new era of minority representation of television. Unfortunately, this is not the case. George Gerbner,
dean emeritus of the Annenberg School of Communication at the University of Pennsylvania, is America's leading researcher on the social
effects of television. While at Penn, he founded the Cultural Indicators
Project, the most sustained effort existing to analyze scientifically the

impact of television on society. Gerbner states that half of all characters on prime-time programs remain white, middle-class males in their prime. Older people, the disabled, and children are underrepresented and overvictimized. Blacks and Hispanics are killed or beaten more than their white counterparts.[11]

Earlier, I cited Weigel's study indicating that the black presence in prime-time programming had increased substantially from 1978 to 1989. As Weigel reminds us, however, even this advance is subject to qualification. The majority of black appearances continue to be confined to a few bursts of programming (e.g., situation comedies) rather than being laced through a wide variety of programming. It can be argued that the increased black presence in television programming may be due in part to pressure from black groups and may not necessarily be a reflection of genuine changes in positive regard. John J. O'Connor's optimistic 1990 statement asserting that the black presence in television is dramatically less separate and more equal was tempered a year later when he expressed some lingering doubts about the regard in which black characters are held:

> So, there are more blacks employed on television these days. But why do so many sitcom fathers ... have to be overweight and jolly when the dads in the white situation comedies can be played by ladies' men types.... And why do so many of the black young people have to appear so dimwitted and ridiculous.... Clowning around is one thing, but these fellows, played by appealing actors, seem positively retarded.[12]

Equally disconcerting is the manner in which cross-racial interactions are depicted on prime-time television. Weigel and colleagues found "that relationships between blacks and whites on television continued [from 1978 to 1989] to be portrayed as cooperative but emotionally detached, particularly when the relationships occurred outside of the work place."[13] In general, the 1989 relationships between black and white characters resembled those of the 1978 sample. In Weigel's description, "Relationships between black and white characters were less multifaceted and exhibited less intimacy, less shared decision making, and fewer romantic implications."[14] The framework of distant, emotional detachment that characterizes many cross-racial interactions in television programming is a significant reflection, and molder, of American society.

News Reporting

Adding to the damage caused by advertising and television portrayals are the ways in which racial minorities are treated by national and local television news and local daily newspapers. Joseph Trimble recalls that 54 percent of the news media photos and virtually all of the political cartoons from the 1973 occupation of Wounded Knee depicted the Native Americans in "traditional" garb (i.e., braids, feathers, and headbands). Only 26 percent portrayed the "militant" Native American (i.e., long hair, beaded, or decorated vests and "Billy Jack" hats). Only 5 percent showed the Native Americans in typical, everyday clothing (i.e., jeans, boots, etc.). As Trimble points out, white journalists present an incredibly biased characterization of the Native American—they seem unable to go beyond stock caricatures and fictitious images.[15]

The stereotypical impact of daily newspapers extends beyond political cartoons to the comic strips. Though we have no research conducted specifically on racial minorities, a recent study examining sexism affirms the possibility that even comic strips may perpetuate negative stereotypes. Camille DeBell of Texas Technological University analyzed six months worth of 13 cartoon strips in 1983 and another six months of 22 strips in 1993. In work settings, men outnumbered women four to one in 1983, and three to one in 1993. Women's occupational roles in cartoons remain primarily relegated to nurses, secretaries, or teachers. Females are often portrayed as emotionally out of control at work, whereas male bosses firmly hold the reins of authority. About 100 million readers see the comics every week and, in DeBell's words, "especially for children, they're perpetrating these awful stereotypes."[16]

A 1994 Los Angeles Times survey found that 65 percent of the respondents received most of their information about crime from the mass media.[17] Unfortunately, mass media depictions of crime have been proven to reveal, and project, a consistent racial bias. Jody Armour, a law professor at the University of Southern California, provides anecdotal support for these findings. When he first asked his students where they got their information about the 1992 Los Angeles riots, most pointed to the mass media. When he asked for their sense of the demographics of those arrested for rioting, most believed the majority were black. The students were shocked to learn that, in fact, about 60 percent of the arrests for "riot-related" violations were of Latinos; 12 percent of those arrested for looting were white.[18]

Can this pervasive racial bias be countered by the increasing prevalence of nonwhite journalists and reporters? A June 1994 Gallup Poll found that a large majority of blacks, Hispanics, and Asian-Americans agreed that using reporters from one's own ethnic group greatly improved the reporting of a story (an unfortunate conclusion, given that 51 percent of the newspapers in the country have no minority employees!).[19] Overall, blacks were the most critical of media coverage and Asian-Americans the least. Specifically, four questions revealed a black alienation from the media not shared by Hispanics or Asian-Americans:

- Only among blacks, by margins greater than two to one, did more people say that television and newspaper reporting worsens, rather than improves, relations among the different racial groups.
- Blacks reported getting upset more frequently about their coverage.
- Two-thirds of blacks said newspapers pay no attention to blacks' criticism of their coverage. Less than half of Hispanics felt so ignored. Among Asian-Americans, more people actually felt the papers respond to their criticisms (40 percent) than feel ignored (37 percent).
- Only among blacks did a majority say that they are unfairly treated in televised crime reports.[20]

The negative impact of media depiction of minorities also is seen indirectly in disparate views of prominent media figures. A June 1992 Gallup Poll, for instance, found that, when asked for opinions of prominent black Americans, whites consistently gave less favorable ratings than blacks. The same was not necessarily true, however, in blacks' evaluation of white leaders.[21]

The media further distort the public conversation about race by placing an inordinate emphasis on the exceptional. A stirring national news report of a white community reaching out to help a black church rebuild its burned-out house of worship deludes us into thinking that racial relations are strong and positive—even while we forget the racist hatred that set fire to the structure the previous Saturday night.

Sports journalists and announcers also have been accused of per-petrating, and sustaining, racial stereotypes. The most public debate of this accusation occurred in 1987, after the Boston Celtics ousted the Detroit Pistons in Game 7 of the Eastern Conference N.B.A. finals. Isiah Thomas and Dennis Rodman, black players on the Pistons, caused a furor by implying that Larry Bird, a white Celtics star, was overrated because of his race. In the ensuing days, Thomas apologized to Bird and maintained that his remarks were misunderstood by reporters, who didn't know his sense of humor. Thomas did not retract, however, his views of how white journalists and announcers perceive black athletes. Referring to those perceptions, Thomas said, "When Bird makes a play, it's due to his thinking and his work habits. It's all planned out by him. It's not the case for Blacks. All we do is run and jump. We never practice or give a thought to how we play. It's like I came dribbling out of my mother's womb."[22]

Is there any evidence that the stereotypes perpetrated by sports journalists and announcers leave an impact on how you and I view black and white athletes? Psychologist Jeff Stone and his colleagues at Princeton University recently showed undergraduates a photograph of either a black or white male basketball player. They were then asked to listen to an audiotape of a college basketball game and evaluate the specific player's athletic abilities, individual performance, and contri-bution to his team's performance. Regardless of the photograph they were shown, each student actually evaluated the same player from the same audiotaped game segment. When rating the player they perceived as black, students reported that he displayed significantly more athletic ability and played a better game. When rating the player they perceived as white, they reported that he displayed significantly more basketball-intelligence and hustle.[23] Clearly, the students applied a stereotype of black and white athletes to guide their evaluations of ability and perfor-mance.

The inordinate emphasis heaped upon our athletic heroes by the media, and advertising corporations, also is problematic. The tremen-dous attention paid black athletes, for example, stands in stark contrast to the complete neglect of blacks' achievement in other areas. As a result, argues John Hoberman, a sports historian at the University of Texas—Austin, it has created an obsession with sports among many young African-American males—often at the expense of the more traditional, if less glamorous, routes to upward mobility (e.g., education). "The whole problem here," states Hoberman in a 1997 *U.S. News & World Report* article, "is that the black middle class is rendered essentially invisible by the parade of black athletes and criminals on television."[24] Frank Deford, a sports columnist for *Newsweek*, made the same point, albeit a bit less sensitively worded:

> By now, a half century later, the most obvious legacy of Jackie Robinson is the utter African-American domination of so many of our most popular sports. But the unintended consequence of the legacy of Jackie Robinson is also the utter African-American domination of so many of our most popular sports, which may well have seduced whole generations of black boys to care only for the body, nothing for the mind.[25]

Similarly, the fact that many black athletic superstars have become commercially palatable to American consumers should not necessarily be taken as a sign of real progress in society's racial arena. As Princeton sociologist Marvin Bressler argues, the social implications of the recent color-blind marketing revolution are minimal:

> It has no implications for race relations as such. It's long been the case that whites have acknowledged the athletic excellence of blacks without giving up a whole series of prejudices in other areas. There's no contradiction there. It has always been possible in the history of race relations in this country to say that some of my best friends are X. Such people are very useful in demonstrating our own benevolence. We must be good people—we love Michael Jordan.[26]

Additionally, the media often overromanticize sports as the ideal to which society should aspire. Following Tiger Woods's victory at Augusta, Michael Wilbon, a columnist for the *Washington Post*, commented on the symbolic significance of an event that "carried us to a time when a kid of African and Asian descent can be mobbed adoringly by a predominantly white audience in Georgia on land that used to be a slave plantation, and when the uniformed sons of the Confederacy are offering a handshake instead of a billy club."[27] Mike Barnicle, a columnist for the *Boston Globe*, reminded us, however, that the rarified air of the athletic arena does not necessarily translate into a societal equivalent: "Put Tiger Woods on the 18th fairway and the crowd bows and applauds. Put him in a project or on a train at rush hour and he gets a whole different look."[28]

QUALITY-OF-LIFE INDICATORS FOR MINORITIES

Nationwide public opinion polls indicate that more than half of African-Americans believe that the quality of life for blacks has gotten worse during the past decade.[29] Jill Nelson wrote a 1997 editorial, responding to a study by the National Center for Health Statistics, that revealed the happiest Americans are, in order, white men, white women, black men—and at the bottom of the happiness barrel—black women. In trying to think of things for black women to be happy about, Nelson writes,

> Children: a blessing, right? Except that when you're a black mother your kids are most likely to be raised in poverty, to be unsuccessful in school, to be victims of violence. What about work, then? Not much hope there. Black women make less than anyone else, often for routine, unrewarding work without benefits.... What about home life? Black women are the least likely to marry, the most likely to divorce and become impoverished, and have the least chance of remarriage.... Is it any wonder we're unhappy?[30]

Nelson's grim portrayal of the quality of life for black women in America is consistent with other relevant quality-of-life indicators. An April 1992, Gallup/*Newsweek* poll of black Americans found 51 percent (compared to 36 percent the previous year) believed their quality of life had deteriorated in the past decade.[31] Substantial gaps in economic, educational, and social well-being between racial minorities and whites persist, and in some cases, are growing.

Economic Indicators

The definition of *poverty* is based on a set of money-income thresholds that vary by family size and composition and do not take into account noncash benefits. In 1993, for instance, the average poverty threshold for a family of four was $14,763.

In 1994, over one-fourth of all black (27.3 percent) and Hispanic (27.8 percent) families lived in poverty. Only 9.1 percent of white families lived in similar economic conditions. In 1989, 27 percent of Native American families lived in poverty, compared to 10 percent of all American families.[32] That disparity is not significantly different from 1970, when nearly 33 percent of Native American families lived in poverty, compared, again, to only 10 percent of all American families.[33]

The rates of persons living below the poverty level reflect similar racial disparities (see Table 5.3). Despite higher educational attainments and median income, the poverty rate for Asian-Americans remains substantially higher than that for whites.

We also should note the wide variation in poverty levels within various racial categories. In 1987, for instance, poverty rates ranged from a high of 38 percent for Puerto Rican families to a low of 14 percent for Cuban-Americans. Because Cubans only make up roughly 5 percent of the Hispanic-American population, however, their statistics have a negligible effect on those of the total group. In general, although the Hispanic-American population is only 8.9 percent of the total U.S. population, more than one in every six persons presently living in poverty in America is of Hispanic origin.[34]

Poverty rates explode in families maintained by women with no husband present. In 1993, although 12.3 percent of all families had incomes below the poverty level, 35.6 percent of families maintained by female householders with no spouse present were poor. The proportion of female-householder families in poverty was substantially higher for blacks and Hispanics than for whites. White families with a female householder, no spouse present, had a poverty rate of 29.2 percent. The corresponding rates for blacks (49.9 percent) and Hispanic-Americans (51.6 percent) were significantly higher. In 1989, 50 percent of Native American families maintained by females with no husband present

Table 5.3. Persons Below Poverty Level by Racial Categories, 1992–1995

Year	Total	Whites	Blacks	Asians	Hispanics
1995	13.8	11.2	29.3	14.6	30.3
1994	14.5	11.7	30.6	14.3	30.7
1993	15.1	12.2	33.1	15.3	30.6
1992	14.8	11.9	33.4	NA	29.6

Source: U.S. Bureau of the Census, *Statistical Abstracts of the United States: 1996* (116th ed.), Washington, D.C., 1996, Table No. 730.

were poor, compared with 31 percent of all families maintained by women with no husband present.[35]

Racial disparities in *net worth and income* also are conspicuous. A 1986 report by the U.S. Bureau of the Census stated that the median net worth (what they owned minus what they owed) of white families was $39,135, compared with $4,913 for Hispanic-Americans and $3,397 for blacks.[36] The most recent U.S. census data reveal that the average black household's net worth is still one-tenth that of whites!

Consistent with the trend in poverty rates, only Asian-Americans enjoy similar (even greater) levels of *median income* to that of whites (see Table 5.4). Even the relative economic achievements of Asian-Americans may be misleading. Many of the poorest Asian-Americans are undocumented or paid under the table at sweatshops or restaurants. In addition, because Asian-American families tend to be larger than average, with more workers per household, comparisons of per capita (rather than median) incomes reveal earnings slightly lower than the U.S. average. Though the small number of Native American households in the 1993 survey render a median-income calculation unreliable, we can note that the median family income of Native Americans in the 1990 census was $21,750, only about 62 percent of the median for all families in that year.[37]

Richard Lacayo, a writer for *Time*, argues that for all the undeniable economic progress obtained by blacks, the gap between black and white median income is still wider now than it was in the late 1970s—largely because blacks did not recover from the 1982 recession as completely as did whites.[38] In every occupation and region of the country, and at

**Table 5.4. Median Income
by Racial Categories, 1993–1995**

Year	All races	Whites	Blacks	Asians	Hispanics
1995	$34,076	$35,766	$22,393	$40,614	$22,860
1994	$33,178	$34,992	$21,623	$41,629	$24,085
1993	$32,041	$32,960	$19,532	$38,347	$22,886

Source: U.S. Bureau of the Census, Current Population Reports, Series P23-189, *Population Profile of the United States: 1995* (U.S. Goverment Printing Office, Washington, D.C., 1995); March 1996 Supplement to CPS.

every education level, the median income for blacks is lower than that for whites.

Economist David H. Swinton also asserts that the relative gaps in income and poverty rates between blacks and whites have not changed much since the early 1970s. Indeed, in some regions, income and poverty gaps have increased since 1970, whereas in the South there has been a modest improvement. Across all regions, however, the income and poverty gaps are still large, even when adjusting for differences in work experience and education.[39]

Rafael Valdivieso, president of the Hispanic Poverty Development Project, and Cary Davis offer evidence that the economic gap between Hispanic-Americans and whites also continues to widen. A survey of eight major metropolitan cities by the Hispanic Policy Development Project compared the Hispanic-American median weekly earnings as a percentage of white median weekly earnings in 1979 versus 1987.[40] Results revealed that in *each* of the eight cities, Hispanic-American median weekly earnings as a percentage of white median weekly earnings actually *decreased* substantially from 1979 to 1987. Today, Hispanic men earn 81 percent of the wages earned by white men at the same education level; Hispanic women earn less than 65 percent of the income earned by white men with the same education level.[41]

The economic disparities continue into the upper echelons of management, decision making, and education. A survey of senior-level managers in Fortune 1000 industrial and Fortune 500 service companies shows that blacks (0.6 percent), Asian-Americans (0.3 percent) and Hispanics (0.4 percent) are significantly underrepresented compared to whites (97 percent).[42] What about the larger picture? According to the Bureau of Labor Statistics, blacks—who comprise over 12 percent of the population—make up just 6.9 percent of the ranks of executives and managers.[43] Less than 10 percent of the country's largest employers have women on their boards, and racial minorities hold only 3.1 percent of total board seats. Black men with professional degrees earn only 79 percent of the salary of their white counterparts. Black professional women earn about 60 percent of the salary of white men.[44]

Evidence for economic disparities is one thing. How we explain those disparities is another. In a 1990 study, James Kluegel, a sociologist at the University of Illinois at Urbana–Champaign, examined a 12-year trend in whites' explanations for the black–white gap in economic status. On the positive side, he found a significant decline in the percentage of whites attributing economic disparities to innate inferiority of blacks (this is consistent with my assertion in Chapter 3 that the general acceptance of biologically based race differences is in decline). On the negative side, however, another form of a dispositional explanation of the black–white gap remained prevalent—the lack of motivation or willpower among poor blacks to pull themselves out of poverty. In other words, whites continued to explain the economic disparities by focusing on perceived deficiencies of blacks rather than societal or institutional barriers. Most significantly, whites' explanations for the racial economic gap influenced their attitudes toward government policies to improve the economic status of blacks.[45]

Lawrence Bobo, a sociologist at the University of California at Los Angeles, refers to such "victim blaming" as "*laissez-faire*" racism. In his words, whites still believe "that the core problem is that Blacks aren't working hard enough, or aren't sufficiently motivated.... It's [blacks'] fault, it's what the free market produced, it's what they chose to be."[46]

Rates of *unemployment* are another economic quality-of-life indicator. Though whites constitute a higher proportion of the civilian labor force, Table 5.5 reveals a consistent pattern that blacks and Hispanics remain about twice as likely as whites to be unemployed. To place Table 5.5 in perspective, the average unemployment for all Americans during the height of the Great Depression was 15 percent. Significant reductions in unemployment rates for both blacks and Hispanics appear

Table 5.5. Unemployment Rates
for Blacks, Whites, and Hispanics,
1990–1995

Year	Blacks	Whites	Hispanics
1995	10.4%	4.9%	9.3%
1994	11.5%	5.3%	9.9%
1993	13.0%	6.1%	10.8%
1992	14.2%	6.6%	11.6%
1991	12.5%	6.1%	10.0%
1990	11.4%	4.8%	8.2%

Source: U.S. Bureau of the Census, *Statistical Abstracts of the United States: 1996* (116th ed.), Washington, D.C., 1996, Table No. 644.

doubtful in the immediate future. Both tend to be overrepresented in low-paying, semiskilled jobs in economic sectors vulnerable to cyclical unemployment and in industries that are threatened with long-term decline.

Disparities between whites and minorities are even more drastic when we examine the *underemployment* rate, which includes those working part time and those making poverty wages. Sociologists Joe R. Feagin and Hernan Vera suggest that at least one-fifth of all black workers are unemployed or underemployed.[47]

Educational Attainment

Table 5.6 summarizes a four-decade trend in the percentage of persons 25 years old and over who have completed 4 years of *high school* or more. Hispanics remain much less likely than whites to complete four or more years of high school. Rates for Native Americans reveal a similar pattern of inequity. In 1980, for instance, 70.5 percent of whites had completed four or more years of high school, compared to 56 percent of Native Americans; in 1990, the rates were 79.1 percent for whites and 65.6 percent for Native Americans.

The relative discrepancies among races in completing four or more years of high school are mirrored in the percentages of those 25 years old and over completing four or more years of *college* (see Table 5.7). The significantly lower rate of Hispanics completing four or more years of college is not primarily related to a limited knowledge of English. Among Hispanic-Americans, Cubans are the most likely to speak Span-

Table 5.6. Percent of Persons 25 Years and Over Who Have Completed 4 Years of High School or More

Year	All races	White	Black	Hispanic	Asian
1995	81.7%	83.0%	73.8%	53.4%	84.8%[a]
1985	73.9%	75.5%	59.8%	47.9%	NA
1975	62.5%	64.5%	42.5%	37.9%	NA
1965	49.0%	51.3%	27.2%	NA	NA

Source: U.S. Bureau of the Census, *Statistical Abstracts of the United States: 1996* (116th ed.), Washington, D.C., 1996, Table No. 241.
[a]Based on 1994 data.

Table 5.7. Percent of Persons 25 Years and Over
Who Have Completed 4 Years of College or More

Year	All races	White	Black	Hispanic	Asian
1995	23.0%	24.0%	13.2%	9.3%	41.2%[a]
1985	19.4%	20.0%	11.1%	8.5%	NA
1975	13.9%	14.5%	6.4%	NA	NA
1965	9.4%	9.9%	4.7%	NA	NA

Source: U.S. Bureau of the Census, *Statistical Abstracts of the United States: 1996* (116th ed.), Washington, D.C., 1996, Table No. 241.
[a]Based on 1994 data.

ish at home yet have the highest educational levels (24 percent with four or more years of college in 1988).[48]

For Native Americans, rates of college educational attainments are fairly similar to those of blacks and Hispanics, depicted in Table 5.7. In 1990, only 9.4 percent of Native Americans had completed four or more years of college.[49] Robert Lorence, president of Northwest Indian College on the Lummi Reservation near Bellingham, Washington, states that 90 percent of Native American students in mainstream colleges and universities drop-out. Over the past three decades, tribal colleges (mostly two-year programs) have blossomed and evidenced tremendous success in preparing Native Americans for four-year schools. According to Lorence, 60–70 percent of students graduating from a tribal college go on to successful careers at mainstream colleges and universities.[50]

In 1993, a whopping 81.7 percent of the bachelor's degrees were awarded to whites. Only 6.7 percent were awarded to blacks, 3.9 percent to Hispanics, 4.4 percent to Asians or Pacific Islanders, 0.5 percent to American Indian or Alaskan Natives, and 2.8 percent to nonresident aliens.[51]

Even the significantly high rates of educational attainment previously discussed for Asian-Americans are subject to qualification by the fact that 6 percent of Asian-Americans have not completed elementary school—three times the rate for whites.[52] The stereotype of Asian-Americans as a "model minority" clearly conceals a wide range of educational experience. Furthermore, a study by Jayjia Hsia suggests that Asian-Americans may receive a lower return on their educational investment than whites. Using 1980 U.S. Census data, Hsia found that Asian-American faculty with stronger-than-average academic credentials and more scholarly publications still were paid less than the average for whites.[53] Similarly, the 1993 mean monthly income for white doctorates was $4,449; for black doctorates, $3,778; for Hispanic doctorates, $2,677.[54]

It can be argued that the figures in Tables 5.6 and 5.7 are overly pessimistic because of the particular sample. Respondents who are 25 years and over include a significant number of elderly people whose window of educational opportunity occurred at a time when such opportunity was severely limited for racial minorities. How different would the data appear if we restricted the sample to a younger generation?

As expected (see Tables 5.8 and 5.9), restricting the sample to those respondents 25–29 years old does raise the level of educational attainment in each year and for every category. Unfortunately, however, restricting the sample does not significantly alter the relative deprivations experienced by blacks and Hispanics.

A recent report from the Frederick D. Patterson Research Institute, part of a consortium of 40 private, historically black colleges and universities, found that the total percentage of college students who are black rose from 8.8 percent in 1984 to 10.1 percent in 1994. Although the increase is encouraging, it still remains significantly lower than the total percentage of blacks in the traditional college-age population (12.6 percent).[55]

Most disquieting, however, is the absence of significant increases

**Table 5.8. Percent of Persons
25–29 Years Old Who Have Completed
4 Years of High School or More**

Year	All races	White	Black	Hispanic
1995	86.8%	87.4%	86.5%	57.1%
1985	86.1%	86.8%	80.6%	60.9%
1975	83.1%	84.4%	71.0%	51.7%
1965	70.3%	72.8%	50.3%	NA

Source: Current Population Survey (CPS) March Demographic Files of U.S. Census Bureau, Washington, D.C., 1996.

**Table 5.9. Percent of Persons
25–29 Years Old Who Have Completed
4 Years of College or More**

Year	All races	White	Black	Hispanic
1995	24.7%	26.0%	15.3%	8.9%
1985	22.2%	23.2%	11.5%	11.1%
1975	21.9%	22.8%	10.7%	8.8%
1965	12.4%	13.0%	6.8%	NA

Source: Current Population Survey (CPS) March Demographic Files of U.S. Census Bureau, Washington, D.C., 1996.

in bachelor's, master's, or doctoral degrees awarded to black males. Deborah Carter, associate director in the Office of Minorities in Higher Education at the American Council on Education (ACE), offers this explanation: "If you look at what happens to African-American men, and it's one of the travesties in this country, the percentage in the prison population is much higher. And it is impacting the college population. Instead of educating African-American men, we lock them up."[56] Carter is right. Though blacks make up only 12–14 percent of the total population, they represent 43.2 percent of those arrested for rape, 54.7 percent for murder, and 69.3 percent for robbery. About 22 percent of the prison population in 1930, blacks were more than 45 percent of that group in 1990.[57]

Disparities in high school and college educational attainment continues in the receipt of *advanced degrees*. In 1993, 75.6 percent of master's degrees went to whites, 5.4 percent to blacks, 2.9 percent to Hispanics, 3.8 percent to Asian or Pacific Islanders, 0.4 percent to American Indian or Alaskan Natives, and 12 percent to nonresident aliens. In that same year, 63.5 percent of doctoral degrees were awarded to whites, 3.2 percent to blacks, 2 percent to Hispanics, 3.8 percent to Asian or Pacific Islanders, 0.3 percent to American Indian or Alaskan Natives, and 27.3 percent to nonresident aliens.[58]

The presence of foreign-born subsets in a given minority population may artificially underestimate statistics of educational attainment and median income. In truth, however, statistics for native-born minorities reveal similar trends and no significant alterations of relative disparity.

Finally class, not race, may be the major contemporary determinant of educational opportunity and achievement. In 1985, however, SAT scores for blacks coming from families earning more than $50,000 per year were still lower than SAT scores of whites coming from families earning less than $6,000 per year.[59] That discrepancy continued in 1990 as SAT scores for blacks coming from families earning more than $70,000 per year remained lower than SAT scores of whites coming from families earning $10,000–20,000 per year.[60] SAT results from 1997 reveal that, across all income groups, test scores by black and Hispanic students remain stubbornly below those of whites. Even after taking class into account, relative educational opportunity and achievement continue to be unevenly distributed across racial groups in America. In the words of the president of the College Board, Donald Stewart, the risk of increased reliance on standardized tests is "simply, the resegregation of higher education."[61]

Although involvement in college-level instruction has increased for each of the American racial minorities, the *racial climate in higher education* remains chilly and, occasionally, outright hostile. As Ellis Cose describes, in recent years, college campuses have become almost synonymous with racial tension.[62] It is not simply that minority students are showing strength and self-confidence by filing more reports and demanding changes. The dramatic increases in intolerance across colleges and universities are disturbing reflections of the discrimination still experienced by racial minorities in America. The University of Massachusetts at Amherst racial explosion following the 1986 World Series between the Boston Red Sox and the New York Mets was the most emblematic recent outbreak, but by no means the only one. According to the National Education Association's 1992 Almanac of Higher Education, 36 percent of institutions reported incidents of intolerance related to race, gender, or sexual preference in the previous year; for doctoral universities, that figure rose to 74 percent.[63] As John Brooks Slaughter wrote in the *Los Angeles Times*:

> Racism and bigotry are back on campus with a vengeance. We can ask any of those black students who were chased and beaten at the University of Massachusetts at Amherst, who were taunted with defamatory posters at Penn State and Stanford, who were subjected to racist jokes on the University of Michigan radio station.... Or ask the Latino students at UCLA about their reaction to the film *Animal Attraction*, which was produced by a UCLA graduate student with

the support of many of his faculty members and portrayed Mexican-Americans in a negative light.[64]

Katherine McClelland and Carol Auster also maintain that specific incidents of racial confrontation continue to rise on college campuses.[65] Supporting this claim, Arlene Smith McCormack compared the results of a 1992 survey study of discrimination against minority undergraduates with a similar study completed in 1988 and concluded that discrimination against black and Hispanic students actually increased over that four-year period. In the 1992 survey, approximately one in every four minority students reported experiencing a personal incident of discrimination at the university; for black and Hispanic students, the rate increased to approximately one in every three students. The most common source of discriminatory incidents remained "other students," followed by incidents involving "faculty" and "campus police." McCormack also notes that the nature of discrimination on college campuses has become more blatant over the four-year period, characterized less by ostracism than by verbal harassment and differential treatment.[66]

In addition, there remains a strong sense of exclusion among racial minorities on our campuses. In a survey of students at 390 colleges and universities, 53 percent of African-Americans felt excluded from social activities as did 24 percent of Asian-Americans, 16 percent of Hispanic-Americans, and only 6 percent of whites.[67] Joined with this exclusion is a scarcity of meaningful interracial contact. Ellis Cose provides some important insights into the hesitations of both whites and nonwhites to engage in such interaction. Cose quotes a black female student at Duke University: "I have lessened my efforts to reach out to others … and I began to be aware of the burden that minorities here have—that is, we have to bear the brunt for establishing positive race relations.… It seems as though the white students feel we have to be responsible for reaching out to them."[68] The burden of minority students is complemented by white students' fear of engaging in interaction that includes the threat of rejection or hostility. Rather than take that risk, many whites choose not to engage. Again, Cose quotes Susan Wasiolek, Assistant Vice-President for Student Affairs at Duke:

> I think one of the greatest fears that I have and that I think I share with a number of people is being labeled or called a racist …

because that's such an ugly word.... It's almost like ... a man being accused of molesting his child or battering his wife. It's one of those accusations or allegations that is so very, very difficult to overcome.[69]

The increased incidence of racial discrimination and exclusion in institutions of higher education, long considered society's vanguards of tolerance and enlightenment, offers a distasteful recognition that racism remains deeply ingrained in American society. It reminds us that the common image of the poorly educated racist is misleading. In institutions meant to suspend ignorance and intolerance, racism remains an integral part of human misrelations. What are the legacies of these experiences for our future leaders? What are they learning about the promise of racial reconciliation? A June 1997 Gallup Poll gave us a disturbing answer. A whopping 76 percent of black college graduates said race relations would always be troublesome for this country; only 56 percent of blacks without a college degree felt that way! As Cose concludes,

Though they [universities] may strive for ivory-tower values, they ultimately reflect the values of the society that spawned them.... Yet, if students have such a difficult time seeing beyond race on college campuses, it seems unlikely they will suddenly become color-blind when they leave—when there is generally less incentive and there are fewer opportunities to forge relationships (or even just to communicate) across racial lines.[70]

General Social Well-Being

One nationwide survey revealed that only 16 percent of blacks (compared to 44 percent of whites) felt that "most people can be trusted."[71] There is even compelling evidence that the mistrust felt by racial minorities for many social structures is deep enough to have taken on a "conspiratorial" tone. Forty percent of blacks, for instance, believe that at least one of the social problems (e.g., unemployment, teen pregnancy, or lack of black-owned businesses, etc.) now afflicting the black community is the result of a racist conspiracy.[72] In a 1990 survey, 64 percent of blacks believed that the government was deliberately encouraging drug use among black people.[73] Thirty-two percent believed that there might be some truth in the view that AIDS had been purposely created by scientists to infect black people. A 1997 survey by the Institute of Minority Health research found that 36 percent of blacks thought it "very likely" they would be used as guinea pigs in medical research. Only 16 percent of whites had the same concern.[74]

Given the reality of the Tuskegee experiments, for which our government only formally apologized in April 1997 (25 years after the experiments ended), such concerns cannot be dismissed as paranoia. They are legitimate attempts to make sense of the fact that bad things happen to a greater number of blacks in America, and with greater frequency than to whites. As summarized by historian Harvard Sitkoff of the University of New Hampshire:

> An increasing minority of African-Americans believed that whites "want to see us dead," and that the mushrooming growth of lethal weapons, AIDS, and crack cocaine in the black inner-city were part of a racist plot, "the plan" of the establishment.... Many more African-Americans assumed that the intertwined problems of black poverty, widespread unemployment, crime, failing schools, and family deterioration were the result of deliberate white disregard, of racist neglect; that if whites had been plagued by the same ills, the society would have acted decisively to cure the malady.[75]

While the majority of blacks and most whites remain relatively hesitant to agree with a distinct "whites to blame" or a conspiratorial scenario, they differ drastically in their rate of agreement that both races are to blame. In a June 1992 Gallup Poll, 30 percent of blacks opted for shared blame, whereas only 18 percent of whites said both races share the blame for racial problems. As expected, whites were much more likely (54 percent) to lay the blame solely on blacks than were blacks (32 percent).[76]

STATUS OF RACE RELATIONS

The story is told of a Greenville, South Carolina, farmer who was experiencing difficulties with a utility pole placed in an unfortunate location near the end of his driveway. After several visitors had run into the pole attempting to back out of the driveway, the farmer finally called the utility service and asked if they would relocate the pole. Several days later, the utility service commissioner visited the farm, took painstaking measurements and concluded that, in fact, the utility pole was perfectly placed. As he backed out of the driveway, waving dismissively to the disgruntled farmer, he crashed into the pole! The next day, utility crews relocated the pole.

Sometimes, similar to the utility service commissioner, we don't know there's a problem until we crash into it. Such is the case with whites' views of the status of race relations. Leonard Pitts, Jr., a columnist for the *Miami Herald*, states, "So many white Americans live in denial that it might as well be the 51st state. They are fond of describing race relations as either hunky or dory, except that black people won't stop caterwauling about imagined injustices. Yet racial animus is worse than it's been in many years."[77]

Unfortunately, much of the research bears out Pitts's comments. A February 1993 Gallup Poll revealed that nearly everyone (98 percent) agreed that our society does not treat all races equally.[78] More than half of the black respondents in a 1989 ABC News survey agreed that black workers generally faced discrimination when seeking skilled jobs. Sixty-one percent gave a similar reply regarding managerial jobs.[79]

Several surveys confirm the strained nature of race relations in America today. As expected, racial minorities view the nature of race relations in America very differently than do whites. A June 1992 Gallup Poll, for instance, found that a majority (51 percent) of blacks agreed that our nation is moving toward two societies, one black, one white— separate and unequal; only 25 percent of whites accepted this view.[80]

An October 1993 Gallup Poll found similar, disparate reactions to the continuing existence of discrimination. Seventy percent of whites believed that a black person now has as good a chance as white to be hired for any job; only 30 percent of blacks agreed; 77 percent of whites believed that blacks overestimate the amount of discrimination in America; only 55 percent of blacks agreed; and 62 percent of whites do not believe new civil rights legislation is necessary to reduce discrimination; only 26 percent of blacks agreed with this view.[81]

Mistrust

The strained nature of race relations in America also is revealed in a persistent level of mistrust between the races. A 1995 Gallup Poll found that 57 percent of whites said that many or almost all blacks disliked whites. Among blacks, 35 percent agreed that many blacks dislike whites. This consistent level of racial mistrust was also found when asking how many whites dislike blacks. Thirty-six percent of whites said that many whites disliked blacks, whereas 35 percent of blacks agreed that many whites disliked them.[82] Though these numbers are not significantly different from previous results in 1992, they do illustrate that a substantial number of Americans believe that racial tensions exist in this country.

These tensions also are manifested in fear. Nearly one-third (31 percent) of whites, for instance, admit to having been afraid of someone of another race.[83] A *U.S. News & World Report* article contends that at one out of three universities, most whites have a physical fear of black students. At less than 1 in 10 universities, however, do blacks report a physical fear of whites.[84]

White Indifference

Adding to the sense of mistrust is the perception that whites are, at best, indifferent to the plight of blacks. In an April 1992 Gallup/ *Newsweek* poll, even in the awkward situation of expressing these views to a white interviewer, 20 percent of blacks said whites want to keep blacks down, and 36 percent said whites do not care much one way or the other, only 28 percent believed that whites want to see blacks get a better break.[85] A June 1992 Gallup Poll found that whites are much less willing to accept the blame; only 9 percent said that whites want to keep blacks down; 27 percent said whites do not care.[86] A 1994 Harris Poll found that 7 in 10 minorities felt that whites were completely insensitive to their aspirations.[87]

The Future

The mistrust and indifference do not lead to very optimistic predictions about the future. A 1995 Gallup Poll revealed that slightly more than half of blacks and whites believed that relations between the races will "always" be a problem for America. Only about 4 in 10 are optimistic that a solution will eventually be worked out.[88] Astoundingly, these figures are significantly higher, and more pessimistic, than responses during the civil rights era more than three decades ago![89]

Neighborhoods

The tenuous status of race relations in America also is mirrored in the composition of our neighborhoods. Lacayo cites a study by two University of Chicago researchers showing that middle-class blacks are significantly less likely than Hispanics or Asian-Americans to live among whites—so much so that an Asian-American or Hispanic with a third-grade education is more likely to live in an integrated neighborhood than a black with a Ph.D.![90] The latest census data reveal that about 30 percent of blacks live in almost complete racial isolation—only a small improvement from the "hypersegregation" of 34 percent of the black population a decade ago.[91]

A 1994 Gallup Poll reveals that blacks continue to desire integrated neighborhoods more than do whites. When asked to describe the racial mix of their own neighborhoods, 74 percent of whites say theirs are all or mostly white. Seventy-one percent of them think the level of integration in their communities is "about right"; only 17 percent wish to see them become more integrated. In comparison, two-thirds of blacks describe the composition of their neighborhoods as 50 percent or more black; 58 percent of them call the level of integration about right; and 40 percent would like to see their communities become more integrated.[92]

Schools

Unfortunately, the reality of continuing neighborhood segregation has led to a return of racial segregation to America's public schools. Researchers at the Harvard Graduate School of Education found that between 1991 and 1994, there was the largest backward movement toward segregation since the 1954 Supreme Court decision declaring school segregation laws unconstitutional.[93] Gary Orfield, a professor of education and social policy at Harvard, estimates that two-thirds of the nation's black children attend schools in which most of their classmates are also members of racial minority groups.[94] Elsewhere, Orfield cites data indicating that Hispanics, now the most racially isolated group, are more likely to attend segregated schools than blacks.[95] Schools have become resegregated as the nonwhite population becomes increasingly concentrated in metropolitan areas—a trend likely to continue.

Resegregation, perpetuated by choice and not mandated by law, is also evident across college and university campuses. At various campuses, racial minorities have their own segregated dorms, student centers, tutorial programs, yearbooks, pages in college newspapers, dances, sororities, and fraternities. Large institutions, where self-segregation is greatest, are more likely than other schools to have had racial incidents. Editorialist John Leo reports that many schools have freshman orientation programs exclusively for minorities, and some even hold separate graduation receptions. As a result, at many universities, it is possible for racial minorities and white students to go through four or more years of enrollment without having any significant contact with each other.[96]

Hate Crimes and Groups

The strain of racial tensions in America boils over in the growing number of "hate crimes"—slurs, vandalism, physical violence—directed against racial minorities. Klanwatch, a project of the Southern Poverty Law Center, documented 126 bias-motivated murders between 1990 and 1994, as well as thousands of assaults, cross burnings, and acts of arson and intimidation.[97] The Federal Bureau of Investigation (FBI) reported almost 8,000 hate crimes in 1995, an increase of 42 percent since 1991.[98] Many other hate crimes undoubtedly went unreported.

Since the early 1990s, black churches in the South have been subjected to several well-publicized attacks. According to the Center for Democratic Renewal in Atlanta, nearly 80 historically black churches have been firebombed, burned, or vandalized since 1990.[99] Most attacks occurred in the middle of the night in poor, rural areas, destroying a joyful refuge and assaulting the soul of the black community.

Ku Klux Klan, neo-Nazi, and Skinhead groups operate in every state of the union. In 1994, there were more than 300 hate groups scattered throughout America. The 1995 linking of three U.S. Army soldiers, accused of harboring Nazi flags and White supremacist literature, with the killing of a black couple in Fayetteville, North Carolina, reminds us that these hate groups permeate all areas of American society. Perhaps most dismaying are the substantial, and increasing, numbers of young people exhibiting racial intolerance. In a 1992 survey of high school students, for instance, 30 percent said they would actively participate in racist incidents, and 17 percent said they would silently support them.[100]

As Hugh Price, president of the National Urban League, states, "The flames of bigotry and intolerance are soaring higher than they have in a generation."[101] Recognizing the urgency, President Clinton has convened a fall 1998 conference of law enforcement officials, members of Congress, and hate crime victims in order to explore ways of dealing with intolerance.

CONCLUSION

Chapter 4 began with a discussion of Myrdal's American dilemma— the dilemma of reconciling the espoused American ideals of equality and justice with the paradoxical realism of individual, institutionalized, and cultural racism. Does the evidence suggest that there remains a striking contradiction between America's promises and the daily realities of American minorities? Is America still struggling for its soul? Is life good for racial minorities?

A black graduate student interviewed by sociologist Joe Feagin commented: "I'd just like to see not only an acknowledgement of differences, but also an acknowledgement that we are still not equal, and that it will take more than lip service to achieve equality."[102] The survey and demographic data reviewed in this chapter clearly acknowledge the fact that whites and racial minorities are not equal. Although, in some cases, racial minorities are better off in absolute terms now than they have been in previous years, racial disparities still exist relative to other groups—especially relative to whites. To accept the myth that life is good for racial minorities is to ignore a wealth of empirical evidence suggesting otherwise. Racist stereotypes and attitudes remain prevalent and influential. Depictions of minorities, both in entertainment and news media, still subtly reinforce many of our dominant images of blacks, Asian-Americans, Hispanics, and Native Americans. Quality-of-life indicators, whether economic, educational, or social, betray the clear and sustained effects of racism in America. The present status of race relations shows no noticeable improvement since the civil rights era of the 1960s. There appears to be little reason for optimism regarding future hopes of racial reconciliation in America.

In addition to this discouraging evidence of the overt racial discrimination and inequities still prevalent in our society, the increasing recognition of more subtle, covert forms of racism adds to the American dilemma and challenges the myth that racism is declining. The changing face of racism in America vastly complicates the ways in which our society must continue to deal with the beast of racism. More subtle variants of individual racism, equally—perhaps even more—insidious, have permeated American society. Chapters 6 and 7 discuss these new faces of racism and their implications for understanding racism-is-declining arguments.

6

The Changing Face
of Racism in America

At its coarsest and most unsophisticated, racism uses violence to enforce explicit laws to subjugate and control.... The evil of such blatant racism is obvious. Racism also assumes sophisticated forms that depend less on brute force than on psychological methods that dissipate resistance. In such forms, racism may in fact create the illusion that it does not exist and therefore be far more difficult to detect and eliminate. Yet its power to oppress is no less than that of open and blatant racism. Iron fist or velvet glove, the results are the same.

—JOSEPH BARNDT, Bronx pastor[1]

During the 1996 study tour, we had the opportunity to spend some time with an African-American father and his 22-year-old son in Atlanta, Georgia. Throughout our conversation, we often returned to their personal experiences with racism in America. The father, an outspoken 65-year-old retired auto mechanic, spoke of the violent and divided South of the 1940s, 1950s, and 1960s. His experiences as a victim of racism reflected the unbelievable reality of living as a black in the American South during those decades: cross burnings, assaults, and racial epithets; eating at the back door of cafes; sitting in the back of buses; drinking at separate water fountains; and being educated with second-hand books and materials cast off from the local white schools. His cousin lived in the same small Mississippi town where Emmett Till was murdered in 1955 for "wolf whistling" at a white woman. For this father, being black in America was, literally, a daily life-and-death struggle.

His son was a recent engineering graduate of Georgia Tech University. His experiences as a victim of racism were markedly different. The assaults, legalized segregation, and overt racism, though a piece of his legacy through his father's history, were not part of this young man's experiences. Rather, he spoke of more subtle forms of racism: white clerks "tailing" him in a local music store; restaurant managers checking repeatedly on the satisfaction of other patrons while ignoring him and his dining partner; people expressing surprise at how "articulate" and "well-spoken" he was; and white women who, when passing by him on a downtown Atlanta sidewalk, would shift their purses to the opposite side of their bodies.

It became clear that the father was becoming increasingly agitated at his son's descriptions of racism. Finally, the father blurted out, "That stuff you're talking about ain't nothing! *Real* racism is what I went through! Your stuff is just a trifling—just an inconvenience!" In the awkward moments that followed, it became apparent that father and son had endured this particular conversation more than once. The son admitted the difficulty of discussing his experiences with his father, or other blacks from that generation, because the faces of racism are so manifestly different. As the son pointed out, however, the consequences are remarkably similar. Both father and son believe that racism did— and still does—negatively impact their self-esteem, limit employment and housing opportunities, decrease lifetime financial earnings, lead to increased levels of stress and related health problems, and make bitterness and resentment a constant companion. As impossible as it is for them to find common ground in the faces of racism they have endured, they easily discover such ground in the debilitating consequences of those different embodiments of racism.

WHAT IS "REAL" RACISM?

Our inability to recognize the changing face of racism in America lies at the heart of our second myth: that racism is declining. Still, today, the blatant face of racism is most often considered the *only* face of racism by the media and public. The timing of Tiger Woods's victory in the 1997 Master's golf tournament, coupled with the fiftieth anniversary of Jackie Robinson's entry into major-league baseball, invited many comparisons between the two trailblazers. One person who resisted the comparisons, however, was columnist Bob Ryan of the *Boston Globe*.

Ryan, in an April 15, 1977, editorial, described Robinson as a "true" pioneer and a "true" hero, because his achievements came during a time of blatant racism. In Ryan's opinion, Woods does not merit the comparisons with Jackie Robinson because the prejudice, if any, endured by Woods pales in comparison to that facing Robinson in 1947.

On one hand, Ryan is correct. When Robinson broke the professional baseball color line, there was no civil rights movement; it was a year before President Truman desegregated the armed services; the *Brown v. Board of Education* decision was still seven years away; it would be eight years before Rosa Parks's courageous decision to remain unmoved; Martin Luther King, Jr. had not even graduated from Morehouse College; it was 10 years before President Eisenhower found it necessary to send federal troops to Little Rock to desegregate a local high school; 16 years before Governor George Wallace pledged to "stand in the schoolhouse door" to preserve segregation in Alabama. Robinson opened the door for generations of racial minorities when he began the process of restoring the conscience America had routinely ignored.

It does not minimize Robinson's accomplishments, however, to acknowledge the pain of racism and exclusion experienced by Tiger Woods. His singular achievement at Augusta occurred on a course that was still successfully opposing the mere appearance of black golfers a full decade after the passage of the Civil Rights Act of 1964. The Augusta National Golf Club did not even accept its first black member until 1991; it still has only two black members today. Yes, Tiger Woods was born into a better world than that of Robinson. It must be recognized, however, that the face of racism experienced by Woods—though less direct and more subtle than that experienced by Robinson and other early pioneers—results in debilitating consequences and obstacles that are just as legitimate.

The general public is led to similarly troubling conclusions regarding the relative impotence of contemporary racism. The endless string of nondescript television talk shows continues to showcase blatant racism for its entertainment value ("On today's show, people who are proud to be racist!"). My local newspaper recently ran a diversity writing contest in which readers were to recount stories of racial and ethnic discrimination. The winning entries did not deal with the more subtle expressions of racism. Rather, as you might guess, they recalled particularly odious and dramatic cases of segregated lunch counters and hotels. They were stories illustrating what the father in Atlanta would call "real" racism.

Such incidents, when they occur today, are sensational and headline grabbing. To believe these exemplify the *only* face of racism, however, is shortsighted and dangerous. A recent tragedy reiterates the importance of acknowledging the different faces of racism in America. On March 21, 1997, a 13-year-old black child, Lenard Clark, was riding his bike through the Bridgeport section of Chicago. Three older, white teens, vowing to "take care of the niggers in the neighborhood," attacked Clark and beat him so fiercely that he went into a coma, from which he only began to emerge one week later. This violent example of blatant racism galvanized the American public and prompted numerous calls for task forces and community leadership to address race relations. In the midst of this, however, President Clinton reminded us that

> racism in America is not confined to acts of physical violence. Every day, African-Americans and other minorities are forced to endure quiet acts of racism—bigoted remarks, housing and job discrimination. Even many people who think they are not being racist still hold to negative stereotypes, and sometimes act on them. These acts may not harm the body, but when a mother and her child go to the grocery store and are followed around by a suspicious clerk, it does violence to their souls.[2]

Such "everyday racism" does not minimize violent racial incidents such as those involving Lenard Clark. As discussed at the end of Chapter 5, crimes and violence spurred by hatred remain a serious problem in all segments of American society. We must understand, however, that a focus on overt persecution as the only legitimate and significant face of contemporary racism distracts us from the emergence of other, subtle manifestations of the "quiet acts" of racism.

THE DISTRACTION OF BLATANT RACISM

Often, white Americans welcome the distraction of blatant racism. By only focusing on the assaults and other egregious racial incidents, we can affirm our belief in the myth that racism in America is declining.

After all, the mere fact that a race-related assault makes a mammoth media splash—including being part of a presidential address—indicates the rarity with which racism rears its ugly head in contemporary America.

We also welcome the distraction of blatant racism because it gives us a chance to salve our conscience by responding with righteous indignation. Recently, my community was shaken by the publication of a hate letter delivered in response to an opinion column in our local newspaper. In the column, a black woman confessed to the psychological loneliness and isolation she felt as a minority in this community. The next day, she received the following letter:

> You niggers really piss me off. Bitch & complain is all you worthless assholes are good for. Why don't you maintain your ethnic authenticity by going back to Africa & swing with the baboons. Spokane was a nice place till you niggers started moving here esp. the Crips & Bloods from Compton Ca. Black is not beautiful—its worthless.[3]

Our community was incited to action. The Spokane Task Force on Race Relations made an immediate response. Dozens of businesses and institutions repledged their allegiance to Spokane's Commitment to Action for Racial Equity (CARE). We planned, and successfully carried out, a spring community congress on race relations. I was proud of our decisive, quick, and significant responses.

In the back of my mind, though, I wonder if we have simply bought ourselves some short-term "good conscience credits." We've done the right thing in a horrible situation. Will we be tempted to pretend that racism is no longer an issue in our community? Do our decisive, quick, and significant responses mean that we don't have to address this issue again for 5 or 10 years? Do we run the danger of allowing our "good conscience credits" to distract us from the reality of the daily, not so sensational burdens of living as a racial minority in this community? Can we somehow, in the midst of our response to a crisis of old-fashioned racism, open new lines of communication for addressing the more subtle, long-term problems of "everyday" racism? Or have we redeemed our conscience with the "quick fix" of some strong responses and a race-relations summit?

Columnist Leonard Pitts, Jr. wonders if the recent bill proposing a national apology for slavery might have similar redemptive consequences for the American conscience. The bill, forwarded by representative Tony Hall, a white democrat from Ohio, would correct a glaring omission. It might also, however, lead to "a post-apology scenario in which whites declare race matters resolved and become unreceptive to substantive measures to improve the lot of blacks." Pitts adds, "I'm still trying to figure out how, exactly, that scenario differs from the one we already face."[4]

There is yet a third way that blatant racism comfortingly distracts us from the "quiet acts" of everyday racism, namely, that we convince ourselves that discussions of racism in America are really discussions about hate groups in America. When I lecture, audiences invariably ask about hate groups as if they are synonymous with the general issue of racism in America. They do not recognize these groups as the extreme end of a continuum of racism along which most of them can be placed as well. If we pretend that hate groups are the only problem, we avoid facing the reality that it is mostly nice, nonhating people who perpetrate racism in America. I do not mean to minimize the emerging threat imposed by such groups. As Morris Dees and James Corcoran have recently argued in *Gathering Storm: America's Militia Threat*, the internal existence of hate groups potentially poses a far greater danger to the peace of America than any foreign enemy.[5] We cannot, however, allow a national dialogue about racism in America to be relegated to a fringe element in our society.

Why do we so easily allow ourselves to be distracted from the "quiet acts" of racism? Why are we only stirred to action by blatant racism? Why is it so tempting for us to isolate the problem of racism to extremist hate groups? First, I would argue that the distraction of blatant racism puts an *emotional and psychological distance* between us and the real problem. There is something oddly comforting about blatant racism. It reminds us that a problem still exists, but, at the same time, it reminds us of our own relative goodness. Be honest—when you read the hateful response to the opinion column, one of your first thoughts was likely "Spokane is a terrible place! I'm glad my community doesn't have rednecks like that!" You took a bizarre comfort in how our example of blatant racism contrasted with your rose-colored perception of your community. By focusing on the evil in someone else, we can avoid facing our own stereotypical beliefs, prejudicial attitudes, and discriminatory behaviors.

Sociologists Joe Feagin and Hernan Vera recall a lengthy interview with a white woman during which she referred to blacks as "apes," criticized affirmative action, and expressed a strong preference for racially segregated neighborhoods. For all of that, however, she still did not have to see herself as a racist, because she could draw a comforting distance between herself and "real" racists: "I don't consider myself racist. I, when I think of the word racist, I think of the KKK, people in white robes burning black people on crosses and stuff, or I think of the skinheads or some exaggerated form of racism."[6]

Second, the distraction of blatant racism allows us to *escape our responsibility* for addressing the "quiet acts" of everyday racism. When we relegate an evil thing to only its most blatant manifestation, we don't have to be responsible for it. Perhaps our most useful defense mechanism in thinking about race is our inclination to confine the discussion to blatant racism. By doing so, we dodge the responsibility of dealing with everyday racism in our communities.

How do we respond to the myth that racism in America is declining? The previous chapter documented some of the continuing racial inequities in America. The "footprints" of these racial inequities reveal the continued presence of an intruder. In earlier decades, this intruder was overt, conspicuous, and flagrant. Today, however, the intruder is more covert, stealthy, and pernicious. Because the intruder has adopted a new strategy, however, does not mean that the consequences of the intrusion are any less severe or crippling. This more subtle form of racism, while not sensational and headline grabbing takes a substantial toll on racial minorities in America.

Racism is alive and well in America. To understand the extent to which racism survives in America, and to combat the myth that racism is declining, we must distinguish between blatant and "quiet acts" of everyday racism; or what psychologists have termed "old-fashioned" and "modern" racism.

OLD-FASHIONED RACISM

At one time, many people felt no qualms about expressing openly racist beliefs. They would state that they were against social desegregation, that they viewed members of racial minority groups as inferior in various ways (e.g., intelligence, ambition, honesty), and that they would consider moving away if minority members took up residence in their neighborhoods. This is the more traditional, blatant, form of racism.

Such blatant racists have been described under many names—dominative, true, or substantive racists. The common thread underlying all of the descriptions, however, is that the bigoted beliefs of these persons represent the open flame of racial hatred. Psychologists have called such bigoted beliefs "old-fashioned racism." Old-fashioned racism subsumes three sets of beliefs. First is a belief in white racial superiority, especially intellectually and morally. Second is a belief in sanctioned racial segregation in such areas as housing, schools, public accommodations, interracial social contacts, and marriage. Third is a belief in justifiable racial discrimination in such areas as employment and higher education. As you can tell, old-fashioned racism takes its name because its beliefs are no longer considered socially acceptable in most circles. By and large, our conversations and interactions strive to give every appearance of being models of tolerance and understanding.

Measuring Old-Fashioned Racism

How have psychologists measured old-fashioned racism? Table 6.1 lists the seven items from the Old-Fashioned Racism Scale.[7] Rate your agreement or disagreement with each of the following beliefs on a scale from 1 to 5. The parentheses following each question indicate the

Table 6.1. Old-Fashioned Racism Scale

_____ • Black people are generally not as smart as whites. (Strongly agree = 5)
_____ • I favor laws that permit black persons to rent or purchase housing even when the person offering the property for sale or rent does not wish to rent or sell it to blacks. (Strongly disagree = 5)
_____ • Generally speaking, I favor full racial integration. (Strongly disagree = 5)
_____ • I am opposed to open or fair housing laws. (Strongly agree = 5)
_____ • It is a bad idea for blacks and whites to marry one another. (Strongly agree = 5)
_____ • If a black family with about the same income and education as I have moved next door, I would mind it a great deal. (Strongly agree = 5)
_____ • It was wrong for the United States Supreme Court to outlaw segregation in its 1954 decision. (Strongly agree = 5)
_____ Total score

appropriate point allotment. For some, *Strongly agree* = 5; for others, *Strongly disagree* = 5.

Total the scores of your seven responses. Your score can range from 7 to 35. As you can probably tell, lower scores indicate a lower level of old-fashioned racist beliefs; higher scores, a higher level of old-fashioned racist beliefs. Most of you probably scored toward the lower end of the scale (i.e., less than 15 points). Two factors explain this. First, the fact that you are reading this book indicates that, most likely, you have a sympathy for reducing racism in America. Second, even though you are reading this book alone, you are still influenced by strong normative pressures not to endorse blatantly racist remarks.

THE DECLINE OF OLD-FASHIONED RACISM?

Over the past three decades, researchers have unveiled a dramatic decline in old-fashioned racism, at least at the level of publicly expressed attitudes. Though this was discussed in Chapter 4, it bears repeating as evidence for the decline of old-fashioned racism. The perception that blacks are generally not as smart as whites has drastically decreased. In 1933, 38 percent of whites described blacks as ignorant; by 1967, that figure had dropped to 11 percent; and by 1990, 5 percent. Similarly, 22 percent of whites described blacks as stupid in 1933; the figure was 4 percent in 1967; and only 3 percent in 1990.[8] Whites' views of racial integration have evolved in similarly positive ways. Seventy-five percent of whites favored full racial integration in 1965; by 1978, 95 percent favored full racial integration.[9] Whites' views of interracial marriage also are consistent with this positive trend. An August 1991 Gallup Poll found that, for the first time in survey history, more Americans approved (48 percent) of interracial marriage than disapproved (42 percent). These figures represent a dramatic increase in tolerance from those recorded in 1968 (20 percent approved), 1973 (36 percent approved), and 1983 (43 percent approved).[10]

These are real advances. It is no small achievement that people are actually less openly racist and discriminatory than they used to be. But what are the reasons for these changes? How genuine are the declines in old-fashioned racism? There are four different answers to this question.

The Decline in Old-Fashioned Racism Is Genuine

Based on the evidence in the preceding paragraphs, one could argue that old-fashioned racism—whether manifested in stereotypes, attitudes, or behaviors—is actually declining. Moreover, one could argue that this decline is likely to continue in the future. This is primarily due to the fact that its main supporters are (1) whites over the age of 60, and (2) whites (especially those living in the South) who never finished high school. Such groups are dwindling in numbers and, as they dwindle, so may the legacy of old-fashioned racism.

The Decline in Old-Fashioned Racism Is Genuine but Limited

A second position argues that the decline in old-fashioned racism is genuine but does not extend to the really important issues. Whites may be more willing to endorse vague and abstract principles of equality than they were three decades ago. They may be less willing, however, to accept programs and policies that would produce real change with costly implications for them (e.g., losing jobs to blacks with the implementation of affirmative action programs). In other words, there is a gap between the *abstract principles* of egalitarianism and an *applied commitment* to programs or policies to achieve those principles. S. M. Lipset and W. Schneider, for instance, found that laws prohibiting racial discrimination in housing are generally accepted as fair and desirable. Specific proposals from local governments or private groups encouraging blacks to buy homes in the suburbs, however, received relatively little support.[11]

The power of consistency between abstract principles and an applied commitment is the power of conviction and courage. As sociologist Mary Jackman wrote in 1978,

> Commitment should extend beyond vague adherence to relatively general, abstract principles into the application of those principles to specific contexts that more closely approximate real-life settings. Whether the central issue is interracial harmony or democratic stability, adherence to general principles of tolerance is of little practical value if those principles are not successfully applied to specific settings.[12]

Lerone Bennett, Jr., a biographer of Martin Luther King, Jr., argues that the defining and pivotal moment of the civil rights movement was the 1956 jailing of King in Montgomery, Alabama, and a subsequent bombing that shattered the front of his house. Standing on his demolished porch, King reasserted his policy of love and forgiveness. Though he had spoken of these *abstract principles* before, their *application* in the direct face of persecution, fleshed out by pain, paid for by anguish, made King a living symbol.[13]

Unfortunately, the inconsistency between abstract principles and an applied commitment is the impotence of indifference. Historical examples of this inconsistency are found in the beliefs of Thomas Jefferson and Abraham Lincoln. As described by sociologist Lawrence Bobo, Jefferson's writings indicated a conviction that black enslavement was at striking odds with the U.S. Constitution; yet he personally owned 267 slaves in 1822. He was capable of punishing these slaves with great cruelty. He recognized the contradiction in principle—and even agonized over it—yet kept most of his slaves. Similarly, Lincoln, while holding to the principles of slave emancipation, did not believe that whites and blacks could exist as civil equals in the same country.[14]

These examples illustrate that the acceptance of some progressive, abstract principles does not necessarily guarantee a deep commitment to applications necessary for a racially equal and integrated society. As psychologist Thomas Pettigrew states, "White Americans increasingly reject racial injustice in principle, but are reluctant to accept the measures necessary to eliminate the injustice."[15] As early as 1967, Martin Luther King, Jr. echoed similar sentiments when he argued that the attitudes of most whites fell between the polar extremes of segregationist and a deep commitment to racial justice. King said that many whites were "uneasy with injustice, yet unwilling to pay a significant price to eradicate it."[16]

Early research, buttressed by intuition, suggested that whites' reluctance to accept an applied commitment to redress racial injustice was motivated by *self-interest*. In other words, my hesitancy to commit to such programs stems from a fear that they would have a negative impact on *my* quality of life. Several studies, however, question this suggestion.

Researchers have found, for instance, that white opposition to affirmative action is normally *not* based in the individual's fear that it will cost him or her a job, promotion, or related opportunity. Similarly, white support for more restrictions on immigration seems not to arise from any feared personal costs. Rather, it appears that the reluctance is motivated by perceived *group interest*. In other words, my hesitancy to commit to such programs stems from a fear that they would have a negative impact on my *group's* quality of life. Blacks' support for restricting immigration, for example, is closely linked to their sense of its negative impact on blacks as a group—but not to any impact it might have on them personally.[17] Similarly, Derrick Bell has argued that whites will support the cause of racial justice only when it is in the interest of whites as a group to do so.[18] There are many other examples suggesting that it is the power of perceived group interest that underlies the inconsistency between abstract principles and applied commitments.

We see a similar inconsistency in examining responses to interracial social contact. Survey questions concerning *intimate* interracial contacts still detect prejudice. As psychologist David Myers describes, the statement "I would probably feel uncomfortable dancing with a black person in a public place," reveals more racial feeling than, "I would probably feel uncomfortable riding a bus with a black person."[19] A 1988 *Life* survey found that only 3 percent of whites said they would not want their child to attend an integrated school, but 57 percent admitted they would be unhappy if their child married a black person.[20] The fear of the most intimate interracial contact is reflected in the following comments left by an audience member after one of my lectures. "How would you feel if your little girl was dating a colored boy? Or what if she got pregnet [*sic*] by him?"

The phenomenon of greatest prejudice in the most intimate social realms is consistent with the abstract principles–applied commitment inconsistency. Full racial integration is perfectly acceptable as long as it does not hit too close to home. As William Pannell, author of *The Coming Race Wars?* writes "Most Americans are people of good will. Most of us really do like other people, even those who are not like us. We prefer that they not be too close, however. We like those people in the abstract, not in the concrete."[21]

The Decline in Old-Fashioned Racism Is Not Genuine

On a more pessimistic note, it may be argued that the reported declines in old-fashioned racism are more apparent than real. This illusory change stems from the fact that changes in societal norms and the enaction of antidiscrimination legislation have made it socially undesirable to openly express racism. Thus, it may be argued, people still firmly cling to racist beliefs and attitudes while only paying lip-service to greater tolerance. Consistent with this, Mary Jackman reviewed national survey data and found that well-educated people are the most likely to hide their true racial prejudices because they have more thoroughly learned that overt expressions of racism are socially undesirable.[22]

The issue of social desirability is crucial in considering responses to overt self-report measures such as the Old-Fashioned Racism Scale. The items on the Old-Fashioned Racism Scale are extraordinarily reactive. In other words, the items are easily recognized as measuring racial prejudice. The reactions of respondents can be easily censored to appear to themselves and others as less racist. The scale's reactivity creates the potential for faking and often results in people refusing to answer the questions—sometimes in a hostile fashion. This poses critical methodological problems for the researcher. Do the respondents' answers accurately reflect their true beliefs and behavioral intentions, or do they more accurately reflect what respondents believe are the socially desirable answers?

There is a plethora of real life cases that illustrate the tendency for respondents to give socially desirable answers that end up being inconsistent with their eventual behaviors. In 1982, for instance, Californian Tom Bradley was running to become the first elected black governor in American history. Though he had been comfortably ahead of his white opponent in the polls, and whites had expressed strong support for his candidacy, he lost the race. In 1989, Virginian Douglas Wilder, ahead by as much as 15 percentage points in the gubernatorial polls, watched his supposed lead evaporate on election day. Though Wilder eventually won by a fraction of the vote, his experience reminded us that answers to a poll may be influenced by social desirability more than actual behavioral intentions.

How do we see beyond such hypocrisy? Fortunately, there are other clever research strategies that can more accurately reveal the existence of individual racism. These include (1) measures of nonverbal behaviors, (2) situations of behavioral ambiguity, (3) physiological recordings of facial muscles, (4) priming and response-latency measures, and (5) other measures of related behaviors.

Measures of Nonverbal Behaviors

Our covert and more spontaneous nonverbal behaviors reveal very different information than do controlled, overt responses on attitude scales. In one of the initial attempts to study this, psychologist S. Weitz asked white college students to tape-record a message for someone of whom they had been given a brief description. Among other things, this description contained information about that person's race (black or white). In addition to collecting overt measures of friendliness (e.g., ratings of liking), Weitz analyzed the voice tone of the recorded message for more covert features such as voice warmth, admiration, and so forth. Consistent with social desirability norms of the early 1970s, white students who were anticipating interacting with a black person typically reported a high degree of overt friendliness and liking. In contrast to their overt claims of friendliness, however, the same white students actually came across as less than warm and admiring in the voice tone of their recorded messages.[23]

Another similar disparity between overt and covert reports was found by psychologists M. Hendricks and R. Bootzin. In their experiment, white females arrived at a laboratory and were casually invited to take a seat in a room. One of the nine seats was already occupied by a black or white female. The most covert measure was simply which of the eight vacant seats was chosen by the subject. Following this, a more overt measure was taken as subjects were asked to stand at increasingly close distances from one another and rate how uncomfortable they felt. On this latter overt measure, where social desirability norms were very strong, race of the other subject made no difference in the ratings of uncomfortableness. In the covert seating measure, however, white subjects chose to sit approximately one seat further away from the black woman than from the white woman.[24] Other research confirms that whites chose to sit closer to a fellow white interviewee and talk longer, and with fewer speech errors, than they did to a black interviewee.[25]

Situations of Behavioral Ambiguity

More recent experimental studies affirm the value of data from covert measures of racism. These studies reveal that situations of behavioral ambiguity can reveal underlying levels of racism. Behavioral ambiguity refers to circumstances in which (1) appropriate (and thus inappropriate) behavior is not obvious, or (2) a negative response can be justified or rationalized on the basis of some factor other than race. For example, a white survey respondent might express the intention to vote for a conservative white candidate running against a liberal black candidate. In this context, the political ideology of the candidate may be used as a very plausible explanation for the voting intention, and the respondent is protected from having his or her candidate choice attributed to racism.

Political ideology is not the only factor that can create an ambiguous behavioral context. In one experimental study of helping in an emergency, white bystanders were as likely to help a black victim as a white victim when they were the only witness to an emergency and their personal responsibility was clear. In a condition in which the bystanders believed there were other witnesses to the emergency, however, whites helped the black victim half as often as they helped the white victim. The lack of helping was justified by the belief that someone else would intervene. In other words, racial bias was expressed in a way that could be rationalized on the basis of a non-race-related reason—the belief that someone else would help.[26]

In the previous study, behavioral ambiguity was created by a diffusion of responsibility. Behavioral ambiguity also may be created by situations without clear norms or guides for behavior, by situations low in racial salience, or by actions initiated by black actors who are then the target of the negative behavior. In each of these contexts, appropriate (and thus inappropriate) behaviors are not obvious, and negative responses can be justified or rationalized on the basis of some factor other than race. In other words, discriminatory behavior surfaces not when a behavior would look like racism, but when it can hide behind the screen of some other motive. In these cases, ambiguity provides an opportunity to observe covert levels of racism.

Physiological Recordings of Facial Muscles

Paralleling the adage that "the eyes are the mirror to the soul," some psychologists have even demonstrated that activity of certain facial muscles reveals disparities from overt self-report measures of liking. In 1990, psychologist E. J. Vanman and colleagues measured the electrical activity of (1) the muscles above the eye, which are used when we frown; and (2) the muscles in the cheek, which are used when we smile. White subjects were then asked to view slides of white or black people with whom they were to imagine interacting in a cooperative setting. After each slide, subjects rated the person on various scales, including an overt self-report measure of how well they liked them. Again, consistent with social desirability norms, these overt self-report measures revealed that white subjects liked the black persons more than the white ones. The covert physiological readings, however, told a very different story. Whenever a slide of a black person appeared, there tended to be more activity from the "frown" muscles and less from the "smile" muscles.[27]

Priming and Response-Latency Measures

The most recent experimental strategies to supplement overt self-report measures reveal an advanced level of sophistication and complexity. These studies utilize priming and response-latency measures, techniques commonly used in the field of cognitive psychology. In these studies, a prime could be the face of a white or black person, or a house. After seeing this prime, participants are asked to make a judgment about a trait that follows (e.g., "Can this trait ever describe the category of objects represented by the prime?") The response latency, or the amount of time it takes participants to respond, reveals the degree of association between the trait and the prime.

In studies by Dovidio and Gaertner, participants were first presented with the primes "black" and "white," representing racial groups. These primes were then followed by positive and negative traits. The participants' task was to decide if the trait could ever describe a member of the primed racial group. Faster response times were assumed to reflect greater association. Consistent with social desirability norms, negative traits were *not* more associated with blacks than with whites. Positive traits, however, were more associated with whites than with blacks.[28] The differences in response times "gave them away."

Results from priming and response-latency studies also predict other indirect and unconscious expressions of bias, such as negative nonverbal cues (e.g., lower levels of eye contact) by whites engaged in interracial interaction. Such findings confirm that many whites, even those who appear nonprejudiced on overt self-report measures, still find other indirect and subtle ways to express anti-black bias.

Other Measures of Related Behaviors

Finally, other measures of related behaviors reveal some strong inconsistencies relative to responses on the Old-Fashioned Racism Scale. In other words, responses to the Old-Fashioned Racism Scale do not correlate very well with what should be racially relevant behavior, such as reported voting intentions or behavior in elections where racism should have been a factor. For instance, McConahay reports that measures of old-fashioned racism have been shown to be only very weakly related to actual patterns of white voting.[29]

Summary

Each of these experimental reports, and scores of other studies, affirm the difficulty of establishing the accuracy of overt self-reported measures of racism (e.g., the Old-Fashioned Racism Scale). Social desirability constraints against overtly racist expressions are the norms in most segments of contemporary American society. Because of these norms, any overt measure with the reactivity of the Old-Fashioned Racism Scale is bound to reveal low levels of individual racism. Such self-report measures of racism are susceptible to conscious efforts to appear unbiased and are not effective at distinguishing nonprejudiced from prejudiced whites. As these studies suggest, however, more nonreactive and covert measures reveal that the decline in old-fashioned racism is not genuine. The sustained presence of racism in human relations is clearly documented by such measures.

Old-Fashioned Racism Has Mutated into a New Face of Racism

As we have seen, specific research strategies reveal that individuals appearing nonracist on the surface may secretly harbor negative thoughts or feelings about racial minorities. These in turn may lead to discriminatory treatment. These findings raise the possibility that any supposed decline in old-fashioned racism is irrelevant, because the beast of racism in American society has taken on a new face. Like any clever virus, old-fashioned racism has not graciously succumbed to the emerging social mandates of egalitarianism and equality. Rather, it may be argued that old-fashioned racism has mutated into new, more subtle manifestations.

Social scientists have been relatively late coming to this "discovery." Minorities have recognized the new racism for years. A black woman in Washington, D.C., expressed this sense that racism has changed, not declined, to our 1996 study tour group: "It [new racism] is more dangerous because it is so subtle. Individuals will smile in your face and throw roadblocks in your way. Dye your face black and walk in one of the shops. Suddenly, you become the invisible man or woman."

CONCLUSION

In *The Screwtape Letters*, written by the Christian apologist C. S. Lewis in 1943, the devil (Screwtape) offers the following advice to one of his lackeys (Wormwood):

> I do not think you will have much difficulty in keeping the patient in the dark. The fact that "devils" are predominately *comic* figures in the modern imagination will help you. If any faint suspicion of your existence begins to arise in his mind, suggest to him a picture of something in red tights, and persuade him that since he cannot believe in that (it is an old textbook method of confusing them) he therefore cannot believe in you.[30]

By focusing the attention on "old-fashioned" depictions of himself, Screwtape hopes to delude humanity into believing that he no longer exists. If the question of his existence can be compromised, then his more subtle, indirect means of manipulation are easily achieved.

In a similar vein, old-fashioned racism is the "picture of something in red tights" of which contemporary white Americans have difficulty in believing exists. Part of the power of the newer face of racism, similar to the power of Screwtape, is to create the illusion that it no longer exists. It deludes both perpetrators and victims into believing that there is little need for change.

How genuine are the declines in old-fashioned racism? Despite the well-publicized advances in racial tolerance as revealed on self-report measures, the wealth of evidence directs us to some disturbing conclusions. Even if we assume some genuine decline in old-fashioned racism, it is clear that these more tolerant and progressive beliefs and attitudes have not extended to the really important issues. More disconcertingly, there is substantial evidence to indicate that the declines represent an illusory change. Other, more subtle and covert measures reveal the continuing existence of racist thoughts, feelings, and behaviors. Finally, the subtleties observed in research settings appear to have their parallel in newer, more sophisticated faces of racism. It is essential that an enlightened discussion of the role of racism in American society acknowledge the emergence of its newer, more subtle faces. It is to these newer faces of racism that we now turn in Chapter 7.

7

Modern Racism Unmasked

And White people call me paranoid and stuff, because I guess they look at things like the sixties when Black people were like being beaten up every damn day, and crosses [were burned] in front yards, and it was so blatant. But, now it's changed. And just because it's not blatant anymore doesn't mean it's not there. In fact, I think it's worse.[1]

—Black interviewee, 1992

As I discussed in the previous chapter, most contemporary understandings of racism have been overly influenced by the aggressive, overt, and blatant face of old-fashioned racism. Though it still exists, our society has drawn a line against such hateful behaviors. Although we cannot legislate beliefs and attitudes, we have implemented clear legal prohibitions against the behavioral manifestations of old-fashioned racism. Those who wish to be in the American mainstream have embraced social prohibitions against it as well. So has racism in America receded? Or has it simply changed its face? This chapter argues that new mutations of racism have supplanted old-fashioned racism.

The first social scientific suspicion that a new face of racism might be afoot came from a study of voting behavior in the 1969 Los Angeles mayoral election. The election was contested between a conservative white incumbent mayor (Sam Yorty) and a liberal black city councilman (Tom Bradley). Surprisingly, psychologists David Sears and Donald Kinder found that the white vote was not dominated by old-fashioned racism. For example, strong opposition to a belief in black intellectual inferiority or strong support for school integration did not predispose voters to prefer the black candidate over the white. Rather, the white vote was best predicted by responses to a new set of abstract, moralistic, racial resentments. More subtle questions concerned with economic and social advances made by minority groups and specific social policies aimed at redressing past inequities related quite strongly to voting against the black candidate.[2]

Findings such as these led to increasing dissatisfaction with the concept, and measurement, of old-fashioned racism. Psychologists began to grapple with questions of how to measure individual racial attitudes in the general public when the issues, the climate, and the structure of public opinion had changed so significantly. As we saw in Chapter 5, it's clear that racial discrimination in America still exists. How do we reconcile that fact, however, with documented declines in old-fashioned racism and surveys revealing that only 6 percent of whites and 10 percent of blacks consider themselves prejudiced?[3]

MODERN RACISM

Eventually, psychologists proposed that new faces of racism were supplanting old-fashioned racism. Researchers differ in their labels for this newer face of post–civil-rights-movement racism and in its specific characteristics and causes. For simplicity, however, I use the general categorical term *modern racism* to refer to the new faces of racism prompted by the changes in societal norms and the enaction of anti-discrimination legislation.

Psychologist David Sears outlined three interconnected beliefs underlying modern racism.[4] The first belief includes a denial that there is continuing discrimination against racial minorities. Modern racists maintain that racial discrimination is a thing of the past. Since America now has a level playing field, the second belief of modern racism includes a clear antagonism toward the demands of racial minorities for equal treatment. In the perspective of a modern racist, why must minorities continue to demand something that they already have? The third belief underlying modern racism is a resentment about special favors for minority groups. Following the first two beliefs, a modern racist believes that special favors for minority groups are not necessary, and are only given because these groups "whine" so much. Most significantly, such favors give an unwarranted advantage to racial minorities.

Living my professional life in higher education, I most often encounter resentment surrounding financial aid targeted for minorities. Last year, following a lecture I gave at a community college, one student expressed strong resentment (and equally strong need for remedial education) in the following note:

> What about the United Negro College Fund? Why is it that scolarships [sic] are offered to colored kids and there are no scolarships [sic] offered to just white kids. That is racist in itself. Because the general scholarships to college offered to any children are for everybody and the most quilified [sic] ones get it, regardles [sic] of color. So why is there additional money offered to just colored kids?

Modern racists do not define their own beliefs and attitudes as racist. Racism, as defined by modern racists, refers exclusively to the tenets and practices of old-fashioned racism—negative beliefs about black intelligence, ambition, honesty, and other stereotyped characteristics, as well as support for segregation and acts of open discrimination. Modern racists clearly believe that racism, as defined by old-fashioned racism, is immoral. They abhor, and avoid, any expressions of old-fashioned racism.

Modern racists prefer beliefs that are relatively ambiguous and amenable to being defended on moral, empirical, or other nonracial grounds. For example, modern racists believe that the statistical fact that black men are more likely than white men to be involved in violent crime means that potential crime victims are reasonably justified in treating all black men with suspicion. Such "reasonable racism," based on empirical grounds, has been defended by economist Walter Williams, columnist Richard Cohen, neoconservative analyst Dinesh D'Souza, and others. Similarly, many modern attitudes toward homosexuals are not based entirely on negative stereotypes, but rather on beliefs that gay men and women violate fundamental religious and family values.

Measuring Modern Racism

As I have discussed, the accuracy of the Old-Fashioned Racism Scale is hindered by the presence of strong normative pressures not to endorse blatantly racist remarks. How have psychologists measured modern racism? Table 7.1 lists the seven items from the Modern Racism Scale.[5] Rate your agreement or disagreement with each of the following

Table 7.1. Modern Racism Scale

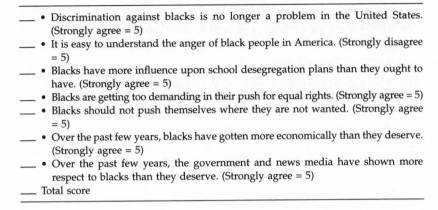

___ • Discrimination against blacks is no longer a problem in the United States. (Strongly agree = 5)
___ • It is easy to understand the anger of black people in America. (Strongly disagree = 5)
___ • Blacks have more influence upon school desegregation plans than they ought to have. (Strongly agree = 5)
___ • Blacks are getting too demanding in their push for equal rights. (Strongly agree = 5)
___ • Blacks should not push themselves where they are not wanted. (Strongly agree = 5)
___ • Over the past few years, blacks have gotten more economically than they deserve. (Strongly agree = 5)
___ • Over the past few years, the government and news media have shown more respect to blacks than they deserve. (Strongly agree = 5)
___ Total score

beliefs on a scale from 1 to 5. The parentheses following each question indicate the appropriate point allotment. For some, *Strongly agree* = 5; for others, *Strongly disagree* = 5.

Total the scores of your seven responses. Your score can range from 7 to 35. As you can probably tell, lower scores indicate a lower level of modern racism; higher scores indicate higher modern racism. In most cases, you will notice that your scores on this scale are noticeably higher than your scores on the Old-Fashioned Racism Scale from Chapter 6. Why?

As described by John McConahay, the Modern Racism Scale is much less reactive than the Old-Fashioned Racism Scale. In other words, the items on the Modern Racism Scale are *less* easily recognized as measuring racial prejudice than are the items on the Old-Fashioned Racism Scale. Two factors lead to the decreased reactivity. First, the items on the Modern Racism Scale tap into current issues about which there is no clear consensus on the racist and nonracist position. Second, for each item, there is a plausible, nonracist explanation for endorsing the position scored as racist on the scale—though the same explanation cannot be used for the racist response across all items. The one thing that can be used to explain the racist response to each and every item is negative racial feeling or prejudice. As McConahay states, "It [negative racial feeling or prejudice] is the common thread that holds all of the items together in the scale."[6]

We should note, however, that the Modern Racism Scale still remains tainted with social desirability. It is usually fairly obvious what the socially "correct" response should be. The tremendous public attention focused on racial issues may be causing the Modern Racism Scale to become a less subtle, and more reactive, measure of racism. Several studies showing that the average scores are skewed toward the non-racist end of the scale affirm the susceptibility of such scales to social desirability. McConahay acknowledges this and expects that new items will have to be generated for the Modern Racism Scale as new issues emerge in American race relations and some of the current scale items become more reactive.

Psychologists Paul Sniderman and Philip Tetlock further argue that high correlations between scores of old-fashioned and modern racism justify their consideration as a single construct.[7] In other words, old-fashioned and modern racism are simply the same thing. Though these high correlations do not prove that old-fashioned and modern racism are the same thing, they do provide a clear reminder that the two have much in common and may be difficult to distinguish empirically. As Donald Kinder points out, however, McConahay has pursued the possibility of an overlap between these two constructs in studies over the course of a decade. As a result of those studies, he finds clear and clean separation between responses to questions intended to assess old-fashioned racism and to those intended to assess modern racism.[8] As further support, scales of modern racism correlate with attitudes toward such issues as school busing, affirmative action, and conservative political candidates in ways that old-fashioned measures simply do not. David Sears, for instance, found that modern racism was a better predictor of choosing an African-American mayoral candidate over a European-American mayoral candidate than was old-fashioned racism.[9] In summary, ample evidence suggests that old-fashioned and modern racism are related but empirically distinct components of racial prejudice.

FACES OF MODERN RACISM

As mentioned previously, researchers have differed in their labels for the new form of racism. Some are even offended by the application of the term *racism* to these beliefs and prefer a term such as *sophisticated prejudice*. Though I have chosen to use the categorical term *modern racism* as the broad contrast with old-fashioned racism, two specific faces of modern racism should be discussed. These faces, each possessing some subtle clarifications and distinctions, can be classified on a continuum of racism (see Figure 7.1).

The continuum illustrates that racism is a cumulative dimension that begins with avoidance of minorities in private contexts. Such *aversive racism*, the mildest form of racism, is most strongly associated with political liberals. The continuum advances through beliefs that minorities receive more social and economic benefits than they deserve. This face of modern racism, termed *symbolic racism*, is most commonly associated with political conservatives. Finally, anchoring the most severe end of the continuum of racism is old-fashioned racism. As we discussed in Chapter 6, old-fashioned racism, representing the open flame of racial hatred, includes beliefs in white superiority, sanctioned racial segregation, and justifiable racial discrimination.

Let's now turn to a discussion of the two faces of modern racism—aversive and symbolic racism.

Aversive Racism

Psychologists John Dovidio and Samuel Gaertner, and their colleagues at Colgate University and the University of Delaware, suggest *aversive racism* as characteristic of many white Americans. This pattern

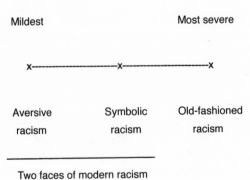

Two faces of modern racism

Figure 7.1. Continuum of racism.

of modern racism assumes that the historically racist culture of America has led most white Americans to develop negative beliefs and feelings regarding racial minorities. These culturally socialized negative beliefs and feelings are held in uneasy contrast to positive beliefs and feelings associated with a sincerely egalitarian value system. Because of the importance of the egalitarian value system to their self-concept, aversive racists typically cut off the negative beliefs and feelings from conscious awareness. By so doing, they fool themselves into believing that their racial attitudes are largely positive.[10]

The contrary existence of both unconscious negative racial biases and the expressed conscious desire to be egalitarian forms the basis of the internal discomfort and uneasiness experienced by aversive racists. The internal conflict experienced by aversive racists influences their social judgments and impacts their interactions with minorities, betraying itself in avoidance and coolness rather than hostility and hatred. In other words, to elude facing these negative racial biases, and to protect their self-images as nonracist individuals, whites simply avoid interactions—sometimes phobically—with racial minorities. In situations where interactions are unavoidable, and there are no strong normative guidelines, the interactions are often characterized by an emotional detachment, lack of appropriate feedback, and the absence of pertinent reinforcement.

Due to the unconscious nature of the negative beliefs and feelings, and the expressed conscious desire to be egalitarian, there are inherent difficulties in directly measuring aversive racism with a questionnaire. The conscious desire to appear egalitarian is too strong to allow the unconscious negative beliefs and feelings to surface in a situation with clear, normative guidelines. So, aversive racists score low on self-report measures of prejudice and racism. As a result, aversive racism researchers eschew the use of self-report and questionnaire measures, and seek support for their theory in other, often more creative, avenues.

Classic studies from the early 1970s by Gaertner and Dovidio, for example, illustrated the tendency of some "liberal" whites to exhibit racial discrimination in the absence of strong normative guidelines. Gaertner and Dovidio had confederates make a bogus "wrong number" telephone call and say that their car had broken down, they had just used their last dime, and they needed the recipient of the call to contact a local garage for a tow truck. Whenever a person with an identifiably black voice made the call, the respondents were six times more likely to hang up prematurely than when the call came from someone who sounded white.[11]

A 1995 experiment by Dovidio asked white students to select dormitory advisors for the coming semester—prestigious and competitive student positions. When the information provided about candidates was unambiguous (i.e., uniformly positive or negative), black and white applicants were treated equivalently. When the candidate's record was more ambiguous, however, white applicants were treated more favorably than black applicants. Again, in a situation without strong normative guidelines, racial discrimination was evidenced.[12]

Psychologist Thomas Pettigrew describes additional experimental research revealing that, in interactions with blacks, whites tend to sit farther away than they do with other whites, use less friendly voice tones, make less eye contact, and terminate interactions more quickly.[13] Patterns of social relationships also reveal the cautious awkwardness of black–white interactions. A June 1997 Gallup Poll found that only 59 percent of blacks reported having close friends who are white; 75 percent of whites reported close friends who are black.[14] Although it is unclear how respondents to the June 1997 Gallup Poll defined "close friends," it remains clear that Americans are still hesitant to voice widespread approval for that most intimate of interracial relationships— marriage. An August 1991 Gallup Poll, for instance, found 42 percent of Americans still disapprove of interracial marriage.[15] The June 1997 Gallup Poll found that a significant number of whites (30 percent) polled still voice disapproval of interracial marriage.[16]

Symbolic Racism

As a term, *symbolic racism* emphasizes that many of the beliefs of the new racism are a reaction to certain post–civil-rights-era policies, such as busing or affirmative action, that symbolize to many whites the unfair gains or demands of blacks. Symbolic racism specifically refers to the resentment focusing on special treatment for racial minorities. Symbolic racists do not pine for the days of a segregated society. They also do not feel, however, that minorities should be given special treatment by the government. The resentment of special treatment is thought to stem from a combination of (1) negative emotional responses to racial minorities (e.g., disgust, fear, or anger) and (2) traditional American values that have little to do with race (e.g., values of self-reliance, equality, and fair play). Symbolic racism is a very complex species of modern racism. On one hand, the resentment could be indicative of some underlying racist attitudes and, thus, be morally indefensible. On the other hand, however, the resentment could simply reveal a strong reliance on traditional American values and, thus, be morally defensible.

Almost all old-fashioned racists are also symbolic racists. Consistent with the power of the new racism to delude, however, there is a fairly large group of people who are symbolic racists but not old-fashioned racists. They truly believe both in integration and that blacks should not push themselves where they are not wanted. These are people who are opposed to racial segregation and discrimination, but are also opposed to special programs or policies for racial minorities. Symbolic racism toward immigrants to America (or Hispanics or Asians), for instance, predicts opposition to bilingual education, support for English as an official language, and support for restricting immigrants' rights.[17]

Affirmative Action

In America, the prominent point of resentment for symbolic racists is affirmative action. During the past year, affirmative action has been debated more intensely than at any other time in its 30-year history. It is a hard issue, with the potential virtue of being morally defensible, about which reasonable people can differ. Some people view it as a milestone, others as a millstone, and still others regard it as a necessary, but imperfect, remedy for an intractable social disease. What is meant by the term *affirmative action*? How does affirmative action differ from *equal opportunity*? Why the vehemence of public reaction? What should be the future of affirmative action?

What Is Meant by the Term Affirmative Action? Psychologists Faye Crosby of Smith College and Diana Cordova of Yale University surveyed three leading national newspapers and found 176 articles on affirmative action published between June and August of 1995. Of those 176 articles, fewer than 6 percent offered a definition of affirmative action! A wide range of government documents even acknowledges that the words have come to have different meanings in different contexts.[18] For the general public, affirmative action can mean anything from the demeaning use of quota programs for supposed incompetents to the meritorious practice of extending a hand to eminently qualified people previously held back by racial, ethnic, or gender bias. Is it any wonder the public debate is so confused?

The term *affirmative action* has been traced to Franklin Roosevelt's presidency. Officially, the policy of affirmative action, however, was set in motion by two forces—the Civil Rights Act of 1964 and Executive Order 11246. Title VII of the Civil Rights Act outlawed discrimination on the basis of race, religion, sex, or national origin. Executive Order 11246, signed by President Lyndon Johnson in 1965, required the federal government and its contractors to take "affirmative action" to ensure fairness in selection decisions with respect to race, religion, sex, and national origin.

In its classical definition, affirmative action occurs whenever people go out of their way (take affirmative or positive action) to increase the likelihood of true equality for individuals of different categories. As Crosby and Cordova point out,

> Whenever an organization expends energy to make sure that women and men, people of color and White people, or disabled and fully abled workers have the same chances as each other to be hired, retained, or promoted, then the organization has a policy of affirmative action in employment.[19]

In practice, affirmative action policies and programs focus on recruiting, hiring, retaining, and promoting more of certain *under*represented groups of people into an organization. By consciously taking race, ethnicity, and gender into account, affirmative action promotes the inclusion of a group that has had a history of exclusion and the establishment of positive relations among all group members.

In recent years, affirmative action has taken on a new meaning. The well-intended "numerical goals" and "timetables" have come to mean unjustified set-asides, arbitrary preferential treatment, or "quotas." Though the general public is most familiar with this new meaning of affirmative action, the reality is that federal laws and regulations continue to use the classical definition of affirmative action. In other words, quotas are not the main means by which affirmative action operates.

The logic of affirmative action is no different than the logic of treating a nutritional deficiency with vitamin supplements. For a healthy person, high doses of vitamin supplements may be unnecessary or even harmful. For a person whose system is out of balance, however, vitamin supplements are an efficient way to restore the body's balance. As Chapter 5 demonstrated, American society is out of balance. In its classical form, affirmative action—although not a cure-all—is one of many supplements that remain necessary in our continual attempt to restore this balance.

How Does Affirmative Action Differ from Equal Opportunity? A policy or program of affirmative action means more than simply ending discriminatory recruiting, hiring, retention, and promotion practices. Affirmative action policies and programs rest on the assumption that non-discrimination alone is not sufficient to overcome the effects of past discrimination. Active policies and programs must be implemented, and evaluated, to ensure fair representation. Equal opportunity employers, however, can adopt a more passive stance. They prohibit intentional discrimination but do not necessarily require anyone to discover whether certain policies or programs are producing unintended discriminatory effects.

Why the Vehemence of Public Reaction? In addition to a growing number of judges who believe the Constitution does not allow government to categorize people by race, even to benefit those who have long been disadvantaged, there is an increasingly vocal public resistance to affirmative action programs. The resistance is often viscerally and violently expressed. Affirmative action has now joined politics and religion as the triumvirate of things one ought not to discuss in polite company.

What is the nature of the public reaction to affirmative action? Although the public is evenly divided on giving special treatment to women, it is generally opposed to giving such treatment to racial minorities. As you might expect, opposition to affirmative action for racial minorities is split along racial lines. Polls reveal that whites generally oppose, and blacks generally support, affirmative action programs. A June 1997 poll found, for example, that 53 percent of blacks thought we should increase affirmative action programs, compared to only 22 percent of whites; 29 percent of both blacks and whites believed we should keep affirmative action programs as is; only 12 percent of blacks opted for a decrease in affirmative action programs, compared to 37 percent of whites.[20] Similarly, a *Washington Post*–ABC News survey found that only 17 percent of whites polled think blacks and other minorities should receive preference in college admissions; 49 percent of blacks think minorities should get preferences.[21]

It is a gross misstatement, however, to categorically assert that the public doesn't support affirmative action anymore. The myth that the public opposes affirmative action is based largely on public opinion polls that offer an all-or-none choice between affirmative action as it currently exists and no affirmative action whatsoever. In truth, most members of the public oppose extreme forms of affirmative action (e.g., quotas, set-asides, reverse discrimination) that violate norms of procedural justice. They do not oppose, however, the concept of affirmative action itself. When intermediate choices are added, surveys show that most people want to maintain some form of affirmative action.

Much of white America's negative reaction to affirmative action is based on three "sincere," though misguided, objections. First is the objection that affirmative action promotes reverse discrimination. If preferential treatment for racial minorities is so widespread as to engender reverse discrimination, then why do we still see the vast racial inequities in unemployment and earned income, as described in Chapter 5? As Tim Wise states, "If [people of color] are reaping the benefits of a vast, iniquitous system of racial preference, one can only wonder where said benefits are hiding."[22]

In addition, the misguided objection of reverse discrimination ignores the fact that discrimination against whites is *illegal*. Whites who believe they have been the victims of reverse discrimination can go to court like anyone else and make their case. Despite this legal avenue, actual claims of reverse discrimination are remarkably rare. A 1995 Labor Department draft report reviewing opinions by U.S. District Courts and Courts of Appeal found that between 1990 and 1994, of the 3,000 discrimination cases filed, only 100 (less than 4 percent) were charges of reverse discrimination. Of the 100, only 6 were found to have merit.[23] If reverse discrimination is so prevalent and unbearable, then why—in a society enamored with legal redress—are its legal manifestations so incredibly scarce?

A second misguided objection is that affirmative action violates the great American ideals of (1) advancement by pure merit and (2) color-blindness. The fallacy in the "pure merit" objection is whites' convenient amnesia regarding the arrangements that have always gone beyond considerations of "pure merit" in the American job market. Some of the best jobs are not advertised. Rather, they are circulated by word of mouth and filled through networks of friends and associates. Many of us have benefited from such informal "buddy" or "good old boy" networks or assistance from upper-class status networks or cliques. We have recruiting and hiring preferences for veterans, special economic incentives for purchase of U.S.-made products, import quotas against foreign goods and agricultural and textile subsidies.

One of the most striking examples of preferential assistance supplementing "pure merit" is in the special consideration given "legacies" in college admissions. The percentage of legacies, the children of alumni, accepted at many selective colleges is often more than twice that of the general pool of candidates. Their applications are clearly earmarked for preferential treatment and are occasionally even routed through different admission committees. In an incredible twist of hypocrisy, a *Los Angeles Times* investigation revealed that several regents of the University of California, as well as state politicians vocally opposed to affirmative action, used their influence to get relatives, friends, and the children of their business associates into the University of California at Los Angeles.[24] These are the same regents who, in 1995, denounced affirmative action in higher education and voted it out of existence in the California system!

In short, pure merit has played less of a role in all of our advancements than we would like to admit. Though it may not jibe with our cherished family stories of great-grandfather Ned's rugged individualism, we have all benefited from preferential assistance, or "nonperformance criteria," at some point in our professional lives.

The objection that affirmative action violates the ideal of color blindness has drawn spurious support from—of all places—Martin Luther King Jr.'s 1963 "I Have a Dream" speech. In that speech, King remarked, "I have a dream that my four little children will one day live in a nation where they will not be judged by the color of their skin, but by the content of their character." Some conservative pundits have commandeered this comment for their argument that government agencies—instead of following King's admonition to demolish distinctions of race—have emphasized them over and over.

The reality of King's views, however, is much more complicated than the "content of their character" sound bite. In that same "I Have a Dream" speech, King also insisted that America had presented blacks with a "bad check," and that the country had an obligation to make that check good. In a 1965 *Playboy* interview, King made clear his advice for making the check good—multibillion-dollar programs of preferential treatment for blacks and the disadvantaged of all races.[25] While holding color-blindness as the ideal to which America should aspire, King recognized that privileged groups historically have not volunteered to give up their privileges. When columnist James Glassman of the *Washington Post* claims that King would be philosophically opposed to affirmative action, he is simply wrong.

Third, and finally, is the misguided objection that discrimination is dead, and affirmative action is simply no longer necessary. Some critics of affirmative action argue that the time has come to revise, scale back, or abandon the temporary imposition of affirmative action goals and timetables because the procedures that require fairness have, in large measure, been institutionalized. In other words, today's playing field is fairly level, and affirmative action is no longer necessary.

National polls reveal that a majority of whites certainly believe the playing field is now level, and no further government intervention is necessary. A March 1995 Gallup Poll, for instance, found a strong agreement (86 percent) that when affirmative action was initiated, it was needed by both women and racial minorities to overcome discrimination. Nearly three-fourths of the respondents also indicated a belief that affirmative action had helped women and racial minorities over the past 30 years. Only 41 percent, however, agreed that affirmative action is still needed to overcome discrimination in present-day America.

Affirmative action has, indeed, helped women and racial minorities achieve more equitable representation in the past 30 years. Business professors Audrey Murrell and Ray Jones at the University of Pittsburgh, for instance, document substantive gains in racial and gender equality as a direct result of affirmative action.[26] Scott Plous, a psychologist at Wesleyan University, cites data from the Labor Department indicating that affirmative action has helped 5 million minority members and 6 million white and minority women move up in the workforce. Likewise, a study by the Office of Federal Contract Compliance Programs showed that between 1974 and 1980, federal contractors added black and female officials and managers at twice the rate of noncontractors. In addition, Plous cites a number of well-publicized cases in which large companies (e.g., AT&T, IBM, Sears–Roebuck) increased minority employment as a result of adopting affirmative action policies.[27] Finally, a study by the *New York University Law Review* dramatically illustrates the power of affirmative action policies to grant a window of opportunity to the disadvantaged. Their comprehensive study of law-school admissions found that 73 percent of the black students who would not have been admitted under a pure scores-plus-grades formula went on to graduate and pass their bar exams.[28]

Despite these gains, however, a wide variety of evidence suggests that the ultimate goals of affirmative action—eliminating the consequences of past discrimination and likelihood of future discrimination—have yet to be reached. The effects of affirmative action across education, employment, and business are fragile. Women continue to earn 72 cents for every male dollar. White males make up only 29 percent of the workforce but hold 95 percent of senior management positions.[29] As Chapter 5 revealed, most racial minorities continue to suffer from twice the unemployment rate of whites, half the median family income, and half the proportion of individuals who attend four years or more of college.

How much more dire might the picture be if affirmative action programs were removed? Recent lessons from two prestigious law schools provide us with a glimpse of the unpleasant answer. The elimination of affirmative action in the University of California systems took effect with graduate students entering in 1997; it won't apply to undergraduates until 1998. For the 1997 entering class at the University of California's Boalt Hall law school, 27 percent fewer blacks and 24 percent fewer Hispanics applied. Of those, only 14 blacks were admitted, down 81 percent from 1996. Only 39 Hispanics were admitted, down 50 percent from the previous year. Amazingly, only *one* black student and 14 Hispanic students were expected in the incoming class of 270 at Boalt Hall law school!

At the University of Texas law school, where several white students filed a lawsuit to block any additional preferential treatment for minorities in law school admissions, minority applications also are significantly down. Thirty-eight percent fewer blacks applied (225 vs. 361) and 14 percent fewer Hispanics (306 vs. 354). Of those, only 11 blacks and 34 Hispanics were admitted, down from 65 blacks (83 percent drop) and 70 Hispanics (51 percent drop) last year.

The impact of affirmative action rollbacks is echoing through the nation. The Association of American Medical Colleges released a November 1997 study indicating an 11 percent drop in blacks, Native Americans, and Hispanics applying to medical schools. In addition, 6.8 percent fewer of those minority students were accepted for 1997 than in 1996.[30] The lesson seems clear. The removal of affirmative action programs is serving to effectively choke off minority access to higher education and, ultimately, severely restrict progress toward racial equality in all areas of life.

On April 14, 1997, the Association of American Universities responded to these events by adopting a statement expressing strong support for continued attention to diversity in university admissions. The closing lines of that statement read:

> We therefore reaffirm our commitment to diversity as a value that is central to the very concept of our institutions. And we strongly reaffirm our support for the continuation of admissions policies, consistent with the broad principles of equal opportunity and equal protection, that take many factors and characteristics into account— including ethnicity, race, and gender—in the selection of those individuals who will be students today, and leaders in the years to come.[31]

What Should Be the Future of Affirmative Action?   The immediate future of affirmative action is cloudy. Generally, polls show that nearly two-thirds of Americans prefer stabilizing, or reforming, affirmative action rather than eliminating it altogether. Reflecting this sentiment, social scientists have recently focused their energies on linking research to the reform of affirmative action policies and programs. While recognizing the flaws of the current program, these researchers affirm the necessity of affirmative action as a remedy to institutional racism. As psychologist James Jones argues, "Retrenchment of affirmative action can only be seen as throwing in with those who intentionally, or out of ignorance, fail to understand the depths of institutional racism and the cumulative effects that such discrimination has on the development and possibility of a people."[32] Ira Glasser of the ACLU echoes this sentiment when he states that it is clearly too idealistic to assume that the "habits of discrimination and preferential systems for the hiring and promotion of whites, nurtured and institutionalized for generations, would not reemerge, at least in part, if affirmative action pressures were removed."[33] Reflecting these convictions, psychologists Anthony Pratkanis of the University of California, Santa Cruz, and Marlene Turner of San Jose State University have described 12 proactive principles for making affirmative action more effective.[34]

Affirmative action is not a cure-all. It does recognize, however, that racism is self-perpetrating, not self-correcting. It makes us "do the right thing" when we are not naturally disposed to do such a thing. It is not a pretty sight. It reminds us of some ugly things about human nature. It is, however, the lesser evil. The options of merit-based selection and equal opportunity policies are limited in redressing the continuing existence of racism. The present concept of affirmative action needs to be stabilized and, perhaps, reformed. It must not, however, be eliminated. As Pratkanis and Turner conclude, "Affirmative action is one step for ensuring a healthy economy and nation, free of discriminatory barriers that prevent us from reaching our national goal, 'that all people are created equal and endowed with certain inalienable rights.' "[35]

THE TAX OF MODERN RACISM

> I don't think white people, generally, understand the full meaning of racist discriminatory behaviors directed toward Americans of African descent. They seem to see each act of discrimination or any act of violence as an "isolated" event. As a result, most white Americans cannot understand the strong reaction manifested by blacks when such events occur. They feel that blacks tend to "overreact." They forget that in most cases, we live lives of quiet desperation generated by a litany of *daily* large and small events that, whether or not by design, remind us of our "place" in American society.[36]

This quotation, from Joe Feagin and Melvin Sikes's *Living with Racism: The Black Middle-Class Experience*, captures the reality of modern racism. Jody Armour incorporates this reality into his concept of the "Black Tax." In Armour's words,

> The Black Tax is the price Black people pay in their encounters with
> Whites (and some Blacks) because of Black stereotypes. The con-
> cept of a "tax" captures several key characteristics of these stereo-
> type-laden encounters: like a tax, racial discrimination is persistent,
> pervasive, must be dealt with, cannot be avoided, and is not gener-
> ally resisted.[37]

The tax of modern racism differs from that of old-fashioned racism.
The toll of old-fashioned racism is the clear, painful images of hatred
and persecution seared on the minds of its victims. The vicious letters,
violent slanders, and hostile behaviors take their impact from their
vividness. The footprints left in the lives of the victims of old-fashioned
racism are like craters left by gigantic meteors. Experiences of old-
fashioned racism are, for many of its victims, unforgettable life crises,
defining moments in their lives.

Modern racism, however, takes its toll in a more subtle and insidious manner. Modern racism leaves few defining moments for its victims. Rather, it leaves a legacy of "minor" and "forgettable" slights and
maltreatments that result in similar debilitating consequences. The tax
of modern racism is seldom dramatic and immediate. Rather, its tax
is cumulative, draining, energy consuming, and, ultimately, life consuming.

On our 1996 study tour, for instance, a black professional in Atlanta
told us of his recent move from Washington, D.C. "I couldn't sell my
remodeled and newly landscaped house in an affluent suburb for a
year. Finally, at a friend's suggestion, I took down all family pictures
and avoided the house when it was being shown so that buyers
wouldn't know the owners were Black. In a week, the house was sold."

The tax of modern racism also is seen in clerks and security personnel who watch every move minorities make in stores; the redlining of
minority neighborhoods by banks and delivery services; the hesitancy
of whites to sit by minorities on buses, in theaters, or stand by them on
elevators; the extensive discrimination by police officers in choosing
whom to arrest, in sentencing, and in executions; the inferior service at
restaurants and hotels. A black college dean, for instance, reflects that
the overt 1950s display of "No Negroes" signs has been replaced by a
more subtle form of racial discrimination:

> When you're in a restaurant and ... you notice that blacks get seated
> near the kitchen. You notice that if it's a hotel, your room is near

the elevator, or your room is always way down in a corner somewhere. You find that you are getting the undesirable rooms. And
you come there early in the day and you don't see very many cars
on the lot and they'll tell you that this is all we've got.[38]

As difficult as it is for white Americans to recognize the new face of
modern racism, it seems doubly difficult for us to comprehend its
impact. We must come to recognize that the sum of modern racism's
impact on its victims—cumulating over weeks, months, years, and
lifetimes—is greater than its individual instances. In other words,
minor instances—considered one at a time—cannot reveal the enduring depth of those instances cumulated over the course of a lifetime.

Sometimes, white Americans believe that minorities are oversensi-
tive to these instances. Let me give one example from our 1996 study
tour. We were speaking with an African-American female student from
a large, prestigious university. We asked her about her everyday experiences with modern racism. She told us of her first day in a large
freshman-level philosophy class. Her professor asked a question, and
she responded with the correct answer. After the class ended, the professor called her down to the front of the class to express how impressed, and surprised, he was with her articulateness and knowledge.
The first reaction from many of my students was to say, "Wow, I would
love to have a professor tell me those things!" Her reaction, though, was
different. She was devastated and brought to tears. In his comments,
she heard: "I am impressed, and surprised, by your articulateness and
knowledge because you are (1) black and/or (2) female." Some of my
students, like most white Americans, felt that her reaction was oversen-
sitive. Her response, however, flowed from a lifetime of experiences
with modern racism that brought a different spin to the professor's
comments.

We must learn that minorities' behaviors and their life perspectives
are powerfully shaped by their repeated experiences with modern
racism. Over the past few years, I have shared our study tour experiences and my research with dozens of audiences across the country. The
most common reaction from white audience members runs along these
lines: "Why are minorities so angry? Why can't they forget what was
done to their ancestors? I want racial reconciliation, but they seem too
bitter to work on it! They should remember that they can be just as racist
as we can be!" Each of these thoughts illustrates the inability of white

Americans to acknowledge how someone's behaviors and life perspective can be shaped by living under the shroud of modern racism. As I'll
discuss in the final chapter, racial reconciliation will not progress until
whites recognize the existence of modern racism as an everyday experience and understand its impact on minorities in America.

THE RANGE OF MODERN RACISM

The notion that racism has taken on a new face is not confined
either to the United States or to the racial context from which it origi-
nated. The Modern Racism Scale, for instance, has been found to predict
the degree of positive and negative attributes associated with Austra-
lian whites' attitudes toward aboriginal Australians. Social psychologist Rupert Brown reports that a similar modern racism measure, used
in a British context, also correlated with other measures of intergroup
bias.[39]

Psychologists Thomas Pettigrew and R. W. Meertens also demonstrated the existence of modern racism toward immigrants in four
major Western European countries: France, the Netherlands, Germany,
and Great Britain. Those members of the native populations who scored
high on a measure of "subtle" (i.e., modern) racism but low on a
"blatant" (i.e., old-fashioned) scale tended to reject immigrants in ways
that were more covert and socially acceptable. For instance, although
not wanting to take action to send immigrants back to their home
country, they were willing neither to do anything to help improve their
relations with the immigrant population nor to go along with special
programs or policies to increase that population's civil rights.[40]

In gender studies, modern racism has its parallel in modern sexism
(or neosexism). The core beliefs, with a different target, remain the
same: (1) denial that women are still discriminated against, (2) antagonism toward women's demands, and (3) feeling that women have
gotten more than they deserve.[41] Research demonstrates that, compared
to measures of old-fashioned sexism, scales of modern sexism more
reliably predict attitudes toward affirmative action.

Finally, psychologist C. S. Crandall has even devised a measure of
antifat prejudice, which he believes is conceptually similar to scales of
modern racism! His research has found that a measure of "subtle anti-

fatism" reliably identifies those who negatively stereotype and discriminate against those who are overweight, because they believe that overweight people have low willpower, set a bad example, and violate other values about personal responsibility and restraint.[42] It is very likely that, as social psychologists continue to push the envelope of modern racism, similar patterns of subtle prejudice will emerge toward groups such as the elderly, people with AIDS, those with disabilities, and others who are identifiably different from the majority.

CONCLUSION

It is a measure of the progress against racism that it is more difficult today for the racists to propagate and peddle their wares openly and in the old crude ways. This is the positive side. But in some ways, it is more difficult to fight racism that is camouflaged, racism that is attached as a rider to other complex issues.

—GUS HALL, columnist[43]

What is the legacy of research on modern racism? Some find offensive the notion that racism lurks behind attitudes seemingly innocent of manifest racial content. Others view modern racism as a progression in our inevitable evolution toward a prejudice-free society. Nevertheless, research suggests that modern forms of racism are an important social force. This same research offers the disquieting reminder that racial exclusion and hatred is a deep virus within the human psyche, possessing the incredible capability to adapt its expression to external demands. Richard Delgado has proposed a Law of Racial Thermodynamics in which racism is neither created nor destroyed. Racism changes from one era to another, but its net quantum remains exactly the same.[44] Faced with increasingly tolerant changes in societal ideals, old-fashioned racism has mutated into newer forms of modern racism. Though now camouflaged by a more pleasant exterior, racial stereotypes, bias, and resentment still lurk beneath the surface.

It is unlikely that modern racism can be alleviated by the conventional techniques of attitude change combined with legal and social pressures. Modern racists already believe that they are egalitarian, nonracist, and nondiscriminating. Attempts to educate them genuinely to accept these ideals would have little impact—they sincerely believe they already embrace them. In this way, modern racism poses an impenetrable wall. It is a wall that cannot be conquered until we choose to believe it exists.

Above my desk is a picture of Martin Luther King, Jr. I often wonder how he would react were he alive today? I think he would see a race-relations landscape that has grown and changed beyond recognition but, in many ways, is still much the same. He would be initially heartened by the tremendous strides made by racial minorities in America. The fact that the legal doors of opportunity are open to all men and women of any color would be tremendously encouraging.

Were he to walk the streets of America for a few days, however, I think his encouragement would slowly fade away. In the absence of the old-fashioned racism that he so heroically fought against, King would find a new foe in its place. He would see in modern racism the rebirth of what he hoped to destroy. He would come to recognize that modern racism is no less burdensome simply because it is less blatant than old-fashioned racism. The tremendous psychological, physical, and financial costs, to be presented in Chapter 8, still exacted from the victims of racism in America would rend his heart yet again. He would remind us that the struggle is not yet—and perhaps never will be—completed. Above all, he would remind us that to accept the myth that racism is declining is to ignore the new face of racism in America.

8

The Costs of Modern Racism
What Are We Losing?

The only thing they could do to me was to kill me and it seemed like
they'd been trying to do that a little bit at a time ever since I could
remember.
—FANNIE LOU HAMER[1]

The opening quotation by Fannie Lou Hamer, a great heroine of the civil
rights movement, is in reference to her decision to attend a mass meeting to register to vote. Her courage stemmed from the fact that she had
faced so many costs of old-fashioned racism that the ultimate cost—
losing her life—wasn't that terrifying. Today, because of her courage
and the steel resolve of countless others, racial minorities less frequently
suffer the pains of old-fashioned racism. As we have seen, however, this
"good news" is countered by the "bad news" of modern racism.

Modern racism, though different in appearance, remains costly to
American society. Modern racism continues to rob us of valuable human talent and energy and many social, economic, and political resources. Recognizing racism as a societal waste reminds us that all
Americans pay a heavy price for the persistence of racism.

Clearly, the net costs of modern racism are not equal across racial
groups. The psychological and material costs are obviously far greater
for the victims of racism. These costs are direct, heavy, and immediately
painful. The costs to whites, while more indirect and less easily recognized, must also be acknowledged, however, if racial reconciliation is to
become a reality.

COSTS OF MODERN RACISM TO THE VICTIMS

The "bad news" of modern racism is amplified by "worse news"—
the persistent toll it exacts from its victims. An analysis of these costs
lends additional weight to discrediting the myth that racism in America
is declining. The reality of painful psychological and material costs to
the victims clearly betrays the continuing presence of racism in America.

Psychological Costs of Modern Racism to the Victims

Perhaps the greatest costs to victims of racism come in the psychological realm. How one thinks about oneself and one's opportunities,
abilities, and self-esteem are tremendously influenced by social relations and misrelations. At the turn of the century, sociologist Charles
Horton Cooley suggested that we use others as mirrors to evaluate
ourselves. In his "looking-glass" theory, the appraisals of others reflect
back to us our own self-image. In other words, we learn who we are by
what others think and say of us.[2]

This theory was borne out in an experience on our 1996 tour. A
black college student in San Francisco shared an entry from his journal
with our group. This particular entry dealt with an experience he had in
a downtown department store. While shopping for a gift for one of his
sisters, he noticed a clerk tailing him. There was no attempt on the
clerk's part to hide her intentions. The student was, as he had been in
previous similar situations, shocked and saddened. One line of his
journal, however, stands out vividly in my mind. He wrote, "I feel,
despite myself, like the thief she takes me to be." Clearly, his sense of
self was shaped strongly by what someone else thought of him.

We recognize this "looking-glass" concept intuitively. During part
of my childhood, we lived in Bluefield, West Virginia. Like other grade-
schoolers, I spent a lot of time at my best friend's house. I vividly
remember one day when my friend had done something to make his
father angry. I don't remember my friend's specific action, but the
father's reaction is seared in my mind. I remember him slamming the
refrigerator door and yelling to my friend: "You'll never amount to
nothing! You're too damned sorry!" Only years later would I understand that his father's anger, like that of many abusive parents, stemmed
more from his own failures, inadequacies, and disillusionments. At that

time, however, I could intuitively recognize the long-lasting damage of his father's words. I hurt for my friend that he had to live in such a situation. Similarly, it's why I can always count on my wife crying when she overhears parents verbally abusing their children. She didn't have the misfortune of growing up in a household where such verbal abuse was commonplace. It's all too easy for her, however, as it was for me, to look into the future and see the devastating impact of such treatment.

My wife and I, similar to anyone else, make intuitive judgments about the future psychological costs of a damaging behavior simply based on one occurrence at one point in time. What must these costs be like, however, for people who suffer societal abuse, at worst, or slights, at best, every single day of their lives? What does social psychological research say to us about such costs? We will explore the psychological costs of modern racism to its victims by looking at the (1) threat of stereotypes, (2) cumulative damage of modern racism to self-esteem, and (3) cognitive burden of coping with modern racism.

The Threat of Stereotypes

Earlier, in Chapter 2, I discussed the work of a Stanford social psychologist, Claude Steele, on the power of cultural stereotypes to influence individual behavior (specifically, academic achievement). Steele argues that minorities are aware of powerful cultural stereotypes, mostly negative, regarding their performance on various tasks. They recognize that failing in those tasks will only perpetuate these collective beliefs. As a result of this threat, they experience extra pressure to defy the stereotypes. Ironically, however, the extra pressure itself may be so great as to sabotage their performance.

Steele and others have performed several experiments detailing the legacy of "stereotype threat." In an original experiment Steele, Steven Spencer, and Diane Quinn gave a series of tests under various conditions to male and female students. Some students were told that women generally performed as well as men on these tests. Others were told that, in the past, performance on the tests appeared to be related to gender. For this latter group, the researchers assumed that the cultural stereotype of women as inferior mathematically would lead most women to infer that females had generally done worse on these tests. Furthermore, the activation of this cultural stereotype was hypothesized to be threatening enough to undermine the performance of women—even those who had a high aptitude for math. Results supported this hypothesis. As the researchers concluded,

> When subjects were explicitly told that the test yielded gender differences, women greatly underperformed in relation to men, replicating the stereotype threat effects in the earlier experiments and suggesting that ... women had assumed a male advantage on the test. But when the test was purported not to yield gender differences, women performed at the same level as equally-qualified men. This happened, of course, even though the test in these two conditions was the same.[3]

So simply the threat of fulfilling a powerful cultural stereotype that "girls are bad in math" led women in this study to underperform in relation to men. Would stereotype threat similarly impact blacks relative to whites? In a 1995 experiment, Steele and Joshua Aronson gave two groups of black and white Stanford undergraduates the same test involving difficult questions from the Graduate Record Examination (GRE). Prior to the test, one group was told that the exercise was nondiagnostic and meant only to examine "psychological factors involved in solving verbal problems." The other group was told that the exercise was judgmental and meant to be "a genuine test of your verbal abilities and limitations."

In the first group of students, who thought they were merely solving verbal problems and, thus, their ability was not being judged, blacks scored the same as whites. In the second group of students, however, the exercise, perceived as a genuine test of their verbal abilities and limitations, was significantly more threatening, because it had the potential to perpetrate a cultural stereotype of black inferiority. As a result of this stereotype threat, black students in this second group scored significantly lower than whites.[4] In effect, blacks in the second group were saying, "If I perform poorly on this test, it will reflect poorly on me and my race." This extra burden of apprehension interfered with their ability to perform as well as blacks in the first group of students, for whom apprehension about stereotype confirmation was removed.

The costs of stereotype threat on standardized tests are incalculable. GREs, Medical College Admission Tests (MCATs), and Law School Admission Tests (LSATs) are the keys to the doors of upper-middle-class society. As Steele argues, however, the cumulative impact of stereotype threat on academic achievement may be even more pronounced. Blacks begin school with test scores that are fairly close to the test scores of whites their age. The longer they stay in school, however, the more they fall behind. By the sixth grade, blacks are often two full grade levels behind whites in achievement—a pattern than holds true for the middle class nearly as much as in the lower class. The increasing disparity in achievement remains throughout high school. In college, the grades of black students average nearly half a letter below those of whites.[5]

In Steele's analysis, background disadvantages (e.g., poor schools, broken families, drug-infested communities, economic poverty, etc.) cannot fully explain these increasing disparities in academic achievement. Blacks underachieve academically, relative to whites, even when they have ample resources, strongly value education, and are well-prepared in terms of knowledge and skills. Something else has to be involved. That something else, he believes, is captured in the concept of stereotype threat—the burden of living "down" to an unfavorable racial stigma.

The apprehension associated with stereotype threat may even become paralyzing. In other words, the threat of confirming an unfavorable racial stereotype may be so severe as to leave racial minorities afraid of taking chances for achievement. It's like the children's game where a coin is hidden in one of two clenched fists. Guess the right one and you win; guess the wrong one and you can try again. For racial minorities, however, the rules of the game are different. Guess the right one and you win; guess the wrong one, and you lose and never get to try again.

Several years ago, Steele and several colleagues launched an experiment at the University of Michigan, the "21st Century Program," designed to make racial minority students less vulnerable to stereotype threat. The program is a racially diverse (both white and nonwhite students), live-in experience. Students enrolled in the program live in the same dorm wing their first year and attend workshops that emphasize collaborative projects. The program's intention to blunt the impact of racial stereotypes seems successful. In 1995, Steele reported that blacks in this program maintained a 2.80 grade point average (GPA)—the same as whites. The GPA for blacks not in the program was only 2.30. In addition, dropout rates for blacks in the program were significantly lower than those for blacks not in the program (10 percent compared to 30 percent).[6]

Stereotype threat can work in the opposite direction as well. For Asian-Americans, for example, the stereotype threat often lies not in living "down" to an unfavorable racial stigma, but rather in living "up" to an overly favorable one. The "model minority" stereotype says that Asian-Americans are overachievers, gifted in math and science, study and work harder, get better grades, and consistently outscore other students on standardized tests. This stereotype has been perpetrated by television news programs and splashed on the cover of national magazines.

Though such positive expectations may sound like a good stereotype to have, many Asian-Americans bristle at the "model minority" label. They grow weary of the threat of unreasonable expectations from peers, teachers, and society. This threat is especially debilitating for newer immigrants, who may be pushed too hard by school systems or organizations that automatically assume they will do well.

In addition, some Asian-Americans harbor a sense that their accomplishments are rarely appreciated, because everyone expects them to succeed. Last year, a Japanese-American student came to my office for an advising appointment. It became clear that she was at a fragile place in her life. Finally, she broke into tears. The tears didn't come from a well of unfulfilled expectations. Rather, they flowed from the universal futility of being underappreciated. I, like most of her other teachers, saw this student as extremely capable and gifted. She completely fulfilled the "model minority" stereotype. Perhaps because of that, I did not adequately recognize her achievements. Other students, of whom I probably expected less, received a lot more strokes for similar—even inferior—work. For her, however, I must confess that the "model minority" stereotype led me to expect superior work from her. As a result, the primary feedback she received from many of her instructors came only when she failed to meet their high expectations.

Finally, the greatest threat of the "model minority" stereotype may come from the supposed example it sets for other racial minorities. For whom are Asian-Americans a "model"? Most often, they are a model held up to discipline other racial minorities. If Asian-Americans can succeed economically and educationally, the model screams, then the failures of other racial minorities to grasp the Great American Dream are easily explainable. "You aren't disciplined enough, don't work hard enough, and aren't self-reliant enough! Look at the Asian-Americans! They did it by pulling themselves up by their bootstraps!" This particular threat of the model minority stereotype strains relations between Asian-Americans and other racial minorities.

The Cumulative Damage of Modern Racism to Self-Esteem

As a parent, one of the most moving moments in Martin Luther King Jr.'s *Letter from a Birmingham Jail* comes when he tells of the pain involved in explaining

> to your six-year-old daughter why she can't go to the public amusement park that has just been advertised on television, and see tears welling up in her little eyes when she is told that Funtown is closed to colored children, and see the depressing clouds of inferiority begin to form in her little mental sky, and see her begin to distort her little personality by unconsciously developing a bitterness toward white people.[7]

What do we know about the cumulative impact of racism on someone's self-esteem, or "little mental sky"? Black psychologists Kenneth and Mamie Clark gave us some disturbing insights more than four decades ago. Much of the Clarks's professional life had been spent comparing the effect of segregated and racially mixed schools upon black children. One of their research techniques involved showing black children four identical dolls—two of them brown and two white. Children were then asked to point out the doll they would most like to play with, they liked best, was nice, looks bad, or was a nice color. The majority of the black children tested in the 1940s and 1950s, some as young as three years old, indicated an unmistakable preference for the white doll and a rejection of the brown doll. In Kenneth Clark's words, "What was surprising was the degree to which children suffered from self-rejection, with its truncating effect on their personalities, and the earliness of the corrosive awareness of color. I don't think we had quite realized the extent of the cruelty of racism and how hard it hit."[8]

The Clarks's research dramatically revealed the impact of old-fashioned racism on blacks's self-esteem. It ultimately proved a pivotal piece of testimony in the 1954 *Brown v. Topeka Board of Education* case. As Chief Justice Warren stated, the soon-to-be-outlawed policy of separate but equal "generates a feeling of inferiority as to their [blacks] status in the community that may affect their hearts and minds in a way unlikely ever to be undone."[9]

But surely, one might argue, the removal of segregation and subsequent decline of racism has ameliorated this problem. As we have seen, however, racism has not declined. Racism has mutated into new expressions. Does modern racism still take a toll on self-esteem? Incredibly enough, the Clarks conducted a set of nearly identical studies in the late 1980s. At a national conference of psychologists in 1987, they reported that the self-esteem of black children was as poor at that time as it was 40 years earlier! Again, Kenneth Clark: "What the children are telling us is that they see their color as the basis of self-rejection. We've tried to hide the damage racism does to black children, but the damage is there, and will continue as long as racism continues."[10]

The Price of Low Self-Esteem: Self-Hatred.   For some, the damage inculcated by racism can lead to a disabling self-hatred. I recall a story of Branch Rickey's days as a baseball coach at Ohio Wesleyan University. In the spring of 1904, Rickey's team traveled to South Bend, Indiana, to play Notre Dame. The hotel at which the team had reservations refused to allow Charlie Thomas, a black first baseman, to lodge there. Rickey finally convinced the management to place a cot in his room for Thomas to sleep on, as they would for a black servant. Rickey recalls later entering the room to find a weeping Thomas rubbing his hands as if trying to rub off the color. "Black skin! Black skin!" he said to Rickey. "If I could only make them white!"[11] Though the significance of this episode may have been exaggerated as the basis for Rickey's later action to integrate professional baseball, it remains a vivid, real-life example of what was hinted at in the Clarks's research: The impact of continual exposure to racism can go beyond lowering self-esteem and even lead to a self-hatred.

The Twisted Face of Self-Hatred.   Occasionally, we vent our self-hatred in ways meant to protect our self-esteem. Most commonly, we turn our self-hatred to hating others in order to make us feel better about ourselves and less threatened by other groups of people. Venting self-hatred in this way poisons our capacity for meaningful relationships. James Baldwin's *The Fire Next Time* speaks of racism as inculcating a "hatred for white men so deep that it often turned against him [black man] and his own and made all love, all trust, all joy impossible."[12] Hatred, even if justified, can be a heavy burden to carry.

On the 1996 tour, we spoke with a black man in Memphis, Tennessee, who, early in his life, had learned to deflect his self-hatred outward to whites, homosexuals, and Jews. Hating those groups somehow preserved his own fragile self-esteem. As Baldwin warned, however, it also made "all love, all trust, all joy impossible" in this man's life. Though he recognized other factors, he believed that the downfall of his recent marriage was at least partly attributable to hatred's choking influence on his ability to engage in meaningful relationships.

In a 1997 article, psychologists Steven Fein of Williams College (MA) and Steven Spencer of the University of Waterloo examined the hypothesis that stereotyping and prejudice may be a common way to protect one's self-esteem. The results of three separate studies disclosed that individuals were less likely to evaluate a person stereotypically if their self-esteem had been recently bolstered. Conversely, they were more likely to evaluate that person stereotypically if their self-esteem had been recently threatened by negative feedback. These results indicate that when our self-esteem is threatened, we may call on negative evaluations of others to make us feel better about ourselves. In other words, prejudice can be self-affirming.[13]

Affirmative Action Revisited. Today, some of the most violent discussion surrounding self-esteem of racial minorities centers around the impact of affirmative action. Clearly, whites attach a stigma of incompetence, based on some of the misconceptions discussed in Chapter 7, to minorities or women who are the beneficiaries of affirmative action programs. Minorities are painfully aware of this stigma. Whites often generalize this stigma to an argument that affirmative action actually undermines the self-esteem of its recipients by implying that they can't make it on their own. Is this argument true?

In truth, interview studies and public opinion surveys suggest that such reactions are rare. For instance, a recent poll asked employed blacks and employed white women whether they had ever felt that others questioned their abilities because of affirmative action. Nearly 90 percent said "no."[14] These findings shouldn't be surprising. After all, white men, who have traditionally benefited from preferential hiring, don't often feel hampered by a loss in self-esteem! We don't even ask them this question! As Philip Green notes, "It would be interesting to ask them [white males]—or to ask the same question of those doctors who managed to get into good medical schools because there were quotas keeping out Jews, the skilled tradesmen who were admitted to the union because two members of their family recommended them and so on."[15] The ridiculous lesson is that it is not detrimental to your self-esteem to be rewarded because you are in the majority or an established elite; it's only detrimental when you are in the minority or a marginal group.

In addition, why would the damage to self-esteem from affirmative action be greater, or of more concern, than the damage caused by old-fashioned racism and discrimination? Can we really believe that a person's self-esteem would be made stronger by unemployment and suffering than by being able to feed his or her family? An argument more easily supported would be that affirmative action actually *raises* the self-esteem of minorities and women by providing them with employment and opportunities for advancement.

(By the way, isn't it interesting that—for decades—whites couldn't have cared less about the self-esteem of racial minorities. But when "caring" about their self-esteem became a plank in the platform of dismantling affirmative action, suddenly there's a long line of people wanting to make sure that racial minorities feel good about themselves!)

The Cognitive Burden of Coping with Modern Racism

The final psychological cost to explore relates to the burden of cognitive effort that victims of racism must bear. Sociologist Joe Feagin, in a 1991 article, describes a revealing interview with an older black woman. In that interview, she spoke of living six decades with having to put on her "shield" just before she left the house each morning. The "shield," trying to prepare herself for insults and discrimination, is an extraordinary cognitive burden that whites simply do not have to worry about. Similar remarks were evident in most of the 135 interviews conducted by Feagin.[16]

In that same article, Feagin describes how another respondent articulates this additional cognitive burden:

> If you can think of the mind as having one hundred ergs of energy
> ... a black person ... uses fifty percent the same way a white man
> does, dealing with what the white man has [to deal with], so he has
> fifty percent left. But he uses twenty-five percent fighting being
> black.... Which means he really only has twenty-five percent to do
> what the white man has fifty percent to do, and he's expected to do
> just as much.[17]

Clearly, the psychological costs of coping with racism are great. In a vicious cycle, the drain of those costs is yet one more additional burden with which racial minorities are loaded.

Material Costs of Modern Racism to the Victims

> They sort of felt like baby turtles left to crawl from birth nest to
> ocean all by themselves, while predators of all varieties came to be
> part of the baby turtle beach buffet. They sort of felt like Indian
> children of Indian parents.[18]

This quotation, from Sherman Alexie's novel *Reservation Blues*, is a striking analogy of the purely material, even life-threatening, costs that racial minorities continue to endure in America. In Chapter 5, we reviewed some of the costs of racism reflected in quality-of-life indicators such as economic status, educational attainment, and general social well-being. The data revealed vast and significant racial disparities across these areas. Sometimes, that much aggregate data can make our eyes glaze over and cause us to lose an understanding of the *daily* toll inflicted by racism. So, I want to supplement that discussion by reviewing some additional material costs in (1) the financial costs of modern racism, (2) modern racism's toll on life and death, and (3) the uneven scales of justice.

The Financial Costs of Modern Racism

Several years ago, I was at a faculty assembly meeting where we were discussing the implementation of an active minority student recruitment and retention program. Like many discussions in higher education, we were stalled because we wanted to implement a great program without having to take money and resources from other areas. Finally, one of my colleagues, who was getting quite perturbed, stood up and shouted, "The color of commitment is green!" His point, that money speaks louder than words, can be mirrored in an analysis of some of the specific financial costs of racism.

Chapter 5 reviewed a wealth of data on economic disparities between whites and racial minorities. We didn't have to look hard to uncover those disparities. For instance, prior to the 1964 Civil Rights Act, black men earned 60 percent as much as white men; still, today, black men earn only 74 percent compared to white men.[19] Across sexes, blacks still receive less than 62 cents for each dollar of income received by whites, and are still roughly three times as likely to be poor across the country.[20] As Chapter 5 demonstrated, quality-of-life indicators, whether economic, educational, or social, betray the clear and sustained effects of racism in America.

At times, however, the financial costs of racism are more subtle and occur outside our immediate awareness. For instance, a 1992 *Prime-Time Live* report, entitled *True Colors*, reported that blacks pay on the average $1,010 more for a car than do whites. In a 1991 *Harvard Law Review* article, Ian Ayres confirmed that finding with the results of a clever and painstaking study of 90 car dealerships in the Chicago area. He found that the sale prices of the cars offered to white men were significantly lower than the prices offered to women or to men of color. Using a carefully rehearsed, uniform strategy to negotiate the lowest possible price on a new car (one that cost the dealer about $11,000), Ayres found that white males were given a final price averaging $11,362, compared to white females, $11,504; black males, $11,783; black females $12,237. These drastic differences withstood any statistical controls that the researcher placed on his data.[21]

Economist Walter Updegrave likewise contends that modern racism still prevents middle-class black families from earning as much as whites; lowers their access to mortgages, business loans, and other financial services; retards their homes' rates of appreciation; prevents them from increasing their wealth effectively; and deprives them of the economic well-being enjoyed by their white middle-class counterparts.[22] A lack of financial assets means that even most middle-class racial minorities are living on the economic edge. Sociologists Melvin Oliver and Tom Shapiro document that middle-class blacks possess only 15 cents for every dollar of wealth (including assets) held by middle-class whites.[23]

Updegrave's assertions are supported by a 1995 *U.S. News & World Report* article examining banking and insurance industry data for racial discrimination. Blatant discrimination—in which financial institutions literally drew a red line (that is, "formal redlining") around entire neighborhoods deemed off-limits for loans and homeowner's insurance— was rare. The report found, however, that other practices were in place that effectively impeded lending to poor neighborhoods. Middle-income black mortgage applicants from mostly minority areas were more than twice as likely to be rejected for loans (37 percent rejection rate) as middle-income whites living in mostly white areas (18 percent rejection rate).

Obtaining full-coverage home insurance is nearly as important as finding mortgage financing. The National Association of Insurance Commissioners reports, however, that only 57.6 percent of the houses in high-minority, low-income areas were insured at all, compared with 81.5 percent in white, high-income areas. Insurance redlining is widespread and continues to impact adversely residents of minority and poor neighborhoods.[24]

Finally, we even find financial costs of modern racism in places where we don't normally expect to find racial minorities. On August 29, 1997, a $512.8 million federal lawsuit was filed on behalf of 641 black farmers who are accusing the Agriculture Department of denying loans because of race—some dating back 12 years. The number of black farmers, presently fewer than 1 percent of the nation's 1.9 million farmers, is dwindling at nearly three times the rate of other farmers. In the words of lawyer Alexander Pires, Jr., "The lives of nearly 700 Black farmers were nearly ruined, and no one paid any attention."[25]

Modern Racism's Toll on Life and Death

A few dollars out of the pockets of racial minorities are one thing. Even if they add up to thousands of dollars over the course of a lifetime, at least they still have their health. Or do they? Is physical health even spared the ravages of modern racism? One disturbing answer came from a series of studies by James Jackson of the University of Michigan. Jackson found that racial and ethnic groups reporting the highest number of experiences with prejudice also had the most doctor-verified health problems and disabilities. This link was independent of income.[26] Specific information regarding racism's toll on life and death can come from a wide variety of areas—racial disparities in AIDS, sudden infant death syndrome (SIDS), and teenage pregnancies, for instance, are well documented. In the next few pages, however, we will focus on racial disparities in (1) hypertension, (2) cancer, (3) syphilis, and (4) mortality.

Hypertension. The high prevalence of hypertension among blacks, relative to whites, has long been recognized. In an exhaustive 1989 review article, Norman Anderson of Duke University Medical Center reported that the incidence of hypertension in the American black population is among the highest of any group in the world. It is approximately twice that of white Americans.[27] As a consequence of the near-epidemic prevalence of hypertension, blacks experience correspondingly high rates of hypertension-related sickness, coronary heart disease, and kidney failure. It is not a stretch to say that hypertension is the number-one health problem of black Americans. All told, about one-third of the excess mortality of American blacks over nonblacks can be explained by their greater burden of hypertension.[28]

The sources of hypertension are many—genetic, biological, nutritional, and behavioral factors among them. Some of these factors exist independently of racism. Black newborns, for instance, already evidence faster resting heart rates in comparison with those of white newborns, though most studies report no racial group differences in blood pressure. In addition, black adults appear to be more sensitive to the effects of sodium.[29]

As Maya McNeilly of Duke University Medical Center asserts, however, "Genetics is far from the whole story." For example, lower income blacks, who more often must fight urban crowding, higher crime rate, and higher unemployment, are at a greater risk for hypertension than are higher income blacks. Researchers now recognize the existence of psychological, social, and environmental factors (including racism) that contribute to the prevalence of hypertension among blacks. McNeilly's laboratory studies, for instance, found that racist comments from whites triggered significant rises in blood pressure and heartrate in 30 black women. As she concluded, "Racism can act as a potent stressor that may contribute to hypertension and heart disease."[30] In an October 1996 article, Nancy Krieger and Stephen Sidney of the Harvard

School of Public Health summarized the research on black–white differences in hypertension by referring to these differences as the literal embodiment of racial discrimination.[31]

A 1996 *Time* health report found that one's pattern of response to racism may even influence hypertension. For instance, blacks who must suffer discrimination in silence were found to have higher blood pressure than those who could afford to challenge racist treatment.[32] In short, there seem to be health advantages to dealing with a painful issue, such as racism, straight on rather than having to suffer in silence and internalize the hurt.

Cancer.   Cancer affects Americans of all racial groups and kills more people annually than AIDS, accidents, and homicide *combined.* The rate of cancer occurrence (called the *incidence rate*) does, however, vary considerably from racial group to racial group. Among men, African-Americans have a higher overall cancer incidence rate than any other racial group. They are followed by whites, whose rates are about 16 percent lower. Cancer incidence rates for Native Americans in New Mexico (a very small cross-section of the Native American population) are the lowest. Cancer rates among Asian-American men are also quite low. Among women, the differences in rates across racial groups are less pronounced than among men.[33]

Now, for the first time in history, overall cancer deaths are dropping, and less-toxic, less-disfiguring treatments are available. But that good news is countered by alarming rises in deaths among women from lung cancer (more women and girls smoke today than decades ago) and black men from prostate cancer. Among black men, deaths from prostate cancer have risen about 50 percent since 1973, compared to only a 23 percent increase among white men.[34] American blacks have the highest prostate cancer incidence rates in the world. Finally, we know that tobacco is a risk factor for some 25 diseases, including various forms of cancer. Today, smoking rates are higher among Native Americans than any other racial group (42 percent of Native Americans smoke, compared to 25 percent of the U.S. adult population). They begin smoking earlier than other Americans. As a result, cancer and heart disease are on the rise and partially explain why the average lifespan of Native Americans is 13 to 16 years shorter than that of other Americans.[35]

The relatively direct link between racism and hypertension is impossible to demonstrate with cancer. It is, however, clear that, again, genetics is far from the whole story. To the degree that race impacts a person's chances for a good education, occupation, income, and living conditions, it also impacts cancer, since each of those factors are related to a person's cancer-risk profile. Unfortunately, national data are not available to evaluate the direct impact of race, and racism, on cancer.

Syphilis.   Syphilis, a sexually transmitted disease, is an infection caused by a bacterium (*Treponema pallidum*) that can damage tissues in many organs of the body, producing a wide range of problems. Syphilis has been treatable, and curable, with penicillin since 1947. Untreated, the infection can pervade all parts of the body, causing pain and eventually leading to paralysis and death.

During 1996, new cases of syphilis in the United States fell to their lowest rate in 40 years. That decline, however, has only exaggerated the black–white racial disparity that has persisted at least since the 1930s. At present, the syphilis rate in blacks is almost 60 times higher than that in whites![36] Again, though racism has no direct physiological tie to syphilis, we see its indirect influence through blacks' reduced access to health care and a lack of awareness of the disease and the availability of treatment.

Mortality.   Given the racial disparities in general health, it should come as no surprise that we find corresponding disparities in mortality. At one end of the spectrum, we find that nearly 40 percent of all black mothers have no prenatal care in the first trimester of pregnancy. This leaves them twice as likely as whites to have babies with low birth weights—often the cause of permanent impairment or infant death. In fact, the black infant mortality rate of 18.6 per 1,000 births (again, twice that of whites) is higher than that for Bulgaria or Costa Rica![37]

According to the National Center for Health Statistics, the average white person lives seven years longer than the average black person.[38] If you are a black man living in New York's Harlem, you are less likely to reach age 65 than a resident of Bangladesh! Black men have a three times greater chance of dying of AIDS and outnumber whites as murder victims by a factor of seven.[39] Most discouraging is the fact that the life-expectancy gap between blacks and whites—as well as the infant mortality gap—had narrowed for several decades, only to increase in the mid-1980s and continue to widen today.

Every day in America, an average of 83 people take their own lives. Blacks, the people whose ancestors survived slavery and segregation, have historically been remarkably resistant to suicide. In the last decade, however, the Centers for Disease Control report that suicide rates have jumped 300 percent among blacks ages 10–14, and 164 percent among those ages 15–24. Among the contributing factors are increasing rates of depression, access to firearms, broken families, and fragmented communities. As Kenya Napper Bello, a suicide-prevention activist in Atlanta, states: "We [African-Americans] characterize ourselves as being able to get through most things because of faith, strong community and our relationships with the church."[40] Unfortunately, those supports are disintegrating as a result of many social forces—including racism.

Conclusion. It would be an irresponsible overexaggeration to claim that modern racism is the only necessary, and sufficient, cause of elevated rates of hypertension, cancer, syphilis, and mortality among racial minorities. Racism's tie to these, and other diseases, must be understood in the light of other genetic, biological, nutritional, behavioral, psychological, social, and environmental factors.

It would also be a mistake, however, to assume that modern racism plays no part in the etiology of disease among minorities. The shorter, and more painful, life of racial minorities results in at least some significant measure from the reality of modern racism. In the most recent illustration of this, a 1997 survey of 1,140 Detroit-area adults by David Williams of the University of Michigan's Institute for Social Research examined the relationship between modern racism and general health. He found that it was the frequency of "everyday" discrimination, chronic hassles, that's most strongly linked to health. As Yale University psychologist Mahzarin Banaji reminds us, "our stereotypes may have some impact on other people's health. ... These 'minor' events of stereotyping can add up, and the effects may be destructive for other people."[41]

Uneven Scales of Justice

From arrest to sentencing to imprisonment to parole, America's justice system is trampled with the footprints of racism. At every stage of the criminal justice process, racial minorities are subject to disadvantages. Your darker color means that you are perceived to be more threatening and, therefore, are an easier target to stop and detain. Our courts of justice seem like alien terrain for most racial minorities. Usually, the judge and prosecutor are white, as are most members of the jury, as well as your attorney. The scales of justice, upon which your life depends, are predominately white. Only in imprisonment do you find similar faces of color.

Blacks' perception of the criminal justice system is very reflective of the mistrust felt by many racial minorities. A 1992 Gallup Poll, for instance, found that nearly one-third (31 percent) of blacks believed that recent criminal prosecutions brought against prominent, black public officials reflect a plot to drive African-American leaders from public life.[42] A 1995 Gallup Poll revealed that nearly two in three blacks (66 percent) accept the statement that the American justice system is biased against blacks. In that same poll, blacks also were much less likely than whites to believe the testimony of police officers, and clearly think that crimes involving white victims are prosecuted with more zeal than when the victims are black.[43]

Arrest Rates. In 1990, more than 10 million criminal counts were logged. Although only comprising 12 percent of the general population, arrest rates for blacks were disproportionate for every offense except drunken driving. Blacks, for instance, accounted for 61.2 percent of all robbery arrests, 54.7 percent of the suspects arrested for murder and manslaughter, and 43.2 percent in cases of rape. (Interestingly enough, the annual victimization survey conducted by the Census Bureau found that only 33.2 percent of the women who said they had been raped identified their attackers as black. Because the race of the rapist does not seem to affect whether a report will be forthcoming, this disparity suggests that attacks by whites are less apt to lead to arrests.)[44]

The racial disparity in arrest rates is clear. How do we explain it? Some of the disparity reflects the tragic reality that desperate circumstances often increase the likelihood that an individual will turn to desperate measures. Some of the disparity, however, reflects subtle racial biases in law enforcement. For instance, the decision to fight the war on drugs on the front lines of the inner city is logical, right? Maybe not. In a 1993 opinion piece, Kenneth Johnson, a judge for the Baltimore City Circuit, cited studies indicating that there are more drugs and drug users in American *suburbs* than there are in the inner cities![45] Given the focus of our law enforcement efforts, however, arrest rates will never reflect that reality.

The inordinate focus of law enforcement on racial minorities also is seen in the scores of African-American males—including prominent athletes, members of Congress, actors, and business leaders—who have experienced the humiliation of being stopped on the nation's roads for no other reason than the alleged traffic offense derisively referred to as "DWB"—"driving while black." The extent of this problem has prompted Congressman John Conyers (D–Michigan) to propose legislation to address this unjust practice. The Traffic Stops Statistics Act of 1997 would encourage police departments to keep detailed records of traffic stops, including the race and ethnicity of the person stopped. Such data would help determine the full scope of this problem nationwide. In a 1995 Gallup Poll, both whites (52 percent) and blacks (68 percent) agreed that police racism against blacks is common across the country.[46]

Sentencing. Continuing racial discrimination in sentencing combines with arrest statistics to exaggerate differences in crime patterns between blacks and whites. Jody Armour, a Professor of Law at the University of Southern California, cites a 1996 New York State study revealing that 30 percent of blacks and Hispanics received harsher sentences than whites in New York for comparable crimes. In addition, about 4,000 blacks and Hispanics are incarcerated each year for crimes under circumstances that do not lead to incarceration for whites.[47] There is an ongoing debate over manifest bias in the drug laws themselves. Powder cocaine is purer than crack cocaine and worth more. Yet it takes possession of 500 grams of powder (worth $40,000 in 1994) to equal the five-year sentence that someone possessing five grams of crack cocaine (worth only $250) would receive. The fact that whites are the main users of powder cocaine, whereas blacks primarily use crack, leads to fewer arrests and lighter sentences for whites than for blacks.[48]

The impact of such disparities in sentencing is tremendous. For instance, nearly one in four black men between the ages of 20 and 29 is either in prison or on probation or parole. Although blacks only make up about 12 percent of our general population, they constitute over 40 percent of state and federal inmates. A 1997 report by the Sentencing Project, "Intended and Unintended Consequences: State Racial Disparity in Imprisonment," revealed that one in seven African-American men is permanently or currently disenfranchised as a result of a felony conviction. Specifically, 1.46 million black males of a total voting-age population of 10.4 million have lost the right to vote because of a felony conviction. About 510,000 are permanently disenfranchised because of laws in 13 states. The remaining 950,000 are currently ineligible to vote because of laws in 46 states regarding offenders in prison or on probation or parole.[49]

Calling the new statistics "disturbing," Mark Kappelhoff of the ACLU said that they

> are not entirely unexpected in light of the racial disparity found throughout the nation's criminal justice system where black men are being stopped, arrested, convicted and sentenced in proportions far higher than is right or fair in a democratic society. Disproportionately excluding an entire segment of our society from voting further polarizes our country along racial lines, and laws that target voting, one of the most fundamental features of our participatory democracy, undercut everything for which this country stands.[50]

A 1995 *Oakland Tribune* report on sentencing for cocaine offenders is equally troubling. Earlier, we presented powder cocaine as the drug of choice for whites, crack cocaine for blacks. Clearly, though, some whites do sell and abuse crack cocaine, just as some blacks sell and abuse powder cocaine. Even in these cases, however, racial disparities still occur in sentencing. The *Oakland Tribune* report indicated that, most often, black and Hispanic crack dealers are tried in *federal* courts serving Los Angeles and the surrounding areas. If convicted, federal courts typically levy a 10-year mandatory sentence. Between 1988 and 1994, however, not a single white was convicted of a crack cocaine offense in those same federal courts! Rather, in those few cases when whites were arrested for distributing or using crack cocaine, they were prosecuted in *state* court, where sentences are much lighter. In state court, a convicted defendant can expect to receive a maximum five-year sentence, often serving no more than a year in jail.[51]

Mock jury studies also suggest a tendency for racial bias to affect jury deliberations in death-penalty cases. Psychologist John Dovidio, for instance, described a recent mock jury study in which white participants made recommendations for the death penalty in a murder case. As expected, those who scored high on a racism scale made significantly stronger recommendations for capital sentencing for black defendants than for white defendants—even though the facts in the case were identical. Also as expected, white participants who scored low on the racism scale generally did not discriminate against the black defendant. In a condition where racial bias could be discounted as a motivation because a black juror advocated the death penalty for the black defendant, however, even those white participants who scored low on the racism scale showed racial bias in sentencing.[52]

The results of these laboratory studies are reflected in reality. Blacks represent a strikingly disproportionate percentage (40 percent) of the prisoners currently under sentence of death.[53] A 1987 study prepared for the Supreme Court found that murderers who killed whites faced a 10 times greater chance of a death sentence than did murderers of black victims. Even after taking into account the ferocity of the crime and the social status of the victim, the prospect for the death penalty was still four times higher when the victim was white.[54] Whether such racial bias is the result of own-race favoritism or other-race antagonism is relatively irrelevant to the fact that racial bias in sentencing, even capital sentencing, exists.

COSTS OF MODERN RACISM TO WHITES

The costs of modern racism are obviously greatest for its victims. But does modern racism exact a toll from whites as well? Do whites *only* benefit from the existence of modern racism? Or, do whites suffer some hidden costs? An analysis of the costs of modern racism to whites is important, because it can become a driving force in bringing about positive change. It would be great if whites jumped on the bandwagon of racial reconciliation purely out of moral reasons. In truth, however, many of us won't make that leap until we can be convinced that the costs of perpetrating modern racism may be more significant than we have traditionally believed. In other words, we are driven by the same profit motive that drives corporate America. If the *benefits* of our stereotypes, prejudices, and discriminatory behaviors outweigh the *costs*, then you and I have little reason to change those thoughts, feelings, or behaviors. If we realize the costs to us, however, we finally may be driven to a conversation about the eradication of modern racism. This is, for sure, an ugly way to bring about racial reconciliation. It's no more pleasing than bribing a child to do the right thing when he or she doesn't want to. When so many other strategies have failed, however, it can, at least, get us started on doing the right thing.

We must recognize that this is not a zero-sum racial game of power and resources. In other words, in the game of race relations, when one side wins, the other does not automatically have to lose. For racial minorities to gain, it is not necessary that whites lose. In some cases, all can win, whereas in others, all can lose. Right now, all of us—both victims and perpetrators—are losing.

The costs of modern racism to whites are relatively negligible and difficult to articulate. I already feel "whiny" even writing about this. The costs, such as they are, simply pale in comparison to those suffered by the victims of modern racism. As a white male, I can take a job with an affirmative action employer without having my co-workers suspect that I got it because of my race; I can do well in a challenging situation without being called a credit to my race; I am never asked to speak for all the people of my racial group; I can easily buy posters, postcards, books, greeting cards, dolls, toys, and children's magazines featuring people of my race.[55] Like any perpetrator of a crime that goes un-punished, I am in a position of unearned privilege and not looking to turn myself in.

Regardless, there are costs of modern racism to whites that we have been trained to ignore, deny, or rationalize away. By facing these costs, we can face the reality that racism is a game with no absolute winners. All of us lose and some more than others. How do whites lose? Parallel-ing our previous discussion, let's explore the psychological and mate-rial costs of modern racism to whites.

Psychological Costs of Modern Racism to Whites

Not all whites are racist. Psychologist Thomas Pettigrew estimates that 15 percent of whites are so deeply racist that they should be viewed as seriously mentally *ill*. At the other end of the continuum, about 25 percent of whites are antiracist and consistently support minority rights. Between these two extremes lie the remaining 60 percent of whites who are conforming, or what we have called modern racists.[56] For this group, their racist beliefs, feelings and behaviors are not so deeply rooted. If the social situation should so warrant, they even may actually change their beliefs, feelings, and behaviors to become more egalitarian.

All whites do, however, benefit from modern racism and, to some degree, suffer from its consequences as well. The psychological costs of modern racism to whites can be captured in the three bondages of hate, fear, and guilt.

Bondage of Hate

Perhaps the most significant psychological cost of modern racism to whites is the bondage of hate that it instills. The *freedom* to hate, abused by some whites, often becomes the *slavery* to hate. In other words, our psyches become so soiled by hatred that hatred begins to dictate our thoughts, feelings, and behaviors. In sociologist George Yancey's words, "They [whites] enjoy a false freedom that fools them into thinking that they are free to act as they want to act, but it is the freedom of an addict. It may give some whites the illusion of power and mastery, but all the while the addiction to hatred controls every action and feeling."[57] Martin Luther King, Jr. saw his efforts as not just attempts to free blacks from blatant external oppression but also to help whites relieve the bondage of hate that racism inflicts upon their psyches. Similarly, Cherokee leader John Ross declared that "the perpetrator of a wrong" would never forgive "his victims."[58]

In this way, racism, while taking an undeniable toll on its victims, exacts a paradoxical price from its perpetrators as well—their eventual dehumanization as they are enslaved by the invisible chains of hatred. As Frederick Douglass stated at an 1881 civil rights meeting in Washington, D.C., "No man can put a chain about the ankle of his fellow man without at last finding the other end fastened about his own neck."[59] Over a century later, Nelson Mandela echoed the same sentiment in his autobiography: "A man who takes away another man's freedom is a prisoner of hatred, he is locked behind the bars of prejudice and narrow-mindedness.... The oppressed and the oppressor alike are robbed of their humanity."[60] The bondage of hatred was nicely illustrated in a 1990 political cartoon in the *Christian Science Monitor*. In Danziger's drawing, entitled "Racism's Full Circle," a hooded Ku Klux Klan figure stands holding a burning torch in one hand and a gasoline can, labeled "hatred," in the other. Unbeknownst to the figure, the flame fueled by hatred has circled around him and is igniting the back side of his white robe.

Bondage of Fear

The bondage of hate is joined by the bondage of fear. How abiding and deep-seated are whites' fears of racial minorities? What is the cost this fear brings to whites? To what relationships, benefits, and opportunities does this fear blind us? Answers to some of these questions were to come from a very unique experience on our 1996 study tour.

On the evening of January 14, we arrived at the Amtrak station in downtown Chicago at about 7:00 P.M. The trip from Denver had taken nearly 20 hours, and we were all anxious to reach our rooms at the International House at the University of Chicago as soon as possible. So far on the tour, I had earned my reputation as "the map-master" by steering us, without incident, to every hostel, museum, restaurant, and lecture site without error. Somewhere in my notes, I had bus directions directly to the University of Chicago, but I decided that, rather than wait for the bus, we could take the subway to a stop near campus and then walk to the International House.

The students, without question, followed me into the subway, where we took the Howard–Dan Ryan red line south to Garfield Boulevard. From there, we would take what appeared to be a pleasant little walk east through Washington Park and then directly onto the beautiful University of Chicago campus. We arrived at Garfield Boulevard and began our walk through the Saturday night of the South Side of Chicago. Within minutes, a white sanitation worker pulled over to ask, "Where the hell are you going?" I pulled out my trusty map to show him our route down Garfield, through Washington Park, and over to the University of Chicago campus. He looked at the 16 white, backpack-laden students behind me and laughed. He said, "You can walk that way, but you'll never make it." Undeterred (at least I was), we continued for another 10 minutes or so. In that time, six other cars—each with black drivers and passengers—stopped to warn us of the neighborhood we were in.

At that point, I decided wisdom was, indeed, the better part of valor and herded the students around a check-cashing store in a shopping strip at the corner of Garfield and Indiana. The area was in an exclusively black neighborhood and was very busy. I called the local taxi service and requested four cabs. With the help of the attendant in the store, I gave clear directions of where to pick us up. One hour, then two, passed without the taxis' arrival. In that time, several more people stopped to ask if they could be of help. Finally, after explaining to one person that I had called cabs, she looked at me and said, "Honey, ain't no cabs coming to this part of the city at this time of night on a Saturday!"

I was at the end of my rope. My anxious responsibility for the 16 students entrusted to my care was only heightened when I looked at their fearful faces. A few of them were even expressing their anger at me for getting them into this situation. The check-cashing store was soon to close, and I didn't know where to turn. Just before closing, the attendant— whose patience with our constant presence was surely wearing thin— made the gracious gesture of calling a friend who ran a livery service. Minutes later, four cars—not yellow cabs, but cars nonetheless—picked us up and drove us the short (only in physical terms) distance to the University of Chicago campus.

That night, and the next morning, the students and I discussed our reactions. Some expressed their anger at me for getting them in that situation; others expressed their appreciation to me for getting them out. All, however, expressed their strong sense of fear and life endangerment. For most, they had never been more afraid in their short lifetimes. Some opted out of the next day's activities because of the physical drain of the previous night's fear and the possibility of finding themselves in a similar situation again.

Trying to play the devil's advocate and save some face, I pushed them a bit about their fear. Why were they so afraid? Most responded that their fear was rational and stemmed from the high crime rate that surely was present in that neighborhood. One even said, "I don't think any of us realized how much danger we were *really* in!" I can't begrudge the fact that their initial responses, similar to mine, of being in this neighborhood were fearful. Later, we were to find that we were, indeed, in one of the highest-crime sections of the city. I was struck, however, by the continued irrationality of their fear even in the face of our experiences. Over a dozen people stopped to say something to us. Of those, not a single person said anything threatening, intimidating, or

meanspirited. Every comment was supportive, helpful, and well intentioned. Surely, the reality of this experience could sway them from their
inordinate fear, I argued. For most, however, the fear ran so deep that
all of the contradictory experiences in the world could not have challenged it. It was as if the very acts of kindness somehow oddly reinforced the appropriateness of their fear. Thus is the power of fear born
from the bondage of hate.

Andrew Hacker argues that fear of racial minorities is really fear of
those aspects of ourselves we would prefer not to confront. This is why,
he argues, whites devised the word *nigger* and gave it so charged a
meaning. James Baldwin, in *The Fire Next Time*, wrote that whites need
the "nigger," because it is the "nigger" within themselves that they
cannot tolerate.[61] In a similar way, Jean-Paul Sartre argued that if the
Jew did not exist for the anti-semite to hate, then the anti-semite would
invent him.[62] So minorities become weighted with all of the negative
baggage with which whites are afraid to be tainted—laziness, hyper-
sexuality, stupidity, violence, and so forth. In a tragic cycle, this negative
baggage that whites throw upon minorities then becomes the basis
for our fears.

Demagogues and fringe groups often exploit this deep-seated fear.
One of the most egregious examples of fear exploitation came when
Willie Horton was made part of the campaign by Republican strategists
in George Bush's 1988 presidential campaign again Michael Dukakis.
While on a furlough program, Horton, a black man who was a convicted murderer, broke into a home of a white couple and then pro-
ceeded to tie up the man and brutally rape the woman. White America's
deep, primal fears of blacks, exacerbated by the sexual assault of a
white woman, were stirred by the campaign ads depicting Horton as
evidence for Dukakis's soft stance on crime. It again reminded us that,
deep within our psyches, our bondage of hate has given birth to a
paralysis of fear.

Bondage of Guilt

A final psychological cost of modern racism to whites is the bondage of guilt. Those of us who have been given the long end of the stick
will, at some level, eventually feel guilt for those who have been given
the short end. We don't like feeling guilty. As a matter of fact, most of

us go to incredible lengths to avoid feeling guilty or facing the fact that the value imputed to being white has injured people who are not white.

I am amazed at the lengths to which some whites go to avoid facing this guilt. Consider some of these responses to my lectures across the country: "Today, whites are the persecuted minority!" "Blacks and Hispanics are just as racist as whites!" "Christians are being persecuted in China!" It goes on and on and on. Instead of directly admitting the costs of modern racism to the victims, and their implicit role in those costs, whites bend over backwards either to assert their own victimization or to divert the attention to victimization elsewhere.

Similar to hate and fear, unrepentant guilt is a bondage that enslaves us. Hate, fear, and guilt can eat away at our psyches and make us unable to function well in a changing world. They corrupt our souls, and they spoil our lives.

Material Costs of Modern Racism to Whites

Even though the costs are indirect and relatively minor, a reflective person can still recognize the psychological price of modern racism to whites. The material costs, however, are more difficult to unpack. It is hard to mourn relationships that never began and contributions that were never made—especially when one, as a member of the majority group, does not routinely experience forfeited opportunities. Regardless, let's examine the material costs of modern racism to whites by looking at the dual sacrifices of meaningful relationships and societal benefits.

Sacrifice of Meaningful Relationships

We live in a world where meaningful relationships are at a premium. Technological advancements, changing definitions of community, shifting employment opportunities—all have made it easier for us to dislocate ourselves from family, friends, and neighborhoods. All of my blood relatives, for instance, live in the Southeast—Tennessee, North Carolina, South Carolina, and Virginia. My, and my wife's, decision to base our lives in the distant Pacific Northwest was not done lightly. I knew that the physical distance between myself and my family would harm our relationships. One hundred years ago, I would have never made that decision. Today, however, I make myself feel better about the decision by repeating the mantra, "I'm only a phone call or airplane ride away." I sometimes wonder, however, if I haven't fallen for a lie and sacrificed more in that move than I anticipated.

Most Americans report a similar yearning for more deep and abiding relationships. We're all trying to fill a hole in our heart in some way. One of the many factors cutting us off from such relationships is racism. Think for a moment. How many great friendships have you cheated yourself out of simply because you were afraid to make an initial contact with someone different from you?

Starting any relationship is risky. Starting relationships with members of racial minorities, however, can be even more risky. On one side, we run the risk of alienation from other members of our own racial group. Does our involvement in a cross-racial relationship reflect badly on their lack of such relationships? Will they think we have an ulterior motive for this relationship? On the other side, we run the risk of entering a relationship that promises great rewards but few easy roads. Are the differences between our heritages and cultures too great? Are we sensitive enough to be in this relationship? Can we handle putting ourselves in the position of being called racist if we are insensitive?

Rather than face these risks, even in the face of great potential rewards, many whites prefer simply to not engage in cross-racial relationships. Even though we live in a world where significant relationships are at a premium, we constrain our potential for relationships with members of racial minorities because they are too risky and take too much effort. A white banker in Memphis, Tennessee, spoke honestly of his hesitancy to engage in cross-racial relationships. At the same time in his life that he yearned for deep and abiding relationships, the risk and effort involved in a cross-racial relationship were simply too prohibitive. We have compounded the effort required for cross-racial relationships by hypersegregating our neighborhoods and schools. This is a loss for whites, but it's also a loss for racial minorities. Racism constrains each of our choices for relationships in a world where such relationships are at a premium.

Sacrifice of Societal Benefits

Clearly, racism has produced economic benefits for whites. My ancestors enjoyed opportunities that racial minorities did not. As a result, generations of economic benefits, however meager, continue to be passed along in my family. In the long run, however, racism detracts from the productivity of American society. University of Florida sociologists Joe Feagin and Hernan Vera, for instance, contend that racism takes its toll on whites in several forms. For example, the energy of white activists in combating racism is energy lost for other beneficial pursuits. In communities with well-chronicled tales of racism, new employers who probably would have created new jobs for whites are often driven away. Corporations, stores, and restaurants that engage in racist practices lose talented minority workers and customers. Organizationally, Feagin and Vera remind us that racism negates the rational principle that goals should be achieved by the most efficient means. This abandonment of efficiency is highly wasteful in material terms.[63] Across the nation, large and small businesses are learning that diversity pays.

There are also global sacrifices. American support of democracy and human rights overseas is viewed as hypocritical in light of America's racism at home. Global economic strength is sapped as the ability of white Americans to understand and get along with people different from themselves is questioned. As Feagin and Vera point out, "It is likely that the label 'Made in the USA' will elicit from some of these people reactions similar to those once produced in the United States and around the world by the label 'Made in South Africa.'"[64] In short, racism is bad business for all Americans.

CONCLUSION

This chapter outlined the significant psychological and material consequences of modern racism to its victims. Minorities carry the threat of fulfilling negative stereotypes, must deal with the cumulative damage of modern racism to their self-esteem, and bear the tremendous cognitive burden of coping with modern racism. In addition, modern racism exacts tremendous material costs in financial terms, in its toll on life and death, and in the uneven scales of justice. The persistence of the psychological and material costs as we approach the millennium provides additional evidence against the myth that racism is declining.

We discussed the toll modern racism exacts on the psychological and material states of whites as well. Although not as heavy as that exacted from the victims, the costs of modern racism to whites remind us that it is not just minorities that will benefit from the eradication of modern racism. The abolition of racism can bring substantial benefits for whites as well.

What is the realistic possibility for erasing modern racism? Many activists believe the only hope lies in America becoming a color-blind, race-neutral, or nonracial society. Is this aim realistic? Can America ever become a color-blind society? Chapter 9 answers this question with a psychological analysis of how we categorize, stereotype, and discriminate against others.

9

Can America Become a Color-Blind Society?

The Cognitive Traps of Racism

Can America become a color-blind society? Can we come to see racial-group membership as irrelevant to the ways individuals are treated? As we saw in Chapter 5, the reality of vast racial inequities in economic and educational attainment reveal that 1997 America certainly *is not* a color-blind society. Though racial minorities—in some cases—may be better off in absolute terms now than they have been in previous years, tremendous racial inequities still exist relative to other groups, especially relative to whites. Although blatant discrimination has largely disappeared, traces of a more subtle form of racism are seen in the residue of these racial inequities. Racism remains our "dirty little secret." It is a fundamental social practice embedded in our cultural and political institutions and in the rhythms of daily American life.

So, we recognize what we are not. But to what should we aspire? Should a color-blind, nonracial society be our prescriptive ideal, our "ought to be?" Ellis Cose, drawing on evidence from an American experimental school and international models, contends that the attempt to ignore race only exaggerates its significance. Cose describes the work of Janet Ward Schofield, a psychologist at the University of Pittsburgh. In the early 1980s, Schofield investigated a model desegregated school, pseudonymously named "Wexler," which serves 1,200 children in sixth through eighth grade. The student body was almost precisely 50 percent black and 50 percent white. The teachers, administration, and staff at Wexler, nearly 25 percent of whom were black, were conscientiously color blind. They rarely acknowledged that the students were of different races, and some even claimed ignorance of the children's races. They insisted that they treated their students as individuals and simply did not take their race into account.

Schofield's four-year study, however, revealed that administration, faculty, staff, and students were *not* significantly less prone to use race as a category for processing information about others. Despite their color-blind intentions, there were everyday indications that race remained a prevailing social category. There was a marked tendency, for example, for students to group themselves by race in a variety of settings. Schofield also documented the emergence of a clear racial hierarchy in academic achievement and social acceptance. Finally, the suspension rate for black students was roughly four times that for whites—a fact not noticed, or perhaps denied, by the faculty and administrators.

Ultimately, Schofield concluded, the color-blind perspective, while laudable, was accompanied by a number of other related beliefs which, taken together, led to some significant negative consequences. The color-blind atmosphere, for example, minimized the chances that the racial disparity in suspension rates would become the focus of constructive action. It also failed to take advantage of the diversity of experiences and perspectives of its biracial student body as a resource in the educational process. One white middle schooler, for instance, did not even know that Martin Luther King, Jr. was black! Often, anger festered and stereotypes strengthened because such issues could not be dealt with in a straightforward manner. In short, color blindness did more harm than good. In Schofield's words,

> It [color blindness] may ease initial tensions and minimize the frequency of overt conflict. Nonetheless, it can also foster phenomena like the taboo against ever mentioning race or connected issues and the refusal to recognize and deal with the existence of intergroup tensions. Thus, it fosters an environment in which aversive [modern] racists, who are basically well-intentioned, are prone to act in a discriminatory manner.[1]

On the international front, Puerto Rico is one of several societies that has aspired to color blindness through an official policy of nonracialism. Cose's interviews with Puerto Ricans, however, suggest that color blindness serves as a psychological cover for hypocrisy. In other words, feigning color blindness allows certain racial issues to be swept under the carpet. Fighting racism in a society that doesn't acknowledge it is a difficult task. Color blindness does not ensure that one will see whites and minorities as equals.

The racial discrimination that occurs in such programs or societies—and it does occur—occurs without regret, because people are blinded to their own race-based assumptions. Color blindness is not a racial equalizer but a silencer. Racial discrimination is easier to get away with because racism cannot be targeted as its source. In Cose's words, "It [color blindness] becomes, in short, a way of justifying the very inequality for which it claims to be the antidote."[2] Cose's insightful work questions the notion that color blindness is the prescriptive ideal to which America should aspire.

I find Cose's argument persuasive. Many others, however, will not. Countless thinkers continue to hold color blindness as the prescriptive ideal to which American society should aspire. This ideal is the bedrock of many racial reconciliation programs, either as an official policy or a powerful social norm. Underlying the "color blindness as the prescriptive ideal" model is the assumption that we *can* become color blind. In other words, as individuals, our minds can be transformed so that we are able to ignore race in the context of our daily interactions. What is the validity of this assumption? Is it true or a myth?

To answer this question is to revisit the concept of stereotypes and how our minds work. As we discussed in Chapter 2, a stereotype is a cognitive shortcut that contains beliefs about the attributes of an individual because of his or her membership in a specific group. We also discussed the strong relationships between stereotypes, racial prejudice, and discrimination. To become a color-blind society depends, in part, on eradicating stereotypical thinking. Is this possible? Is color blindness an achievable goal? If not, then the belief that America can become a color-blind society is a myth based in an inadequate understanding of how our minds work.

I contend that the ways in which our minds naturally work render us unable ever to become a color-blind society. In other words, there are certain inherent fundamentals of human psychological functioning that prohibit the possibility of our becoming a color-blind society. Our brains are finely tuned decision-making machines. We use *social categorization* to simplify an incredibly complex physical world and enrich the information we are given. The efficiency of our brains is further demonstrated in our incredible capacity for *automatic cognitive processing* of information. Without recognizing it, we sort and sift through the billions of bits of data bombarding our senses daily. Finally, the fact that we can jump to conclusions in less than 100 milliseconds illustrates that our capacity for assigning meaning, or *explanation*, to events and behaviors is boundless.

These three cognitive tools—social categorization, automatic cognitive processing, and explanation—are essential to our survival as a species. They are, arguably, the greatest strengths we possess. Ironically, however, they may also constitute our greatest weaknesses. These cognitive tools, essential for life and survival, are also traps that foil the dream of a color-blind society.

THE TRAP OF SOCIAL CATEGORIZATION

Biologists are faced with the overwhelming task of understanding the broad range of diversity in human, animal, and plant life. That's why they always look so tired. How do they respond to this task? They begin by classifying people, animals, and plants into different taxonomies, or *natural* categories. If a person, animal, or plant fits the essential characteristics, or "essence," of a particular natural category, he, she, or it is placed into that category. This process of categorization gives biologists a handle with which to approach the natural world.

Similarly, you and I search for handles with which to approach interpersonal relations by assigning people to broad social categories. In other words, we engage in an automatic process of *social* categorization. These social categories can include groups (e.g., blacks, women, homosexuals), roles (e.g., mothers, sons), and occupations (e.g., teachers, maids, ministers). The more conspicuous a group, role, or occupation, the more likely we are to categorize. Without thinking, we immediately notice whether strangers fit the essential characteristics, or "essence," of a particular social category and place them into that category.

Such social categorization is the nature of how the human mind works. It is an inescapable feature of human existence. Though the *content* of social categories may differ, the *process* of social categorization is universal and pervasive across humankind. It is as natural to our minds as breathing is to our lungs. Its universality, however, still doesn't answer "why." A tool used by all humans, and many lower animals, must have some significant evolutionary value. What is the value of social categorization? Why do we rely so heavily upon it?

First, social categorization simplifies an incredibly complex world by filtering the amount of data we must actively process. We are bombarded with billions of bits of information each minute. Reality is simply too complex for any of us to process precisely. Attempting to deal with every person on an individual basis would quickly overwhelm the brain's limited capacity to process information. Even if our brains did have a greater capacity to process information, it would be relatively inefficient, because groups of people *do* possess many shared characteristics with each other as well as traits that distinguish them from others. Every person is not new and unknown. Social categorization allows us to filter our social experiences and draw from a bank of information to help us to determine how to react to a particular person. Without social categorization as a tool of simplification, we would be reduced to stupefied paralysis.

Second, social categorization allows us to go beyond the information we are given, and thereby enriches it. In other words, though we attend only to the most prominent social categories (e.g., skin color and gender), those categories call up additional information from our memory. In this way, we avoid the tedious alternative of processing information about an individual on a piecemeal basis, trait by trait. Instead, in stripping persons of their individuality, we only attend to the traits to determine if they are consistent with the particular social category. By seeing the traits through the lens of a social category, we confirm the category by blocking out the traits inconsistent with the category.

Despite its obvious benefits, social categorization has a significant cost as well. Its most obvious disadvantage is that it leads to the formation of oversimplified stereotypes that serve only to feed prejudices. By itself, social categorization is not prejudice. The first step in prejudice, however, is the creation of groups. By distorting reality to achieve order, social categorization stands as a fundamental foundation for creating prejudice.

The stereotypes activated by social categorization impact the judgments we make of others' behaviors. For example, stereotypes activated by social categorization can lead us to view behaviors by members of certain racial groups as more menacing than the *same* behaviors by members of other racial groups. A classic 1976 study by psychologist Birt Duncan illustrated this tendency. In interpreting an ambiguous shove, 75 percent of white subjects characterized the behavior as "violent" when the protagonist was black and the victim white. When the protagonist was white and the victim black, however, only 17 percent characterized the ambiguous shove as "violent." So the same act performed by a black was much more likely to be characterized as violent than when committed by a white.[3] This finding even has been replicated in studies of schoolchildren![4]

Consequences of Social Categorization: Who's In and Who's Out?

Perhaps the most significant legacy of social categorization lies in its influence upon our perception of who we are and whose we are. Social psychologists often speak about these perceptions in terms of "in-group" and "out-group." The in-group refers to any group to which we belong or with which we identify. In-groups can range from small, face-to-face groupings of family and friends to large social categories such as race, ethnicity, gender, or religion. Out-groups are any groups to which we do not belong or with which we do not identify. Assigning people to in-groups and out-groups has four important consequences.

First, there is the *assumed similarity effect* in which we perceive other in-group members as more similar to us than to out-group members. We solidify this perception by exaggerating the similarities within our own group. Even when we have been randomly, or arbitrarily, assigned to a group, we assume that other in-group members are especially similar to us on a surprisingly wide range of thoughts, feelings, and behaviors.

Defining what the in-group is requires defining what it is not as well. The second consequence of assigning people to groups, defining what the in-group is not, is the *out-group homogeneity effect*. This is our tendency to see members of the out-group as all alike. So, as good cognitive misers, if we know something about *one* out-group member, we are likely to feel that we know something about *all* of them. Similarly, since we assume that out-group members are highly similar, or essentially interchangeable, we can use our handy social group stereotype to quickly interpret an individual out-group member's behavior. They are, after all, all alike. Why waste our cognitive energy on attending to potentially distinctive information about a specific individual in the out-group?

Though the out-group homogeneity effect applies to thoughts, feelings, and behaviors, it resonates most clearly with our physical perceptions of racial out-group members. The tired racist line that "all blacks look alike" is built on this out-group homogeneity effect. Studies have confirmed a tendency for persons belonging to one racial group to be more accurate in recognizing differences among the faces of strangers in their own group than in another racial group.[5] On the international front, for example, many of us see the Swiss as a fairly homogenous people. But to the people of Switzerland, the Swiss—including French-, German-, and Italian-speaking people—are incredibly diverse.

We amplify our assumed similarity of in-group members and homogeneity of out-group members by drawing ever starker lines between "us" and "them." We draw these lines by exaggerating the differences between our group and the out-group. This exaggeration of out-group differentness, termed the *accentuation effect*, is the third consequence of assigning people to groups. It leaves us biased toward information that enhances the differences between social categories and less attentive to information about similarities between members of different social categories.[6]

In a recent study, psychologists L. Huddy and S. Virtanen demonstrated that these cognitive biases also are evident in racial subgroups' perception of each other. Whites and respondents from three Hispanic subgroups (Cuban-Americans, Puerto Rican-Americans, and Mexican-Americans) rated their feelings toward their own group and each of the other three groups. Results revealed that each Hispanic subgroup saw the other two Hispanic subgroups in the same way as whites viewed them—very similar to each other (out-group homogeneity effect) and very different from them (accentuation effect). In addition, each Hispanic subgroup exhibited as much bias against members of the other two Hispanic subgroups as did whites![7] As psychologists Marilynn Brewer and Norman Miller point out, "This motivated bias was exhibited at the expense of the other Latino subgroups, even though they shared with them not only language, religion, and other cultural features, but also, a relatively disadvantaged state with the broader U.S.

society."[8] These findings clearly reveal the pervasiveness of the cognitive biases resulting from social categorization.

So we have different perceptions of "us" and "them." We think in-group members are similar to us, out-group members are all alike, and we overestimate the differences between "us" and "them." What is the danger in these distortions? They are not done out of malice. Rather, they reflect a cognitively determined perceptual bias that should be evaluatively neutral. Unfortunately, however, experience and research has demonstrated that such categorization is seldom neutral. We generally like people we think are similar to us and dislike those we perceive as different. Thus, the mere act of dividing people into groups inevitably sets up a bias in group members in favor of the in-group and against the out-group. We evaluate in-group members more positively, credit them more for their successes, and hold them less accountable for their failures or negative actions, reward them more, expect more favorable treatment from them, and find them more persuasive than out-group members.

In one early study, for instance, employees from a variety of businesses and organizations worked on a number of exercises in groups of 8–12 participants. At certain points in the two-week-long study, they were asked to compare and evaluate the work of their own group with that of other participating groups. In general, all participants displayed a very strong tendency to rate their in-group performance more favorably than other out-group performances. In the words of the researchers, Robert Blake and Jane Mouton, the "own group product was rated higher than the comparison group in 378 of the instances, own group product was rated as equal in quality 19 times, and in *only* [emphasis mine] 13 instances did a group member rate his own group product as inferior to that created by another group."[9] Such in-group bias has been demonstrated across a wide range of groups, ages, contexts, and tasks. This fourth consequence of assigning people into groups, labeled the *in-group favoritism effect*, has the most profound implications for understanding racism in America.

In the mid-1960s, Jane Elliot gave us a compelling illustration of the in-group favoritism effect. Elliot was faced with the dilemma of trying to communicate the importance of the civil rights struggle to white third graders in a small farming community in Iowa. As a class exercise, she grouped children according to eye color and arbitrarily gave blue-eyed children a superior status. Simply on the basis of that categorization, the blue-eyed children stuck together and actively promoted and used their higher power and status in the classroom.

Elliot's classroom experiences were confirmed in the now-famous research program of a British social psychologist, Henri Tajfel. In Tajfel's "minimal group" experiments, complete strangers are divided into groups using the most random, arbitrary, or trivial criteria imaginable. In one experiment, for example, groups were formed on the basis of a coin toss; in others, they were formed on the basis of musical preferences or dot estimation. In the most famous series of studies, participants were asked to express their opinions about indistinguishable abstract paintings by artists they had never heard of and were then randomly assigned to a group that preferred either the "Paul Klee style" or the "Wassily Kandinsky style."

Let's be clear about these minimal groups. The participants were strangers prior to the experiment. The groups were formed using random, arbitrary, or even trivial criteria. The individuals in the groups had no contact or interaction with each other during the experiment. There were no pleasurable interactions with other in-group members, nor were there any unpleasurable interactions with out-group members. Finally, the groups were not competing for a prize or scarce resources. There were no selfish gains to be made.

Despite the "minimalness" of these groups, however, individuals still showed bias, discrimination, and a competitive orientation in favor of the in-group and against the out-group. They rated members of their own group as more pleasant and better workers. They liked the members of their own group better. They allocated more money or other resources to those who shared their label. Though in-group favoritism need not be always mirrored by a negative bias against the out-group, the sequence does often follow. In one experiment, for example, in-group members voted to give themselves only $2 instead of $3 if it meant that out-group members got $1 instead of $4! They voted to take less money rather than let the out-group members make more money! They sacrificed absolute gain for a relative advantage. In other words, in-group members were more interested in beating the out-group than in gaining as much as possible for their own group.

You've got it right. Complete strangers arbitrarily assigned to groups, having no interaction or conflict with one another, and not competing against another group behaved as if those who shared their meaningless label (e.g., "Klee style") were their dearest friends or closest relatives (those two aren't always the same). Such findings have been replicated more than 20 times in several different countries using a wide range of experimental participants. In Tajfel's words,

> The mere perception of belonging to two distinct groups—that is, social categorization per se—is sufficient to trigger intergroup discrimination favoring the in-group. In other words, the mere awareness of the presence of an out-group is sufficient to provoke intergroup competitive or discriminatory responses on the part of the in-group.[10]

If you're surprised, don't feel alone. Social psychologists also were jolted by Tajfel's original findings. Before these experiments, most social psychologists assumed that discrimination was the result of existing prejudice and hostility that developed over time in the course of active, intergroup relations. Discrimination produced by mere categorization into separate groups, in the absence of any previous history of intergroup contact or conflict, simply did not fit our understanding of intergroup behavior. As a result, Tajfel's findings led to a flurry of research questions. Why does the mere act of placing people into groups lead to the in-group favoritism effect? What is the motivational explanation for this cognitive phenomenon? Does in-group favoritism stem from a liking for our own group, a dislike for the out-group, or both?

On the basis of his research program with minimal groups, Tajfel believes that the major underlying motive for in-group favoritism is self-esteem. In his social identity theory, one tool used by individuals to enhance their self-esteem is identification with specific social groups. By allowing the in-group to become an extension of ourself, we open another avenue to enhance our self-esteem. For self-esteem to be enhanced, however, individuals must see their group as superior to other groups. The in-group favoritism effect, rooted in the assumed similarity, out-group homogeneity, and accentuation effects, is the cognitive mechanism that makes it possible for us to see our group as superior to other groups. Thus, according to Tajfel, our natural tendency for in-group favoritism (or out-group dislike) stems from a basic motivational need to enhance our self-esteem.

Unfortunately, much of the strained status of race relations in America stems from the fact that members of *all* racial groups share this same tendency. Each of our groups, aiming to somehow view ourselves as better than the others, has a vested interest in putting down other groups. This tendency is so universal that Zach Hall, director of the National Institute of Neurological Disorders and Stroke, suggests we have inherited "a biological need to divide the world into 'them' and 'us.' "[11] There is even recent experimental evidence suggesting that the concepts "we" and "us" carry positive emotional significance that is activated automatically and unconsciously.[12]

Summary

Social categorization, and its four cognitive consequences, does not represent racism as we have defined the term. Social categorization does not lead us to hate all out-groups. Racism is not an inevitable consequence of social categorization. Social categorization is, however, a universal cognitive propensity that, combined with certain social dynamics, underlies racism.

THE TRAP OF AUTOMATIC COGNITIVE PROCESSING

Automatic cognitive processing is a second universal cognitive propensity from which racism can emerge. Our sensory field scans two billion bits of information per second. We simply cannot attend to the entirety of that information. To process the incoming information, our brain sorts the data and jumps to conclusions in less than 100 milliseconds. Most often, those conclusions are accurate and helpful. Any lengthy processing of the implications of being hit by a fast-moving truck if I *don't* run back onto the sidewalk, for instance, would be life threatening. The ability to automatically process information and make lightning-fast decisions is essential for our survival. Similar to social categorization, however, the gain in cognitive efficiency achieved by automatic cognitive processing is not without its costs. At times, the conclusions reached from automatic cognitive processing are traps that can lead to prejudicial thinking.

Patricia Devine, a leading social-cognitive psychologist at the University of Wisconsin–Madison, offers a distinction between *automatic* and *controlled* processing.[13] This distinction closely mirrors one of the oldest concepts in psychology—the distinction between habits and decisions. A habit is an action that has been done many times and has become automatic. It is done without conscious thought. A decision, on the other hand, involves conscious thought. The limited capacity of our conscious thought is freed up by the allocation of habits to unconscious, or subconscious, awareness.

Devine's theory parallels this historic distinction. Her theory has two basic assumptions. First, each of us learns negative racial stereotypes early in life. No one escapes this curse.[14] Each of us gains knowledge of racial stereotypes as a part of being socialized into American culture. Because we acquire these stereotypes at an early age, we do not have the cognitive ability and flexibility to critically evaluate and decide on their acceptability. In addition, these stereotypes are constantly reinforced through the mass media and other socializing agents. As a result, we use them many times and across many situations. Due to repeated activations, they become ingrained, and we begin to use them automatically over time. As we grow older, we may develop personal beliefs that are inconsistent with those in the stereotypes. We all remain, however, equally knowledgeable of the cultural stereotypes of various racial groups. Some will bristle at the implication that we are all racist. It is not, as Devine maintains, that we are all racist; rather, it is that we are all creatures of habit.

Second, these stereotypes are automatically activated whenever we encounter a person from a different racial group. We assume that the person has the group's characteristics. The activation of these stereotypes—similar to the activation of a habit—is spontaneous, unintentional, and requires no conscious effort. They lead to biased assumptions, emotional reactions, and treatment. In one study, for instance, Devine presented subjects with various words that are stereotypically associated with the category of "blacks"—for example, "ghetto," "lazy," "athletic." These "racial primes" were embedded in a string of meaningless letters and only exposed for 80 milliseconds. As a result, it was virtually impossible for subjects to detect the words at a conscious level. Later, the subjects read a brief scenario in which a person performed some ambiguous actions that could be interpreted as more or less hostile. Results revealed that subjects exposed to a higher proportion of racial primes rated the person as significantly more hostile than those exposed to a much lower proportion of racial primes. Because the racial primes could not be processed at the conscious level, Devine argued that the primes *sub*consciously activated the category "blacks," and that this category was then used to interpret the ambiguous behavior in the scenario as aggressive—consistent with the black stereotype.[15]

Is there any way to avoid the pitfalls of automatic cognitive processing? Can we suppress or override the activation of automatic stereotypes? Can we control our cognitive processing? Such controlled cognitive processing requires time, effort, cognitive capacity, and active attention. Though, as we have seen, our miserly tendencies do not predispose us to such effort, the possibility of controlled cognitive processing does hold out some hope for the future. When we are not mentally lazy, busy, overwhelmed, distracted, or paying much attention, can we control the automatic stereotypes? Is prejudice an inevitable consequence of ordinary cognitive processes? We'll explore the answer to this question in the final chapter. You'll be surprised at how relatively nonpessimistic (not the same as optimistic) Devine's answer is.

THE TRAP OF EXPLANATION

The tools of categorization and automatic processing are complemented by our brain's remarkable capacity to seek, and find, explanation in the events surrounding us, our actions, and the behaviors of people with whom we interact. Like categorization and automatic processing, however, our natural tendencies to search for meaning can be cognitive traps as well.

By nature, each of us is designed to find meaning, or explanation. When I see two students walking across campus and one pushes the other into a pine tree, I seek an explanation. To what should I attribute such bizarre behavior? Was it an accident? A perceptual illusion? Is the "pusher" a mean and violent person? Or, did the "pushed" deserve his or her unpleasant fate?

Social psychology has a rich history of studying our ways of finding explanation. This history shows that, in general, we tend to grant ourselves the benefit of the doubt in explaining our own behaviors but are much harsher in explaining other people's behaviors. Our harshest explanations are reserved for finding meaning in why people suffer. We recognize that victims can be grouped in two broad categories: (1) those who deserve their suffering, and (2) those who do not deserve their suffering. We know that bad things *do* happen to good people. This belief is countered, however, by our need to believe that the world is fair and just. Our need to believe in a just world often overwhelms our recognition that bad things can happen to good people. As a result, we often assume that victims deserve, and can be blamed for, their fates. Indeed, we show a hardy cognitive tendency to search for ways to blame individuals for their own victimization. As individuals, some may hold a strong belief in a just world; others may hold such a belief less strongly. On the whole, however, the general tendency to blame the victim for his or her own suffering is a central truth about human experience.

This concept was captured in a term, the *just-world phenomenon*, originally coined by social psychologist Melvin Lerner.[16] Two other psychologists, Zick Rubin and Letitia Anne Peplau, developed the Just-World Scale (JWS) to calculate the strength of an individual's belief in a just world. Take a moment to read and respond to the questions on the JWS in Table 9.1. To calculate the strength of your belief in a just world, first reverse your scores on items 1, 4, 5, 8, 10, 13, 16, 17, and 20. In other words, change 0 to 5, 1 to 4, 2 to 3, 3 to 2, 4 to 1, and 5 to 0 for these questions only. Then add up the numbers in front of all 20 items. Total scores can range from 0 to 100, with higher scores (i.e., more than 50) indicating a stronger belief in a just world and lower scores (i.e., less than 50) indicating a weaker belief. If your score is below 0 or above 100, (1) run downstairs and dust off your calculator, (2) immediately enroll in a remedial math program, and (3) quit your job as an accountant.

When the JWS was first developed, Rubin and Peplau tested it in relation to the 1971 national draft lottery of 19-year-olds. Although most people responding to the survey expressed sympathy for the "losers" (those who were inducted), those who scored high on the JWS resented the "losers" more than the "winners."[17] It's as if their strong belief in a just world necessitated a need to blame the "losers" for their own misfortune—even though the lottery selections were completely random. Subsequent research with the JWS has found that it predicts a variety of social attitudes and behaviors.

A belief in a just world also has influenced responses in controlled laboratory settings. Lerner and others, for example, have had two peo-

Table 9.1. Just-World Scale

Indicate your degree of agreement or disagreement with each of the following statements in the blank space next to each item. Respond to every statement by using the following scale:

5 = Strongly agree
4 = Moderately agree
3 = Slightly agree
2 = Slightly disagree
1 = Moderately disagree
0 = Strongly disagree

___ 1. I've found that a person rarely deserves the reputation he has.
___ 2. Basically, the world is a just place.
___ 3. People who get "lucky breaks" have usually earned their good fortune.
___ 4. Careful drivers are just as likely to get hurt in traffic accidents as careless ones.
___ 5. It is a common occurrence for a guilty person to get off free in American courts.
___ 6. Students almost always deserve the grades they receive in school.
___ 7. Men who keep in shape have little chance of suffering a heart attack.
___ 8. The political candidate who sticks up for his principles rarely gets elected.
___ 9. It is rare for an innocent man to be wrongly sent to jail.
___ 10. In professional sports, many fouls and infractions never get called by the referee.
___ 11. By and large, people deserve what they get.
___ 12. When parents punish their children, it is almost always for good reasons.
___ 13. Good deeds often go unnoticed and unrewarded.
___ 14. Although evil men may hold political power for a while, in the general course of history good wins out.
___ 15. In almost any business or profession, people who do their job well rise to the top.
___ 16. American parents tend to overlook the things most to be admired in their children.
___ 17. It is often impossible for a person to receive a fair trial in the USA.
___ 18. People who meet with misfortune have often brought it on themselves.
___ 19. Crime doesn't pay.
___ 20. Many people suffer through absolutely no fault of their own.

Source: Zick Rubin and Letitia Anne Peplau, "Who Believes in a Just World?" *Journal of Social Issues*, vol. 31, pp. 65–89.

ple work equally hard on the same task. By the flip of a coin, however, one received a sizable reward and the other received nothing. Later, observers were asked to reconstruct what had happened. In general, the observers convinced themselves that the unlucky person who had lost the coin flip must have worked less hard. The observers knew that the coin flip was the sole determinant of rewards. In their reconstruction of the events, however, their minds drove them to find a reason for the

inequitable distribution of rewards. A random coin flip was not sufficient; the observers reinterpreted events to lay blame on the victim's
inferior work habits. In other experiments, observers denigrated victims who were picked *at random* to be given electric shock. The victims
were held responsible for their chance misfortunes!

The tendency to blame persons for their own victimization is evident outside the experimental laboratory as well. How do we explain,
for instance, the plight of the poor and homeless? For those who display
a strong belief in a just world, they are most likely to blame the poor and
homeless for their own suffering. Similarly, some find it more comfortable to believe that battered spouses must have provoked their beat-
ings; sick people are responsible for their illness; persons involved in a
traffic accident must have been driving carelessly; victims of theft surely
brought it on themselves by not taking adequate security precautions.

At times, our cognitive need to see the world as fair and just results
in some incredible displays of insensitivity. My wife often counsels
women who are recovering from rape or sexual assault. She tells me
that, quite often, the recovery process is complicated by painful experience in which someone close to them asks the victim: "What did you do
to bring this on? How were you dressed? What did you say? How did
you look at him?" My wife's observations as a counselor are reinforced
by a 1985 study by Ronnie Janoff-Bulman and her colleagues. In that
study, college students were given a description of a young woman's
friendly behavior toward a man. The students consistently judged that
behavior as completely appropriate. In another condition of the experiment, students read the exact same description but also were told that
the encounter ended with the young woman being raped by the man.
How did students in this condition judge the young woman's friendly
behavior? You're right. They rated her behavior as inappropriate and
concluded that she was to blame for the rape.[18] More recent experimental research by Linda Carli and her colleagues replicates this troubling
finding.[19] Internationally, these results were confirmed by a national
survey in which 33 percent of Britons agreed that women who have
been raped are usually to blame for it.[20]

Do we see the same pattern in our explanations for the plight of
racial minorities? Martin Delany, a leading black nationalist of the
nineteenth century, certainly thought so. He argued that the inferior and

dependent economic and social position occupied by Northern blacks actually served to reinforce white racism.[21] If blacks don't have what they need, the reasoning goes, then they must be as inferior and deficient as our stereotypes suggest. Even if we can be led to admit that minorities are discriminated against, we often engage in some incredible mental gymnastics to retain our view of the world as fair and just. We depict minorities who are discriminated against as too pushy, unmotivated, or passive and believe them to alienate people with their demands. They, therefore, are seen as deserving their fates.

Still not convinced of the strength of the just-world phenomenon? Perhaps you will be swayed by the fact that even *victims* often go to great lengths to blame themselves for their own victimization. Some rape victims, for example, see their victimization as stemming from inappropriate behaviors (e.g., hitchhiking or leaving the apartment window unlocked). Similarly, victims of robbery may blame themselves for being too passive, careless, or trusting. A Holocaust survivor who spoke to our group in Los Angeles lamented, "Every day, I still try to understand what I, or what the Jewish people, did to deserve such a fate." The fact that many victims of arbitrary suffering find meaning by pointing the finger at themselves attests to our overwhelming urge to see the world as a fair and just place—of necessity implying that victims deserve their fate.

Why are we so harsh in explaining the suffering of others? Why don't we cut each other, and ourselves, some slack? Why is the just-world phenomenon such a prevailing cognitive tendency? Why are we so driven to see the world as a fair and just place, one where people get what they deserve and deserve what they get? The most obvious answer is socialization. Certainly, some of this tendency stems from early childhood, when we are taught that good is rewarded and evil punished. The final five minutes of nearly every Hollywood movie continue to teach us that hard work and virtue ultimately pay dividends.

But is socialization the only answer? Like many "obvious" answers, it is only partially correct. Socialization may explain what reinforces the just-world phenomenon but it doesn't tell us "why." Why is it so important for us to see the world in this way? What motivates our inclination to blame victims for their own suffering? On a cognitive level, social psychologists have focused on our tendency to underestimate the impact of situational factors in producing another's behavior and overestimate the role of personality factors. This cognitive tendency is driven by two underlying motivational factors.

One major motivational source of the just-world phenomenon lies in its use as a self-protective device. Seeing others hurt, want, or suffer is terrifying because it reminds us of our fragile existence. The best way to protect ourselves from this fear is to convince ourselves that the victim must have done something to bring it on him- or herself. In our minds, we remain safe—and in control of our world—because we would always behave more cautiously or wisely than other victims have. In addition to studying racism, a good portion of my time is spent investigating the origins of human cruelty. That investigation often places me in the field of Holocaust studies. I've noticed that both students and teachers in that field occasionally try to make sense of the senseless by implicating the victims in their own destruction. Why such an absurd and offensive notion? It protects us from the painful recognition that the world is *not* a fair or just place.

A second motivational source of the just-world phenomenon is that it can be used to justify our own good fortune. Those of us who benefit from social inequality can justify and rationalize our advantages with this handy cognitive tool.

These two underlying motivational factors have a significant implication. In short, the just-world phenomenon allows us to be indifferent to issues of social justice. The indifference is not because we are without concern for social justice, but rather because we see no injustice. The suffering of victims is just and deserved. Social interventions are not warranted. It's yet another reminder that mere exposure to suffering does not automatically lead to compassion. As Theolic "Fireball" Smith, a character in Mark Winegardner's baseball novel *The Veracruz Blues*, mourned, "It's so much easier to blame than to understand."[22]

CONCLUSION

Psychologist John Duckitt of the University of the Witwatersrand in Johannesburg, South Africa, outlines a historical evolution in the psychological understanding of racism. Before the 1920s, racism was seen as a natural, and justifiable, response to scientifically validated "inferior" people. In the 1920s and 1930s, there was a thematic reversal in which racism was redefined as a problem of white prejudice rather than one of black inferiority. The 1940s saw the application of psychodynamic theory to explain the pervasiveness and irrationality of white racism. Following World War II and the Holocaust, racism was seen as the expression of a pathological need. In the 1960s and 1970s, however, the pervasiveness of racism in the American South, and race riots throughout the nation, forced psychologists to abandon the pathological model. In its place, psychologists focused on the larger social norms and structures that influenced racism. Finally, in the past two decades, psychologists have recognized prejudice as the inevitable outcome of how we think. Today, we continue our search for the normal, natural, and universal psychological processes that underlie prejudice and racism.[23]

This chapter summarized some of the contemporary psychological research on these cognitive processes. In examining the cognitive bases of racism, we discovered that even in the absence of racist social conditioning, pathological motives to displace and project hostilities, or competition for resources, certain universal psychological processes build in an inherently human potentiality or propensity for prejudice. I grant that it is an exaggeration to claim that racial hostility is embedded in a part of the human psyche that cannot be changed by the forces of reason, education, or law. We must also grant, however, that at least some of the origins of prejudice are found in the operation of normal cognitive processes. These processes are common to all persons and account for the pervasiveness of prejudice and its universality as a feature of human social behavior. Clearly, we have never been, and can never become, a color-blind society. So where are we left in regard to the future of racism in America?

Ellis Cose laid out the notions of a race-relations hell (where discrimination is officially sanctioned and animosity flows freely), purgatory (where the legal apparatus of discrimination is dead, but the ugly legacy continues), and utopia (where discrimination is condemned and a color-blind society has risen). Using this allegory, it could be argued that contemporary America is now in a race-relations "purgatory" that is a necessary step in an inevitable progression to a race-relations utopia. In other words, American society still is working through growing pains, though not as severe, that are necessary as we mature to become a color-blind society.

This hopeful and optimistic spin on our current situation is clearly inconsistent with the information reviewed in this chapter. If we have emerged from a race-relations hell, a questionable proposition in itself, it has only been into the uncomfortable purgatory where the tensions of race relations—inherently tied to how our minds work—will continue for eternity. We must not be duped, however, into thinking that the problem of racism in America is impenetrable. Only by recognizing our inherent cognitive limitations can we begin to build meaningful principles, and programs, for racial reconciliation in America. It is to those principles that we turn in the final chapter.

10

Racial Reconciliation in America
How Do We Find Unity in Diversity?

It is not upon you to finish the work. Neither are you free to desist from it.

—Rabbi Tarfon[1]

Some time ago, I met with 21 undergraduates who had read a draft of the first nine chapters of this book and agreed to offer some comments and questions. As I look back on the discussion, the students—many of whom I've had in class—were caught off guard by the bleakness of the realities of race in America. This was compounded by a sense of futility. To recognize there is a problem is one thing. To find a solution is another. Sometimes the *outcome* of a solution is so far off that we don't even know how to begin the *process* of seeking that outcome. In one student's words, "I'm dulled into inactivity because the problem is just so huge! You told us that life still sucks for minorities and that racism is some supervirus that persists by mutating in response to our social, educational, and legal reforms. To top it off, you've said that the ways our minds work will always leave us with this problem! Why try to solve something that is insolvable?"

I agree that, up until this point, I have not been exactly "Pollyanna-ish" about the prospects of racial reconciliation in America. I've been downright pessimistic. I have aimed to convince you that racism is still our most significant social problem and that utopian ideals to develop a color-blind society are simply inconsistent with the reality of how our minds work. With those points laid out, however, I don't want to leave the impression that the problem of racism is impenetrable. There *are* things that can, and must, be done!

Any program for racial reconciliation must be grounded in the realities that (1) negative stereotypes and racial inequities are not disappearing, (2) racism has not declined but has taken on a new face, and (3) we can never become a color-blind society. With that groundwork, I want to conclude this book with seven principles for racial reconciliation. As the opening quotation of this chapter indicates, we will never finish the work of racial reconciliation. We are called, however, to roll our collective sleeves up and do what we can with what we have. As Henri Tajfel wrote, "The choice is between initiating some form of action on a limited scale or waiting until—miraculously—prejudice and discrimination disappear from our social scene."[2]

The following seven principles represent America's best hope for finding unity in diversity:

- Be a good reconciler: Nurture skills of listening and disagreeing.
- Teach yourself to think: Control cognitive processing of stereotypes.
- To thine own self be known: Become more self-aware of story and prejudices.
- Open your mind: Appreciate the panorama of our borderland.
- Get in touch: Engage in personal interaction with racial diversity.
- The power of many: Draw on the strength of community.
- Invest in our future: Teach antiracism early.

BE A GOOD RECONCILER: NURTURE SKILLS OF LISTENING AND DISAGREEING

Reconciling with anyone, whether similar to or different from us, involves basic human relations skills. How we talk, listen, and disagree are all essential components of what it means to be a good reconciler. The two fundamental skills of reconciliation are listening and disagreeing.

The Art of Listening

The art of *listening* is tremendously undervalued in America society. In our ordinary conversations, most of us don't listen. Rather, we simply wait until the other person stops talking so that we can set them straight. We nod our heads to signify our "attention," but, most often, our brains are whirling away to come up with that remarkable rebuttal that would make the Greek philosophers stand up in their sandals and applaud. Be honest. What do you really enjoy most about conversation? Seldom is it listening to what other people have to say. Rather, it's our enthusiasm in telling our own story or opinion. All of us, some more than others, like to hear ourselves talk.

We must reclaim the lost art of listening. In our relationships, can we prevent ourselves from always focusing on our reaction in a conversation? Can we discipline ourselves not to think about what we are going to say while someone else is talking? Can we avoid the temptation to continually frame the other's comments in our experiences (e.g., "That reminds me of a time when I ...")? Try engaging in a conversation in which you are not even intending to respond. How does it change what you hear? When you give yourself permission to not *have* to respond, do you become a better listener?

When we commit to really listen to others, we open up an avenue of understanding and discovery. The Quakers have a saying to illustrate this commitment: "When we listen devoutly, the heart opens." Sometimes, though, our open heart is flooded with the pain, rage, and resentment of the person to whom we are listening. This is especially likely in the pursuit of racial reconciliation and is a situation for which we must be prepared. Catherine Meeks, a professor and director of African-American studies at Mercer University in Macon, Georgia, even contends that rage and reconciliation are two sides of the same coin: "As long as we talk about reconciliation without acknowledging our very real and legitimate rage, we are trying to have a manipulated reconciliation.... White people as well as Black people have a responsibility to be honest about their rage."[3]

In our 1996 tour, we encountered a middle-aged black professional who spoke openly about his rage. In a room adorned with a plaque of Martin Luther King, Jr. and his quote urging all of us to sit at the table of brotherhood, we asked this man about his views on the prospects for racial reconciliation. In reply, we were hit with more than 45 minutes of pent-up rage.

> Why racial reconciliation? I don't want that. All that will do is pacify white guilt. Every time whites talk about reconciliation, I look for the hook behind the worm. I'm as reconciled to whites as I want to be. Let us [blacks] have our own businesses, clubs, and theaters. I don't want any part of what whites are offering! You want to make me happy? Don't reconcile with me—just compensate me for all that you have taken! Just give me what you owe me!

He concluded with a somber warning: "I fear for white Americans. You will reap what you have sown."

The 45 minutes seemed like an eternity. That experience reminded us, however, that a commitment to listen is a commitment to face another person's rage. In other words, our commitment to listen must be unconditional: It cannot be restricted to listening only to that with which we agree, or that which we find comforting. Finally, even though we recognize that not all whites are enamored by racial reconciliation, this conversation also reminded us that some racial minorities are just as disillusioned. Programs and policies aimed at racial reconciliation run the risk of failure if they are based on the assumption that everyone wants this "good" thing.

The Art of Disagreeing

In addition to facing the rage in others, our commitment to listen also is a commitment to *disagree* in ways that continue a conversation. Very few of us yearn for disagreements. Many of us do all we can to avoid them. Racism is a deep-seated and sensitive issue. Our hesitancies to engage in conversations about racism are justifiable. Disagreements, however, can be a significant source of growth. To avoid them is to cut ourselves off from a chance for personal development. We may be swayed by the other's argument, we may sway the other, or we may, at the least, come to know more clearly what we believe by fully understanding an opposing viewpoint. If we remain afraid of the possible tension or conflict, we'll never engage in meaningful and constructive conversation about racism.

Sometimes our fear of disagreement leaves racist words and actions unchallenged. Several years ago, for instance, I was on an elevator going up to the eighth floor of an office building in Texas. Also on the elevator were two black men, two other white men, and a white woman. For the first four floors, we minded our elevator etiquette and remained silent. After the black men exited on the fourth floor, however, one of the white men turned to the other and said: "Damn niggers. They could have jumped all the way to the fourth floor." The woman and I exchanged glances of discomfort. It was clear that we both were made uneasy by the comments. It was equally clear, however, that neither of us was going to say anything. In my (even now it's tempting to write "our" to make my cowardice more becoming) silence, the two bigots assumed companionship. My silence sent the message that I was in agreement with them. They thought I was one of them. I wasn't one of them, though, and they needed to know that. Unfortunately, the fear of disagreement overwhelmed my desire to confront them.

On the 1996 study tour, we met a woman who embodied the courage of disagreement. On a frigid, January morning in Memphis, we left our hostel, caught a bus, and then walked several blocks to the National Civil Rights Museum. The multimillion-dollar museum, built on the site of Martin Luther King Jr.'s assassination at the Lorraine Hotel, was one of the most anticipated stops on the tour. As we approached the museum, we noticed a woman sleeping on a sofa underneath a plastic tarp. She was just beginning to stir, as were the employees inside the museum—both anticipating the start of another business day in 15 minutes. The woman on the sofa, Jacqueline Smith, turned out to be a well-known Memphis protestor. Ms. Smith was a former motel desk clerk who lived at the Lorraine from 1977 to 1988. In March 1988, she was evicted to make way for the construction of the National Civil Rights Museum. Since that time, she has lived on the sidewalk facing the museum and fought, in vain, to have the soil where King fell more accurately reflect his vision by using it as housing for the homeless. In her words, "The National Civil Rights Museum is a disgrace to the life and works of Dr. King, a scam and a land grab that is inflating real estate values and displacing people who have lived in the area for years." Jacqueline Smith is a flesh-and-bones protest of the museum. Twenty-four hours per day, seven days per week, in the frigid cold or the ceaseless heat, she camps across from the museum and continues her one-woman vigil. She explained her protest to our group, gave us pamphlets, and wished us well. She knew we would end up visiting the museum—the museum authorities say that very rarely are people ever turned away by her protest. She also knew, however, that it was incumbent upon her to stand up and be heard. To do any less would be to deny her responsibility. We were moved by her mission and persistence. Mostly, though, we saw a model of the courage of disagreement.

To disagree in ways that continue a conversation is an art. Parker Palmer, a sociologist and renowned teacher, has said,

> Truth is an eternal conversation about things that matter.... And if I want my students to be in the truth, I want them to know how to be in the conversation, not just resting on conclusions. I want them to know how to hang in with a conversation that's increasingly difficult because it's increasingly diverse and it invokes much woundedness, and much anger and much struggle. There are ways to stay in the conversation if you understand that that's what truth is.[4]

Aristotle recognized the problematic nature of disagreement centuries ago when he wrote, "Anyone can become angry—that is easy, but to be angry with the right person, to the right degree, at the right time, for the right purpose, and in the right way—this is not easy."[5] The challenge is to stay in conversations that are difficult and to disagree in ways that keep a conversation going. To do this, we must engage and project love and forgiveness. We cannot preach or be self-righteous. We must communicate—by our words and actions—that racial reconciliation (not personal victory) is the goal.

TEACH YOURSELF TO THINK: CONTROL COGNITIVE PROCESSING OF STEREOTYPES

In Chapter 9, we reviewed Patricia Devine's work on automatic and controlled cognitive processing.[6] In her theory, Devine maintains that each of us learns negative racial stereotypes early in life. These are part of the social heritage of American society and are inescapable. These negative stereotypes (e.g., "Blacks are hostile") are automatically activated whenever we encounter a person from a different racial group. In essence, the activation of negative stereotypes becomes a "bad habit" that leads to biased assumptions, emotional reactions, and treatment. A racist is satisfied with these automatic negative reactions and is seldom willing to exert any cognitive effort to suppress them.

If we pride ourselves on being unbiased, though, is it possible to break the "bad habit" of automatic processing? Can we consciously attempt to control our cognitive processing? When we are not mentally lazy, busy, overwhelmed, distracted, or paying much attention, can we override the activation of our learned, automatic negative stereotypes? Can we teach ourselves to think? Devine's answer is a qualified "yes."

First, we must develop, or be taught, a set of *personal beliefs* about the inappropriateness of stereotypic descriptions. Research suggests that high- and low-prejudice people are equally knowledgeable of the negative racial stereotypes. Low-prejudice people, however, have developed more tolerant personal beliefs than high-prejudice people. Second, having developed these more tolerant personal beliefs, we must then *teach ourselves to consciously suppress the automatic activation of our negative racial stereotypes.* By so doing, we allow our personal beliefs of tolerance to censor, shape, or adjust our assumptions and reactions to other people. For example, we can say to ourselves, "Hey, that stereotype isn't fair and it isn't right. Blacks are no more hostile than whites. Ignore the stereotype and give the person a chance!" Notice that the negative stereotype is not eliminated; rather, we teach ourselves to consciously inhibit its expression.

Typically, the automatic negative stereotypes remain stronger than the personal beliefs because they are older. In other words, each of us has been socialized in negative racial stereotypes since birth. The development of more tolerant personal beliefs, however, is a new cognitive structure typically acquired only years later. The negative stereotypes have a longer history and greater frequency of activation than the personal beliefs. Thus, the "bad habit" of automatic negative stereotyping is much more potent than the acquired "good habit" of tolerant personal beliefs. As a result, when we have not taken the time, effort, or attention to suppress them, even well-meaning people will allow the automatic negative racial stereotypes to bias their assumptions and reactions. Devine calls this "prejudice with compunction" (i.e., with guilt and self-criticism). As we increase the frequency with which our tolerant personal belief structure is activated, however, we decrease the potency of our automatic responses. Our intentionality and resolve make the "bad habit" become weaker as the "good habit" becomes stronger. Clearly, controlling our cognitive processing is not an easy task. In Devine's words, "Overcoming prejudice is like breaking a habit.

As in breaking any habit, it's not easy. It requires a great deal of effort, practice, and relearning."[7]

In what other ways can we teach ourselves to think in directions that encourage racial reconciliation? One strategy is to redirect our innate tendency for social categorization by developing "supercategories" that include members of both the original in-group and out-group in a larger, more inclusive, group. As we have seen, when we have only two groups, the in-group is perceived to have only positive attributes and the out-group only negative attributes (what we have called the in-group bias effect). If some members of both groups share membership in another larger, superordinate group, however, the social split should be less severe and in-group bias less evident.

Utilizing superordinate groups occurs, for example, when nations form with the hope of unifying previously warring groups in a larger, more inclusive category. At times, it works (Catholics and Protestants in the United States); other times, it doesn't (the former Yugoslavia). How has this strategy fared in psychological laboratories? In one experiment, John Dovidio and his colleagues created an in-group and an out-group. Consistent with the in-group bias, each group expressed clear, negative evaluations of the other group. Half of the members of each group were then placed into a positive superordinate group. Contrary to their earlier evaluations, these members—previously separated but now joined in a positive superordinate group—evaluated their new "out-group colleagues" (an apparent contradiction in terms) much more positively.[8]

We should recognize that cognitive and motivational forces may conspire to reestablish subgroup differentiation and subsequent in-group–out-group distinctions. In most cases, large, diverse social categories are less likely to elicit strong social identification and in-group loyalty. Subgroup identities remain more likely to meet our needs for optimal social identification and in-group loyalty. Research on superordinate categories does, however, offer the intriguing potential for racial reconciliation found in creating new superordinate groups and discarding old subgroups. As poet Edwin Markam has written:

> He drew a circle that shut me out—
> Heretic, rebel, a thing to flout,
> But love and I had the wit to win:
> We drew a circle that took him in.

TO THINE OWN SELF BE KNOWN:
BECOME MORE SELF-AWARE

A third principle for racial reconciliation involves increasing our self-awareness in two areas: (1) our personal racial, ethnic, and religious stories; and (2) our personal stereotypes, prejudices, and discriminatory behaviors. As Annie MacGuire, a lead character in Oscar Hijuelos's powerful novel *Mr. Ives' Christmas* states, "The troubles in life were started by people who never looked into their own souls."[9] Why is looking into our own souls an important part of racial reconciliation?

Personal Racial, Ethnic, and Religious Stories

It is important that we become more self-aware of our personal racial, ethnic, and religious stories. This is a central aim as I prepare students for our January cross-country study tours. Each fall, they are required to construct an extensive genealogy examining their personal stories. (The appendix lists several helpful Internet sites related to tracing one's personal heritage.) In addition, they participate in a group-sharing exercise (they really HATE this) in which they respond to questions "How do you identify yourself and what does your identity mean to you?" "What is the significance of your name? Where did it come from?" "Describe a time when you wished you belonged to some other group, or a time when you wished you weren't identified with so visible a group. How did you cope with these feelings?" Both exercises are meant to sharpen the students' sense of identity by more directly connecting them with their racial, ethnic, and religious stories. The potential costs of drawing attention to the very things that divide us are profound. The fact that I require the exercises, however, tells you that the potential benefits are even more striking.

What, then, are the potential benefits? First, becoming more self-aware of our personal racial, ethnic, and religious stories gives us an opportunity to learn about the people who influenced the people who influenced the people who influenced us. The vast majority of my students know little about their heritage beyond their grandparents. In more clearly exploring their past, however, the students come to understand the lingering influence of the past upon their present. It's a matter of education, not exclusion. We can take pride in the good, regret the bad, and abhor the ugly. We get an alternate understanding of who we are and can be. We recognize that our identity does not begin and end with us individually. Rather, our identity is, in part, a cumulative "hand-me-down" from the past as well as a connection to the future. We hurt ourselves if we turn a blind eye to that which nurtures us in our own stories. Identity is at the cutting edge of many disputes between racial groups. We can't solve disputes rooted in identity if we can't talk about our own identity. In the words of Malcolm X: "A race of people is like an individual man; until it uses its own talent, takes pride in its own history, expresses its own culture, affirms its own selfhood, it can never fulfill itself."[10]

In April 1996, Keith Woods, a staff member at the Poynter Institute for Media Studies in St. Petersburg, Florida, went to admirable lengths to help his children grasp the importance of the past in their present identity. Woods and his two teenage children spent their Easter vacation tracing the civil rights movement and Dr. King's life by touring six Southern cities (Atlanta, Tuskegee, Montgomery, Selma, Birmingham, and Memphis). In Woods's words, "I wanted them to learn the truths of history that explain their past, inform their present and inspire their future ... feel what happens when the past pulls you to its bosom and hugs you so tight that it pushes all your pride to your chest and squeezes all the shame from the recesses of your soul." After the trip, Woods acknowledged its impact: "The picture of their past and mine now has more depth, more dimension, more colors and shades than all the stingy American history books I've read in 38 years.... We drove 2,000 miles for that lesson. I'd drive 20,000. Two hundred thousand."[11] Connecting our narrative with our heritage of stories is an important part of full identity.

Second, for most of us, an examination of our personal stories will reveal that—not too long ago—we, too, came from another shore. In a time when restrictive immigration legislation is frequently discussed, it's helpful for each of us to recognize that had such legislation been in place four or five generations ago, our lives today would be drastically different. It's good to be reminded that whites share at least one commonality with blacks, Hispanics, and Asian-Americans. We all came from somewhere else.

Finally, we benefit because we begin to understand why story is so important to people as a source of identity, belonging, or personal place in the large scheme of things. This is as important for whites as it is for racial minorities. We have lost our own "white" cultures and stories. We have no European-American identity. Our ancestors worked extremely hard to dismantle their European identity in favor of what they perceived to be the true "American" identity. As a result, we have become disconnected from the languages, foods, music, games, rituals, and expressions of our ancestors. Often, we fabricate connections by turning to other traditions for our identity. Kathleen Norris's *Dakota: A Spiritual Geography* is a wonderful work on the importance of heritage and story. In that book, she describes white Americans as "seeking the sacred in Native American spirituality, often appropriating it in ways that add to the already bitter experience Indians have of being overwhelmed and consumed by white culture."[12]

Discovering our stories can be invigorating and instructive. Some of my students, for example, discover for the first time that their heritage includes Swedish, German, or Irish roots. Often, as the semester progresses, I notice that they are placing flags of these countries on their car bumpers, taking a stronger interest in World Cup and Olympic games, and so forth. Most important, however, the significance of heritage to racial minorities begins to dawn on them. If it comes to mean so much to my students, how much more must it mean to groups of people for whom their identities and self-esteem have been devastated by American culture? Is it any wonder, for instance, that blacks have taken such tremendous pride in their African heritage when white America has denied them so consistently the opportunities to find identity and esteem in this country? Again, Kathleen Norris notes the state of Native Americans in the Dakotas: "Native Americans have learned through harsh necessity that people who survive encroachment by another culture need story to survive."[13]

Becoming more self-aware of our personal racial, ethnic, and religious stories is crucial to a truly multicultural society. This in-group self-awareness, however, need not automatically preclude membership in superordinate groups. Psychologist Teresa LaFromboise and colleagues, for instance, demonstrated that bicultural individuals (those with mixed racial heritage, or born in one culture and raised in a second) can gain competence within two cultures without losing their primary cultural identity or having to choose one culture over the other.[14] Other experimental research has confirmed that superordinate identities can be achieved without sacrificing identification with distinctive subgroups. Similarly, increasing self-awareness of our own stories need not imply a rejection of our membership in a larger political entity comprising other racial, ethnic, and religious groups—America.

The search for our stories can build bridges between racial groups and actually solidify our connection to the superordinate group of "Americans." It is done as part of, not separate from, improving intergroup relations. We are capable of knowing and understanding ourselves through two or more different groups. We can hold each group in positive, if not necessarily equal, regard. We shouldn't have to lose our heritage in order to become good Americans. If we do, all of us lose. The fact that we use hyphenated names to indicate cultural and social connections to our ancestors has nothing to do with our loyalty to the United States. Short of making it an obsession, recognizing the affiliations that have traditionally helped hold America's communities together need not threaten our sense of national belonging. In Norris's book, she describes a prophetic warning from Ole Rolvaag's *Giants in the Earth* trilogy, in which a country pastor is addressing Norwegian farmers in Dakota:

> If this process of leveling down, of making everybody alike ... is allowed to continue, America is doomed to become the most impoverished land spiritually on the face of the earth; out of our highly praised melting pot will come a dull ... smug complacency, barren of all creative thought.... Soon we will have reached the perfect democracy of barrenness.... Dead will be the hidden life of the heart which is nourished by tradition, the idioms of language, and our attitude to life.[15]

Personal Stereotypes, Prejudices, and Discriminatory Behaviors

Becoming more self-aware of one's racial, ethnic, and religious stories is relatively simple given a certain level of motivation. Becoming self-aware of our personal stereotypes, prejudices, and discriminatory behaviors, however, is much more difficult. How do we become aware of this dark side of ourselves? Though, as Devine maintains, we all are knowledgeable about racial stereotypes, most of us try to consciously prevent those stereotypes from impacting our feelings (prejudice) or behaviors (discrimination) toward another group of people. Unless we are brutally honest with ourselves, we protect our self-esteem by excluding our personal stereotypes, prejudices, and discriminatory behaviors from conscious self-awareness.

How can we become more aware of our personal stereotypes, prejudices, and discriminatory behaviors? How do we inflict insight upon ourselves? Some are self-aware enough to reflect back on their experiences and find unflattering examples of biased thoughts, feelings, and behaviors. Others have close relationships in which a friend or family member can give a constructive "outsider's" perspective of their stereotypes, prejudices, and discriminatory behaviors. For most of us, however, it's only when we actually engage in personal contact with members of different racial groups that we become aware of our most deep-seated biases. As psychologist Thomas Pettigrew describes, "Many [people] have confessed to me ... that even though in their minds they no longer feel prejudice toward Blacks, they still feel squeamish when they shake hands with a Black."[16] When our contact with racial diversity is limited, we should be wary of the false comfort that comes with our belief that we have no negative stereotypes, prejudices, or discriminatory behaviors. It may be that only in the context of actual physical contact do we become aware of our deepest biases. We'll return to the importance of personal interaction with diversity in the fifth principle.

OPEN YOUR MIND:
APPRECIATE THE PANORAMA OF THE BORDERLAND

The "perfect democracy of barrenness" is contrasted with the rich fruits that can come when we appreciate the richness of America's diversity. This fourth principle of racial reconciliation recognizes this is at the heart of a crucial question. How do we live in a place where two or more cultures edge each other? In this "borderland," where people of different races occupy the same territory, how do we meet on communal ground? This is the great question of our age. As we have seen, the ideal of a multicultural society is to maintain and develop group identities in the context of the larger, superordinate identity of "Americans." How does this play out? How do we draw strength from our multiple identities?

First, we must encourage the reality of a truly multicultural society.

We must not force other cultural identities into a homogeneous "American" (read white) identity. The "melting pot" theory suggesting that cultures sharing an economic, political, or geographical space will fuse together until they are indistinguishable to form a new culture always has been problematic. In the early part of this century, for instance, Langston Hughes recognized that there was a "mountain standing in the way of any true Negro art in America—this urge within the race toward whiteness, this desire to pour racial identity into the mold of American standardization, and to be as little Negro and as much American as possible."[17] Native American history, as well, is polluted with egregious examples of forced assimilation. In 1879, for instance, boarding schools for Native American children became national policy. They were run by well-intentioned "liberals" of the time, who were devoted to "saving the savages." With the motto "Kill the Indian and save the man," the boarding school was a place where children were stripped of their past, their family, their spirituality, their culture—a place where they were trained to be "American." After World War II, though no longer national policy, many Native Americans saw the boarding schools as the only option for education and willingly sent their children. The repercussions of these experiences are still felt in the fragmentation of Native American communities today.[18]

Many contend that the "mold" of American standardization is even inherent in the apparently noble enterprise of integration. A black undergraduate interviewed by sociologist Joe Feagin remarked, "To integrate means simply to be White. It doesn't mean fusing the two cultures; it simply means to be white, that's all.... They have no reason to know our culture. But we must, in order to survive, know everything about their culture."[19] Manning Marable, a professor of political science and sociology at the University of Colorado at Boulder, concurs that integration, in practice, has threatened blacks' sense of community and identity—without fulfilling the promise of improving their lives or ending racism.[20]

Today, the "melting pot" theory has been replaced by a model that encourages groups to maintain and develop their group identities. As a result, we must recognize a second strategy for living in the borderland. We must come to appreciate, not lament, the richness of America's racial diversity. We must recognize the beauty of our mélange.

Practically, this means white Americans can no longer remain ignorant of the culture, language, history, contributions, and sufferings of racial minorities in this country. No longer can we suffer remarks that are born out of ignorance, such as those of University of Texas at Austin law professor Lino Graglia, a white, who recently opined, "Blacks and Mexican-Americans are not academically competitive with whites in selective institutions. They have a culture that seems not to encourage achievement. Failure is not looked upon with disgrace." As Clarence Page, a columnist with The *Chicago Tribune*, suggests, Graglia may not be a racist. He is, though, ignorant.[21] Blacks and Hispanics represent not "a" culture but dozens of them. Many of their subcultures are obsessed with achievement. In some of their subcultures, as in some white subcultures, achievement is not valued as it should be. Graglia's comments, however, reveal that it's easy for whites to be ignorant of how racial minorities really live in America.

In addition, it's easy for us to ignore the reflections of racial minorities on their own cultural experiences. We must recognize that racial minorities are experts on their own experiences, and we must listen to those reflections. We must come to appreciate the relevance of those reflections to our collective identity. One person wrote the following statement in response to a lecture I presented: "A major in African-American issues or studies is irrelevant! This type of major, if one can call it that, should only exist at schools with a large black population." Such a comment is a result of a social and educational system in which we have defined America too narrowly. As Carol Hampton, national field officer of the Native Americas Ministry of the Episcopal Church, has written, "You taught me that my history mattered not at all unless it impinged on yours and then you taught my history only from your perspective."[22] Through the omission of information, America's schools can become monocultural environments. We have to go beyond such compartmentalized thinking and realize that "their" story, as told by "them," is an important part of "our" story, as understood by "us." At times, hearing "their" story leads us to the painful realization that our image of America as a free and democratic nation must be qualified. We are forced to revisit our assumptions about our country's past, present, and future. In short, we are challenged to think outside of the narrow and traditional compartments of understanding in which most of us were educated.

This challenge is the heart of our study tour experiences. We operate on the well-established social psychological principle that the greater our familiarity with a social group, the more we see its diversity and, as a result, the less likely we are to stereotype.[23] Daily, the study tour students are exposed to the history, food, celebrations, contributions, sufferings, and traditions of racial minorities. As Paul Kivel writes, "When we aren't remotely familiar with the music, literature and dance of people we live with, we cannot expect to understand what they experience or what moves and guides them. We cannot honor and respect their concerns and life choices."[24] We frame the information in a helpful model developed by psychologist James Jones. Jones's TRIOS model represents five dimensions of human experience—time, rhythm, improvisation, oral expression, and spirituality. The dimensions emerged from Jones's analysis of racial differences in sports performance, African religion and philosophy, Trinidadian culture, and psychotherapy with black clients.[25] These five dimensions reflect basic ways in which individuals and cultures orient themselves to living. They refer to how we experience and organize life, make decisions, arrive at beliefs, and derive meaning. They are valuable educational tools for appreciating the richness of America's racial diversity.

When white Americans care enough to appreciate the richness of racial diversity, a significant step toward racial reconciliation already has been taken. In Hijuelos's *Mr. Ives' Christmas*, the lead character, Edward Ives, is sitting in a bar studying a book of Spanish grammar. Though himself white, Ives had a long-standing interest in Spanish culture, history, and language. The bartender, a Cuban named Luis Ramirez, noticed the book and struck up a conversation. From that conversation, kindled because a Cuban took notice of a white man interested in an aspect of his culture, grew a significant, long-term friendship. Though they had little in common, Ives's humble attempt to understand a group of people different from him sowed the seeds for a relationship with Ramirez.

We experience much the same dynamics on our study tours. As you would expect, people are fairly quick to notice a group of backpack-laden, white college students on inner-city public transportation. Often, we were asked what we were doing. Each of us dreaded that question. Initially, we stumbled and bumbled our way around the most obvious answer—"We're studying you." We quickly got skilled, however, at explaining our desire to study race relations in America from the perspective of racial minorities, to hear about their experiences from their mouths, and to encounter their culture in a firsthand way. In every instance, our goals were met with appreciation. One Asian-American woman in Los Angeles said simply: "I am moved by your mission." Another African-American man in Memphis responded, "That's downright nice of white people to let us tell the story for a change!" A Hispanic-American in Chicago said, "It's flattering that you would take the time to do that." There was a sincere appreciation, and intuitive recognition, that in learning to value America's racial diversity, we were taking a significant stride toward racial reconciliation. That's an important lesson for those of us who feel hesitant to immerse ourselves in the study and life of another group of people.

GET IN TOUCH: ENGAGE IN PERSONAL INTERACTION WITH RACIAL DIVERSITY

A cognitive knowledge of the history, culture, and so forth of another group is important and necessary. It is not, however, sufficient to ensure racial reconciliation. This knowledge must be applied in the context of personal, face-to-face interaction. This cross-racial interaction must be "real," however. Racial reconciliation will not flow from the superficial contacts in formal settings or the "pseudorelating" found in forced interactions. Rather, racial reconciliation will flow only from a sincere, open, in-depth interaction with racial diversity.

Why doesn't superficial contact or forced interaction have more favorable effects? It's common sense that lack of familiarity with others can breed hostility and contempt. It follows that increasing opportunity for personal contact should lead to reduced hostility by increasing mutual knowledge and acquaintance. The idea that direct, individual personal contact with members of disliked out-groups should reduce prejudice toward those out-groups is known as the *contact hypothesis*. Unfortunately, more than four decades of social psychological research demonstrates that simply putting people from different backgrounds together is not enough to ensure positive social outcomes. Mere contact is not a sufficient panacea in itself. Rather, the contact must be structured in some particular ways.

Our country has learned, in a painful way, the parameters of the contact hypothesis. Since the historic 1954 Supreme Court ruling, school desegregation has had a controversial history—legally and socially. On the social science front, the effect of school desegregation on the improvement of interracial relations has been negligible. Only a minority of studies have reported decreases in prejudice following desegregation. Many studies have found that white prejudice against blacks actually increased following desegregation or showed no improvement. The prejudice of blacks against whites increased in about as many cases as it decreased. Most disconcertingly, observational research reveals the existence of "resegregation," where blacks and whites in desegregated schools rarely interact in any meaningful way. Their friendship choices, curricular and cocurricular involvements, and even academic tracking reveal deep racial divisions. In short, only a small fraction of the constructive potential of school desegregation has been realized. Why? Surely mere contact is better than no contact at all? Reconciliation can't begin unless we are actually in the presence of those with whom we need to reconcile. Why hasn't desegregation fulfilled its promise?

The failure of superficial or forced contact in remedying negative racial attitudes has demonstrated that we must be intentional in our preparation for interacting with racial diversity. How does this happen? First, we recognize that the preparation builds on the previous four principles. In other words, we consciously prepare for personal interaction with diversity by nurturing basic human relations skills, controlling our cognitive processing, becoming more self-aware of our personal story and prejudices, and learning to appreciate the richness of America's racial diversity.

Second, we recognize that the interaction must be structured in a certain way. In other words, there are some qualifying conditions to the interaction that must be met in order for positive intergroup relations to develop. What are these conditions that promote true integration? In 1985, psychologist Stuart Cook, late of the University of Colorado at Boulder, suggested five necessary conditions for producing favorable attitudes from interracial contact:[26]

1. The contact situation must promote *equal-status* interactions between members of the racial groups. In many racially-mixed settings, the reality of preexisting status differences renders this condition prob-

lematic. Often, members of higher-status groups may be unwilling to learn from, or be influenced by, members of lower-status groups.

At the end of our 1996 study tour, the students and I met for a final debriefing on our last evening in Washington, D.C. One of my questions to them was "What could I do differently next time? How can I make the next tour better?" Most of their responses centered around the issue of wanting to spend more time in personal interaction with blacks, Hispanics, Asian-Americans and Native Americans. When I pushed them for a picture of what that interaction would look like, they replied with some very noble ideas—working in a soup kitchen, building a shelter with Habitat for Humanity, or passing out blankets to the homeless. In the midst of those noble desires, though, there was hidden an unsettling truth. The truth was that most of my students, similar to most of white America, were only comfortable relating to racial minorities in situations of *un*equal status—where they were the saver and the black, Hispanic, Asian-American, or Native American needed saving. They wouldn't have to learn from or be influenced by a minority. They could do all of the teaching and all of the influencing. This "messiah complex" betrays our hesitancies to engage in equal-status interactions. When status is unequal, interactions follow stereotypical patterns. We must force ourselves, however, to take the necessary steps to promote equal-status interactions between group members.

2.   The interaction must encourage behaviors that *disconfirm stereotypical beliefs* that the racial groups hold of each other. Kathleen Norris, for instance, tells of a dance troupe that visited a school in Lemmon, South Dakota. One dancer was a black man who had been raised on a farm in Indiana and had broken horses for a living. He'd been a bull rider on the rodeo circuit and told the students he had given it up and taken up dancing, because the bull riding wasn't good for his body. In Norris's words, "I felt he'd earned his fee right there" because his power in disconfirming the stereotypical belief of the students was so tremendous.[27] What is crucial is that we must come to believe that the supposedly atypical out-group member is actually rather typical of their group. Otherwise, the stereotypical beliefs can be maintained by labeling one atypical out-group member as the exception.

3.   *Mutual interdependence* among members of both groups is required. Such a mutually interdependent relationship is most often seen

in cooperating to achieve a joint goal that cannot be accomplished without the contributions of members of both groups. In other words, members of both groups are forced to share the same concern, even if only for a short period of time.

In a classic series of studies conducted between 1949 and 1954, social psychologist Muzafer Sherif and his colleagues demonstrated the importance of mutual interdependence in ingenious field experiments at a summer camp. In the summer of 1954, 22 eleven-year-old boys, with no preexisting cultural, physical, or status differences between them, participated in a three-week study at Robber's Cave in Oklahoma. Through an initial period of segregation and bonding, followed by a period of interaction in conditions of intergroup competition, Sherif created two rival groups—the "Rattlers" and the "Eagles." Having created two rival groups with hostile attitudes and negative images of each other, Sherif then was faced with the task of conflict reduction. Simply bringing the two groups together in neutral situations only increased the hostility. It was only by introducing tasks of mutual interdependence (e.g., both groups cooperating to solve the breakdown of the water supply system to the camp) that Sherif was able to restore harmony between the two groups. In other words, group membership was redefined along the boundaries of an interdependent, or superordinate, group. "They" came to be included into "us."[28] By the end of the camp, friendships had formed across group lines, and intergroup hostility had reduced significantly.[29] Sherif's results also have been replicated in experiments among 150 groups of executives from industrial organizations.[30]

Out of this decade's tragedy of the attacks on black churches (nearly 80 have been firebombed, burned, or vandalized since 1990) have emerged some notable stories of racial reconciliation built on the mutual interdependence of blacks and whites to rebuild the churches. On January 29, 1995, the 130-year-old Friendship Missionary Baptist Church of Columbia, Tennessee, was torched by white men who wanted to punish the black race. Responding to that hatred, white churches and neighbors moved quickly to help rewire, remodel, repaint, refurnish, and ready the sanctuary for Sunday services the next week.[31]

Similarly, there was the case in central India in October 1993, in which 30,000 people were estimated to have died from a massive earthquake. Faced with this disaster, the sectarian hatred between Hindus and Muslims was submerged in the common rescue effort.[32] From these acts of mutual interdependence and cooperation blossomed a personalization of out-group members and a positive atmosphere within which reconciliation could progress. As he was organizing a church watch in Eastover, South Carolina, the Reverend Joseph Darby of St. Phillip AME Church reflected on the promise inherent in such cooperation: "We would love to have white volunteers serve on the watch squads. If you stand out in the countryside together in the middle of the night, you are going to have to talk."[33]

4.   The contact situation must have *high "acquaintance potential."* In other words, it must promote intimate contact between participants. Such contact will reveal enough detail about members of the out-group that they will come to be seen as individuals rather than as persons with stereotypical group characteristics. The most successful efforts involve contact over an extended period of time or multiple cooperative interactions. Sociologists Mary Jackman and Marie Crane also suggest that the level of intimacy is less important than the variety of contacts.[34] Contacts that are extended, multiple, and varied increase the chances of generalizing positive racial attitudes across the board. The importance of such contact is illustrated in the challenge laid out by Bill Bradley: "When was the last time you talked about race with someone of a different race? If the answer is never, you're part of the problem."[35]

5.   Finally, the *social norms* in the contact situation must be perceived as favoring interracial acceptance and equality. Social norms are reflected in our laws and customs as expressed by relevant authority figures and institutional supports. Principals, parents, teachers, religious leaders, peers, and social, political, and athletic icons are important channels in the transmission of social norms. We must harness that power to establish racial tolerance and reconciliation as sanctioned social norms. If we can, then group members, when placed in positions of interracial contact, may modify their behavior to fit egalitarian social norms.

It is not enough, however, that we simply *teach* the social norms. We must also make them salient in real-life situations. A study by University of Michigan political scientist Mary Jackman, for instance, found that the well educated are more likely to have learned principles of racial tolerance than are the poorly educated. In an applied situation (e.g., support for government action to promote integration), however, the "learned" principles of the well educated do not translate into significantly different responses from the poorly educated.[36] In short, instruction in social norms must be accompanied by their application in specific settings.

Can We Make the World a Better Place?

In a host of laboratory and field experiments, Cook and others have confirmed that these five qualifying conditions increase the likelihood of friendly interracial behavior, the promotion of cross-racial respect and liking, and more favorable racial attitudes. In an important educational application, now used in some form or another by more than 25,000 teachers, psychologist Elliot Aronson and his colleagues implemented cooperative, interdependent structures in racially mixed elementary school classrooms in Texas and California. These structures, known as "jigsaw groups," place students in six-person clusters that are racially and academically diverse. The day's lesson is divided into six paragraphs, such that each student has one segment of the written material. For example, if the students are to learn about the life of Eleanor Roosevelt, her biography is arranged in six parts. Like the pieces of a jigsaw puzzle, each student has a unique and vital part of the information that is essential to the whole picture. In true cooperative fashion, the student must learn his or her own section and teach it to the other members of the group, who do not have access to that material. Even when used for as little as 20 percent of a child's time in the classroom, results indicate that jigsaw groups increased the self-esteem, morale, interpersonal attraction, and empathy of students across ethnic and racial categories. In addition, the students showed an increase in cross-racial interactions and a reduction in racial prejudice. The jigsaw groups also improved the academic performance of minority students without hampering the performance of whites.[37] The success of such cooperative learning strategies in a cluster of public schools in East Harlem has been documented in Deborah Meier's recent book, *The Power of Their Ideas*.[38]

These five necessary conditions also reveal how *un*structured contact can actually increase or reinforce prejudice. In other words, they tell us what to avoid in contact situations. Prejudice will be increased when the contact is between persons of unequal status (particularly when the person from the out-group is of lower status); when the contact tends to confirm rather than disconfirm negative stereotypical beliefs; when the contact situation involves competition, opposing interests or values, or is unpleasant, tense or frustrating; when the contact involves superficial rather than intimate contact, and when there are no powerful social norms or institutional supports favoring interracial tolerance and equality.

THE POWER OF MANY:
DRAW ON THE STRENGTH OF COMMUNITY

The work of racial reconciliation is long and difficult. We can easily fall into the weariness of "problem fatigue" and resign ourselves to a belief that nothing can be done to improve our lot. The work is not one for short-term enthusiasms. We must draw on the strength of each other to sustain ourselves in the struggle for racial reconciliation. The strength of community is a vital and, too often, untapped reservoir of resolve.

The power of community can play out in several ways. On one level, community frames social norms. In 1993, a series of alarming events escalated in Billings, Montana. First, hate flyers and KKK newspapers appeared. Then, "skinheads" harassed Native American children on their way home from school. This was followed by assaults on gays. Quickly, Billings's Central Labor Council passed a resolution condemning those attacks. Thousands of people attended rallies and signed statements condemning hate activity in Billings. More than 100 local organizations passed similar declarations.

In the face of this emerging social norm, however, the bigots stepped up their attacks. They desecrated a Jewish cemetery, harassed a local black church, and painted swastikas and hate messages on the side of a house of a Native American family. The Painters Union formed a volunteer workforce to paint over racist graffiti, and religious and civic leaders sponsored community watches, marches, and ecumenical services. When a cinder block was thrown through a window displaying a Hanukkah menorah and crashed into the bedroom of a six-year-old Jewish child, the *Billings Gazette* published a full-page color picture of a menorah. An idea swept through the town. By late December, nearly

10,000 homes and businesses in Billings had taped the picture of a menorah to their windows. In the words of a former police chief of Billings, "Hate groups have learned through experience that if a community doesn't respond, then the community accepts."[39] The people of Billings responded. From their responses, a strong social norm emerged that, in the final words of the documentary entitled *Not in Our Town*, said, "Today—not in our town. Tomorrow—not in our country."

Across the nation, communities have learned the power of fighting back in establishing strong social norms against racism. From Great Falls, Montana, to Whitinsville, Massachusetts; from Cedar Rapids, Iowa, to Bloomington, Illinois; from Reno, Nevada, to Los Alamitos, California; and from Cobb County, Georgia, to Sandpoint, Idaho, communities are proclaiming "Not in our town!" In the midst of their response to short-term crises of old-fashioned racism, new lines of communication for addressing the more subtle, long-term problem of modern racism are being opened. Communities are recognizing that responding to racism is like bathing. You can't just do it once in your life. It has to happen regularly to be truly effective.

On an even more direct level, community empowers in the application of concrete programs aimed at racial reconciliation. Communities across the nation have developed citizens' guides and committees to institute programs aimed at establishing climates of reconciliation and tolerance. In Portland, Oregon, the Southeast Uplift Neighborhood Program, as part of its Antiracism Action Plan, publishes a guide on how to establish a "racism-free zone." They offer a selection of activities for groups and individuals to use to establish a climate where racism cannot exist, and where all people feel welcome.[40] In Houston, the Center for the Healing of Racism attempts to foster interracial communication through a multiweek discussion series called "Dialogue: Racism." In my own community, civic leaders have drafted a commitment to action for racial equity that has been endorsed across a wide range of businesses and organizations in Spokane.[41] In some communities, civic leadership has been complemented by religious leadership. This is especially vital, because, too often, the church has intensified racial hatred instead of alleviating it. The fact that Sunday morning remains the most segregated time of the week must not preclude the active involvement of religious leaders in racial reconciliation.

We also can learn from integrated communities that are models of diversity and tolerance. In the Mount Airy section of Philadelphia, about two-thirds of the residents are black and one-third are white. For nearly 30 years, the residents of this urban neighborhood have been making integration work. In the words of their representative, Rep. William Gray III, "This is a very unusual slice of urban America. It works because the people have decided to make it work. They have refused to let fear and division take over."[42] Similar interracial communities in Auburn Park in Chicago, Seven Oaks in Detroit, Cranwood in Cleveland, and South DeKalb in Atlanta offer important lessons in the art of living together.

We must remember that true community means full inclusiveness. In the words of author and environmentalist Wendell Berry, "A true and appropriate answer to our race problem, as to many others, would be a restoration of our communities—it being understood that a community, properly speaking, cannot exclude or mistreat any of its members."[43] The integrity of true community rests on the degree to which all are encompassed in the circle of "us."

INVEST IN OUR FUTURE: TEACH ANTIRACISM EARLY

Last Christmas, my six-year-old son and I were at an advent service. To our left, our pastor was sitting with a guest pastor from California. They both were of the same approximate height, weight, and burly build. They both had tightly curled hair and a rough beard. On this Sunday, they both wore similar dark, pinstriped suits. Our pastor is ivory white. The guest was ebony black. During the beginning of the service, I noticed that my son kept craning his neck to stare at the two men. Finally, during a period of silent prayer (my children's favorite time to speak loudly and provocatively), my son blurted out, "Look, Dad, they're twins!"

In his six-year-old mind, the salience of their similarities in build, hair, beard, and appearance overwhelmed the one striking difference that snares our immediate attention—the color of their skin. At some point in his life, however, he'll come to the unfortunate recognition that the color of one's skin is a fundamental principle (along with gender) around which we organize our perceptions of people. As he "matures," the forest of similarities will be lost for the tree of difference. How does that come about? When do children become aware of social categories? More important, when do they begin to pledge allegiance and loyalty to their own social category?

When do children first become aware of social categories? One popular technique used to answer this question involves presenting children with a series of photographs and asking them to sort them into groups according to how they "belong together" or "look alike." In the photographs, there are usually several cues that the children could use for sorting criteria—race, gender, age, style of dress, hair color, and so forth. Generally, research shows that by two and a half, and certainly by three years of age, race and gender labels can be readily and correctly used. By the age of four of five, race has emerged as the most dominant sorting criterion.[44] By this age, most children living in America can differentiate between blacks and whites, and are at least somewhat aware of the prevailing norms about race.

Other research, using a different experimental strategy, suggests that even infants of a few months old are capable of making categorical distinctions among human faces! At the Institute for Research on Social Problems in Boulder, Colorado, psychologist Phyllis Katz and her colleagues first habituated 100 black and 100 white six-month-old infants to pictures of someone from a different race. In other words, they repeatedly showed the pictures to the infants until they (the infants, not the researchers) had lost interest in the pictures. Following habituation, the research team then introduced a picture of someone from a different race. When the infants saw this new picture, they spent a significantly longer period of time looking at it, thus demonstrating that they noticed the difference. In Katz's words, "The results show that children are sensitive to race cues even before they develop language skills."[45]

At what point do children begin to pledge allegiance or show loyalty to their own social category? When does in-group bias develop? The evidence suggests that children begin to prefer their own social category fairly soon after they become adept at constructing those categories. Psychologist A. Davey, for instance, asked 7- to 10-year-old British children to distribute four pieces of candy between unknown members of different racial groups shown in photographs. Of the 500 or so children in the study, fully 50 percent gave at least three of the four pieces of candy to the in-group photographs (i.e., their own racial category). Less than 1 percent gave at least three of the four pieces of candy to the out-group photographs! Subsequently, Davey found that these children's stereotypical views were almost always more positive about their in-group (e.g., "more clever") than about the out-groups (e.g., "lazy").[46] The work of Henri Tajfel also indicates that by age six or seven, children exhibit a strong preference for their own nationality, even though they don't yet fully understand the concept of a "nation."[47] Similar patterns of bias in young children are seen across a range of other social categories—gender, disabilities, obesity, and people who speak a different language.

So, at an early age, children develop patterns of bias based on their actual membership in a certain social category. How do they respond, however, when their group membership is determined randomly or arbitrarily? Recall from our discussion in the previous chapter that adults are prone to in-group bias even when randomly or arbitrarily assigned to a "minimal" group. Does that same tendency hold true for young children? Studies across a range of cultures answer "yes." Children as young as seven to eight years of age show a propensity for in-group favoritism in the minimal group paradigm. Similar to adults, they reward more allocations to their own group, especially when it establishes a relative difference between their group and the out-group.[48]

In summary, children—at a remarkably early age—evidence the same capacity for social categorization and in-group favoritism that adults do. But, an optimist might counter, the good news is that each succeeding generation is becoming more tolerant than the previous. Unfortunately, research by sociologist Thomas Wilson seriously challenges this widely held hope. In a 1996 article, Wilson empirically examined the thesis that if younger people truly are persistently and permanently less prejudiced than their elders, then as younger members are added to the population and older members are lost, the level of prejudice in American society can be expected to decrease.

Using data from the 1990 GSS, Wilson concluded that Americans born after World War II (1946–1960) *do* tend to be less prejudiced than prewar Americans toward African-Americans, Asian-Americans, and Hispanic-Americans. The most recent generation of Americans reaching adulthood (born between 1961 and 1972), however, show no tendency to be less prejudiced (at least toward Hispanics and Asians) than their immediate predecessors born since World War II. More disconcertingly, the most recent generation of Americans residing *outside* of the South actually tend to be *more* prejudiced (at least toward Jews) than their elders. Wilson's work is the first to show that the youngest American adults are actually more prejudiced than their elders.[49]

This change in climate, in which recent generations can no longer be counted upon to be persistently more tolerant than their predecessors, offers little reason for optimism about future declines in prejudice resulting from generational succession. As Wilson argues, if the most recent generation of American adults are no longer less prejudiced than their predecessors—and if the pattern of people becoming more prejudiced as they age holds true—the clear implication is that American society is facing a continuing increase in overall levels of prejudice. The need to teach antiracism early appears as pivotal now as at any point in American history.

How do we teach antiracism to our children? As we've seen, the use of social categories is inherent in the way our minds work. We cannot change the fact that our children, the same as you and me, actively use social categories as "file folders" in which to order the experiences of their world. Those folders are an essential survival mechanism. We can, however, have some influence over the content of the folders. In other words, socialization processes, while subject to our cognitive limitations, may still hold some promise.

On the most direct level, we must examine the environment of the homes in which our children are raised. Do the calendars, pictures, and posters on our walls reflect the diversity of America? Do our books, magazines, toys, and games celebrate the panorama of our borderland? Do we seek out relationships with families different from ours? Do we recognize, and commemorate, ethnic, cultural, and religious holidays other than our own? Ask your children how your home environment could be made different. Empowering them in the process moves them from being passive spectators to active participants. It's not that our homes should be ethnic museums. Rather, it's that our homes should be the first places where our children are exposed to people of color and to images and information about them. The more they are exposed to these things, the greater will be their familiarity with other racial groups, and the weaker will be their negative stereotypes.

Most important, we must examine what we say, and don't say,

about racism to our children. Do they see us speak out against racism and intolerance? Do we talk openly about racism with our children? We intuitively recognize that racism is often taught by what parents say. Psychologists have discovered, however, that racism also can be caused by what parents do not say. A lack of parent–child dialogue makes racial differences a taboo subject and contributes to children's ideas that differences translate into deficits. Beverly Tatum, a professor of psychology at Mount Holyoke College, illustrates: "A young child, for example, asks his mother why the man in the grocery store is so dark. Instead of answering, his mother tells him to be quiet, which tells the child it's not okay to discuss differences."[50]

At the heart of teaching antiracism is teaching empathy. How do we teach empathy for the victims of racism? Obviously, an individual's personal experience with oppression is the best, though most painful, teacher. Are there other ways in which we can teach empathy to our children—short of making them victims of oppression? Sociologists Tiffany Hogan and Julie Netzer have developed the helpful idea of "approximating experiences." In this perspective, we search for ways to approximate (not minimize) the oppression experienced by victims of racism. We may, for instance, teach our children to *borrow approximations* by listening to stories and personal accounts that minorities tell of their own experiences. We encourage victims of racism to speak and to be heard. In addition, we may rely on *global approximations,* where we examine general values of fairness and equity to relate to an oppressed group's experiences. Here, we draw lessons from one of the favorite phrases of children—"That's no fair!" Drawing on their recollections of being treated unfairly or in an inequitable manner can be a good way of approximating the experiences of racial minorities in America. Finally, we may rely on *overlapping approximations* to connect some aspect of our own oppression to make sense of similar experiences for racial minorities. As children grow, they will, unfortunately, accumulate a bank of negative experiences tied to their gender, religion, ethnicity, or physical appearance. These experiences overlap, to a certain degree, the experiences of victims of racial oppression. In that overlap is an important point of empathy as we draw on our own experiences to understand the experiences of another.[51] Like any approximation, these strategies are, at best, poor mirrors of what minorities actually experience; however, they can be important tools for teaching empathy.

CONCLUSION

America lives under the shadow of racism. It is an undeniable part of our past, present, and future. We need not, however, fall into the trap of believing that it is intractable and insoluble. The seven principles in this chapter remind us that a world of light begins right where the shadow ends. It is to that world of light that we must aspire. Early in my life, my parents—both ministers—introduced me to a biblical passage about relationships. That passage came to hold such great personal meaning that my wife and I included it on the front of our wedding invitations. The passage also speaks to the importance of racial reconciliation. It is fitting that I conclude this book with the wise admonition of the writer of Ecclesiastes:

> Two are better than one, because they have a good return for their work: If one falls down, his friend can help him up. But pity the man who falls and has no one to help him up! Also, if two lie down together, they will keep warm. But how can one keep warm alone? Though one may be overpowered, two can defend themselves. A cord of three strands is not quickly broken. (4:9–12)

Appendix

NATIONAL ORGANIZATIONS

The following list of national organizations, while representing a range of perspectives and activities, are involved in work against racism. Many of these organizations have local chapters in cities and towns across the country. The national office would be very willing to put you in contact with its local affiliates. In addition, many of these organizations provide educational resources or newsletters. Your involvement with, and commitment to, a local or national organization helps build a social norm against intolerance and racism.

African-Americans

Center for Democratic Renewal
P.O. Box 50469
Atlanta, GA 30302
(404) 221–0025

Congress of National Black Churches
1225 I Street, NW, Suite 750
Washington, DC 20005
(202) 371–1091

Martin Luther King Jr. Center for Nonviolent Social Change
449 Auburn Avenue, NE
Atlanta, GA 30312
(404) 524–1956

National Association for the Advancement of Colored People (NAACP)
4805 Mt. Hope Drive
Baltimore, MD 21215
(301) 358–8900

National Urban League
500 East 62nd Street
New York, NY 10021
(212) 310–9000

Asian-Americans

Asian American Legal Defense and Education Fund
99 Hudson Street, 12th Floor
New York, NY 10013
(212) 966–5932

Asian Women United
1218 Spruce Street
Berkeley, CA 94709
(510) 644–0717

Ecumenical Working Group of Asian and Pacific Americans
1824 Selma Avenue
Youngstown, OH 44504
(216) 743–8758

Pacific Asian American Center for Theology and Strategies
1798 Scenic Avenue
Berkeley, CA 94709
(415) 848–0173

Hispanic-Americans

Hispanic Policy Development Project (HPDP)
1001 Connecticut Avenue, NW, Suite 310
Washington, DC 20036
(202) 822–8414

League of United Latin American Citizens (LULAC)
401 West Commerce, Suite 222
Arlington, TX 78207
(512) 223-3377

Mexican American Legal Defense and Education Fund (MALDEF)
634 South Spring Street, 11th Floor
Los Angeles, CA 90014
(213) 629-25112

National Council of La Raza
1111 19th Street, NW, Suite 1000
Washington, DC 20036
(202) 785-1670

Native Americans

Association on American Indian Affairs, Inc.
Tekakwitha Agency Road #7
Sisseton, SD 57262
(605) 698-3998

HONOR, Inc.
2647 North Stowell Avenue
Milwaukee, WI 53211
(414) 963-1324

Indian Law Resource Center
601 E Street, SE
Washington, DC 20003
(202) 547-2800

National Congress of American Indians
2010 Massachusetts Avenue, NW, 2nd Floor
Washington, DC 20036
(202) 466-7767

Native American Rights Fund
1506 Broadway
Boulder, CO 80302
(303) 447-8760

OTHER RELATED ORGANIZATIONS

American Civil Liberties Union (ACLU)
132 West 43rd Street
New York, NY 10036
(212) 944-9800

Common Destiny Alliance (CODA)
Room 4114, Benjamin Building
University of Maryland
College Park, MD 20742
(301) 405-2341

Congress of Racial Equality (CORE)
1457 Flatbush Avenue
Brooklyn, NY 11210
(718) 434-3580

Facing History and Ourselves
16 Hurd Road
Brookline, MA 02146
(617) 232-1595

National Coalition Building Institute (NCBI)
172 Brattle Street
Arlington, MA 02714
(617) 646-5802

National Institute Against Prejudice and Violence (NIAPV)
31 South Greene Street
Baltimore, MD 21201
(301) 328-5170

REACH Center
180 Nickerson Street, Suite 212
Seattle, WA 98109
(206) 284-8584

Sojourners Resource Center
Box 29272
Washington, DC 20017
(202) 636-3637

United States Commission on Civil Rights
1121 Vermont Avenue, NW
Washington, DC 20425
(202) 376–8177

INTERNET SITES ON DIVERSITY AND TOLERANCE

Because it is impossible to regulate, the Internet has been a haven for hate groups and white supremacists. It also, however, offers access to hundreds of organizations that are pledged to the importance of diversity and tolerance. Here are just a few:

http://www.afroam.org/	Afro-Americ@
http://www.aclu.org/	American Civil Liberties Union
http://www.adl.org/	Anti-Defamation League
http://asdg-99.umd.edu/coda/	Common Destiny Alliance (CODA)
http://www.facing.inter.net/	Facing History and Ourselves
http://hatewatch.org/	HateWatch
http://www.webcom.com/~justcaus/	Just Cause
http://www.mecca.org/~crights/ncrm.html	National Civil Rights Museum
http://alabanza.com/kabacoff/Inter-Links/diversity.html	Resources for Diversity
http://www.splcenter.org/	Southern Poverty Law Center
http://members.aol.com/ulcenterlulc1.htm	Urban Life Center (Chicago, IL)
http://humanitas.ucsb.edu/shuttle/minority.html	Voice of the Shuttle

INTERNET SITES ON GENEALOGY

In Chapter 10, I discussed the importance of becoming more self-aware of one's racial, ethnic, and religious stories. There are thousands of Internet sites that can aid genealogists of all levels. Here are just a few:

http://www.switchboard.com	Online Phone Directory
http://www.rootsweb.com	RootsWeb Genealogical Data Cooperative
http://www.usgenweb.com	USGenWeb Project
http://www.nara.gov	National Archives
http://www.lcweb.loc.gov/rr/ genealogy	Library of Congress
http://www.genealogy.org/~ngs/	National Genealogical Society
http://www.firstct.com/fv/ tmapmenu.html	Family History Library, Salt Lake City, UT

Notes

PREFACE

1. F. Cramer, *Chaos and Order: The Complex Structure of Living Systems* (Weinheim, Germany: Verlagsgesellschaft, 1993), p. 116.
2. Internet electronic transmission, February 4, 1997.
3. Heather Knight, "1 in 10 of Us Is an Immigrant," *Los Angeles Times* reprinted in *The Spokesman-Review*, April 9, 1997, pp. A1, A9.
4. William A. Henry III, "Beyond the Melting Pot," in "America's Changing Colors," *Time* 135 (April 9, 1990), pp. 28–31.
5. David W. Moore, "Americans Feel Threatened by New Immigrants," *The Gallup Poll Monthly*, July 1993, pp. 2–16.

CHAPTER 1

1. Ellis Cose, *Color-Blind: Seeing beyond Race in a Race-Obsessed World* (New York: HarperCollins, 1997), p. 14.
2. Joe R. Feagin and Hernan Vera, *White Racism: The Basics* (New York: Routledge, 1995), p. 14.
3. Ibid., p. 154.
4. Nathan Glazer, *Affirmative Discrimination* (New York: Basic Books, 1975).
5. William J. Wilson, *The Declining Significance of Race* (Chicago: University of Chicago Press, 1978), p. 151.
6. Shelby Steele, *The Content of Our Character* (New York: St. Martin's Press, 1990); Stephen L. Carter, *Reflections of an Affirmative Action Baby* (New York: Basic Books, 1991).
7. James L. Robinson, *Racism or Attitude? The Ongoing Struggle for Black Liberation and Self-Esteem* (New York: Insight Books, 1995).

8. Stephan Thernstrom and Abigail Thernstrom, *America in Black and White: One Nation, Indivisible* (New York: Simon & Schuster, 1997).
9. Cose, p. 208.
10. Allan Bloom, *The Closing of the American Mind: How Higher Education Has Failed Democracy and Impoverished the Souls of Today's Students* (New York: Simon & Schuster, 1987); E. D. Hirsch, *Cultural Literacy: What Every American Needs to Know* (Boston: Vintage Books, 1987).
11. Jim Sleeper, *Liberal Racism* (New York: Free Press, 1997).
12. Dinesh D'Souza, *The End of Racism* (New York: Free Press, 1995).
13. Cose, p. 208.
14. Rachel Shuster, "Arthur Ashe: 1943–1993; Ashe Legacy Goes beyond Sports, Race," *USA Today*, February 8, 1993, p. 1C.
15. John Howard Griffin, *Black Like Me* (Boston: Houghton Mifflin, 1960), p. 16.
16. Douglas Brinkley, *The Majic Bus: An American Odyssey* (New York: Anchor Books, 1993).
17. Cose, p. xi.
18. Ibid., p. 228.
19. Derrick Bell, *Faces at the Bottom of the Well* (New York: Basic Books, 1992).
20. Andrew Hacker, *Two Nations: Black and White, Separate, Hostile, Unequal* (New York: Scribner's, 1992), p. xiii.
21. Richard Delgado, "When a Story Is Just a Story: Does Voice Really Matter?" *Virginia Law Review* 76 (February 1990), p. 106.
22. Feagin and Vera, p. 193.
23. Carl T. Rowan, *The Coming Race War in America* (New York: Little, Brown and Company, 1996).
24. Fred Davis, "Clinton's Race Effort Can Help, If We Will Let It," *Spokesman Review*, June 23, 1997, p. A13.
25. Electronic transmission.
26. Feagin and Vera, p. xii.
27. Peter Baker, "Race Relations Commission Off to a Shaky Start," reprinted in the *Spokesman Review*, July 15, 1997, p. A1.
28. Bruce Schoenfield, "The Loneliness of Being White," *New York Times Magazine*, May 14, 1995, pp. 34–37.
29. Paul Kivel, *Uprooting Racism: How White People Can Work for Racial Justice* (Gabriola Island, BC: New Society Publishers, 1996), p. 72.
30. Don K. Nakanishi, "Seeking Convergence in Race Relations Research: Japanese-Americans and the Resurrection of the Internment," in *Eliminating Racism: Profiles in Controversy*, eds. P. A. Katz and D. A. Taylor (New York: Plenum Press, 1988), p. 161.

31. Albert Ramirez, "Racism toward Hispanics: The Culturally Mono-
    lithic Society," in Katz and Taylor, pp. 137–157.
32. Joseph E. Trimble, "Stereotypical Images, American Indians, and
    Prejudice," in Katz and Taylor, pp. 181–202.
33. Joe Lapointe, "Racial Stereotypes: Us vs. Them Exposed Anew,"
    Lexington Herald-Leader, June 9, 1987, p. C1.
34. Daniela Gioseffi, ed., *On Prejudice: A Global Perspective* (New York:
    Anchor Books, 1993), p. xxvi.

CHAPTER 2

 1. James M. Washington, ed., *A Testament of Hope: The Essential Writ-
    ings of Martin Luther King, Jr.* (San Francisco: Harper and Row, 1986),
    p. 623.
 2. Jorge del Pinal, "The Hispanic Population in the United States:
    March 1993," *Current Population Reports, Series P20-475* (Washing-
    ton, DC: U.S. Census Bureau, 1993).
 3. Richard M. Lerner, *Final Solutions: Biology, Prejudice, and Genocide*
    (University Park, PA: Pennsylvania State University Press, 1992),
    p. 11.
 4. Walter Lippmann, *Public Opinion* (New York: Harcourt & Brace,
    1922).
 5. Daniel Katz and Kenneth Braly, "Racial Stereotypes in One Hun-
    dred College Students," *Journal of Abnormal and Social Psychology* 28
    (1933), pp. 280–290.
 6. T. W. Adorno, E. Frenkel-Brunswik, D. J. Levinson, and R. N. San-
    ford, *The Authoritarian Personality* (New York: Harper & Row, 1950).
 7. David J. Schneider, "Modern Stereotype Research: Unfinished Busi-
    ness," in *Stereotypes and Stereotyping*, eds. C. N. Macrae, C. Stangor,
    and M. Hewstone (New York: Guilford, 1996), p. 419.
 8. Richard Ashmore and Frances Del Boca, "Conceptual Approaches
    to Stereotypes and Stereotyping," in *Cognitive Processes in Stereotyp-
    ing and Intergroup Behavior*, ed. D. L. Hamilton (Hillsdale, NJ: Law-
    rence Erlbaum Associates, 1981), p. 28.
 9. Gordon Allport, *The Nature of Prejudice* (Reading, MA: Addison-
    Wesley, 1954).
10. David Myers, *Social Psychology*, 4th ed. (New York: McGraw-Hill,
    1993), p. 391.
11. Allport, pp. 13–14.
12. Steven Fein and Steven J. Spencer, "Prejudice as Self-Image Mainte-

nance: Affirming the Self through Derogating Others," *Journal of Personality and Social Psychology*, 73 (1997), pp. 31–44.

13. Robert C. Gardner, "Ethnic Stereotypes: The Traditional Approach, New Look," *Canadian Psychologist* 14 (1989), p. 134.

14. Claude M. Steele and J. Aronson, "Stereotype Threat and the Intellectual Test Performance of African-Americans," *Journal of Personality and Social Psychology* 69 (1995), pp. 797–811.

15. Claude M. Steele, "Race and the Schooling of Black Americans," *The Atlantic Monthly* 69 (April 1992), pp. 68–78.

16. Stephen J. Gould, *The Mismeasure of Man* (New York: W. W. Norton, 1996), p. 77.

17. Hypertext Webster Interface, electronic transmission.

18. Rupert Brown, *Prejudice: Its Social Psychology* (Oxford, UK: Blackwell, 1995), p. 6.

19. Ibid., p. 8.

20. *The Main Types and Causes of Discrimination* (United Nations Publication, 1949), p. 9.

21. G. Haddock, M. P. Zanna, and V. M. Esses, "Assessing the Structure of Prejudicial Attitudes: The Case of Attitudes toward Homosexuals," *Journal of Personality and Social Psychology* 65 (1993), pp. 1105–1118.

22. R. T. LaPiere, "Attitudes vs. Actions," *Social Forces* 13 (1934), pp. 230–237.

23. B. Kutner, C. Wilkins, and P. R. Yarrow, "Verbal Attitudes and Overt Behavior," *Journal of Abnormal and Social Psychology* 47 (1952), pp. 649–652.

24. Leon Festinger, *A Theory of Cognitive Dissonance* (Stanford, CA: Stanford University Press, 1957).

25. John F. Dovidio, John C. Brigham, Blair T. Johnson, and Samuel L. Gaertner, "Stereotyping, Prejudice, and Discrimination: Another Look," in Macrae et al., *Stereotypes and Stereotyping*, p. 311.

26. D. O. Sears, J. Citrin, and R. Kosterman, "Jesse Jackson and the Southern White Electorate in 1984," in *Blacks in Southern Politics*, eds. L. W. Moreland, R. P. Steed, and T. A. Baker (New York: Praeger, 1987), pp. 209–225.

CHAPTER 3

1. Daniela Gioseffi, ed., *On Prejudice: A Global Perspective* (New York: Anchor Books, 1993), p. 621.

2. Ellis Cose, *Color-Blind: Seeing beyond Race in a Race-Obsessed World* (New York: HarperCollins, 1997), p. 22.
3. Madison Grant, *The Passing of the Great Race* (New York: Scribner, 1916).
4. Cose, pp. 19–20.
5. Marvin Harris, *Patterns of Race in the Americas* (Westport, CT: Greenwood Press, 1964), p. 56.
6. Jefferson M. Fish, "Mixed Blood," *Psychology Today* (November/December 1995), p. 57.
7. Cose, p. 11.
8. Reported by the Associated Press, "It's Not All Genes," *The Spokesman Review* 31 (July 1997).
9. Carol Lynn Martin and Sandra Parker, "Folk Theories about Sex and Race Differences," *Personality and Social Psychology Bulletin* 21 (1995), pp. 45–47.
10. *Report of the National Advisory Commission on Civil Disorders* (New York: Bantam, 1968), p. 203.
11. Joe R. Feagin, "The Continued Significance of Racism: Discrimination Against Black Students in White Colleges," *Journal of Black Studies* 22 (1992), p. 574.
12. For a detailed discussion of these three varieties of racism, see James M. Jones, *Prejudice and Racism* (New York: Random House, 1972) or James M. Jones, "Racism in Black and White: A Bicultural Model of Reaction and Evolution," in eds. P. A. Katz and D. A. Taylor, *Eliminating Racism: Profiles in Controversy* (New York: Plenum Press, 1988), pp. 117–135.
13. Joe R. Feagin and Hernan Vera, *White Racism: The Basics* (New York: Routledge, 1995), p. 7.
14. Harvard Sitkoff, *The Struggle for Black Equality: 1954–1992* (New York: Hill and Wang, 1993), p. 201.
15. James M. Jones, *Prejudice and Racism* (New York: Random House, 1972), p. 6.
16. U.S. Commission on Civil Rights, *Indian Tribes: A Continuing Quest for Survival* (Washington, D.C.: U.S. Government Printing Office, 1981).
17. James M. Jones, "Racism: A Cultural Analysis of the Problem," in *Prejudice, Discrimination, and Racism,* eds. John F. Dovidio and Samuel L. Gaertner (San Diego, CA: Academic Press, 1986), pp. 225–278.
18. Dalmas A. Taylor, "Race Prejudice, Discrimination, and Racism," in *Social Psychology,* eds. A. Kahn, E. Donnerstein, and M. Donnerstein (Dubuque, IA: Wm. C. Brown, 1984).

19. Joseph Barndt, *Dismantling Racism: The Continuing Challenge to White America* (Minneapolis, MN: Augsburg, 1991), pp. 28–29.
20. Paula S. Rothenberg, *Racism and Sexism: An Integrated Study* (New York: St. Martin's Press, 1988), p. 6.
21. Jones, 1972, p. 172.
22. George Yancey, *Beyond Black and White: Reflections on Racial Reconciliation* (Grand Rapids, MI: Baker Books, 1996).
23. Alan Dershowitz, *The Washington Times*, January 29, 1991.
24. Nick Jans, "In Alaska, Racism against Non-Natives Is Fact of Life," *USA Today*, March 12, 1997, p. 13A.

CHAPTER 4

1. Pamela Trotman Reid, "Racism and Sexism: Comparisons and Conflicts," in *Eliminating Racism: Profiles in Controversy*, eds. P. A. Katz and D. A. Taylor (New York: Plenum Press, 1988), p. 206; H. Rap Brown was later known as Jamil Abdullah al-Amin.
2. W. E. B. Du Bois, *The Souls of Black Folk* (New York: Dover Publications, 1903, 1994), p. 9.
3. Gunnar Myrdal, *An American Dilemma: The Negro Problem and Modern Democracy* (New York: Harper & Row, 1944), p. xxi.
4. Darrell Huff, *How to Lie with Statistics* (New York: W. W. Norton & Company, 1954), p. 1.
5. Andrew Hacker, *Two Nations: Black and White, Separate, Hostile, Unequal* (New York: Scribner's, 1992), p. 6.
6. Edward E. Jones and Harold Sigall, "The Bogus Pipeline: A New Paradigm for Measuring Affect and Attitude," *Psychological Bulletin* 76 (1971), pp. 349–364.
7. H. Schuman, C. Steeh, and L. Bobo, *Racial Attitudes in America: Trends and Interpretation* (Cambridge, MA: Harvard University Press, 1985); Rupert Brown, *Prejudice: Its Social Psychology*, (Oxford, UK: Blackwell, 1995).; data from *USA Today*, June 11, 1997, p. 9A.
8. G. D. Jaynes and R. M. Williams, Jr., *A Common Destiny: Blacks and American Society* (Washington, DC: National Academy Press, 1989), pp. 155–156.
9. Tom W. Smith and Paul B. Sheatsley, "American Attitudes toward Race Relations," *Public Opinion* 7 (October/November 1984), pp. 14–15, 50–53.
10. Burns W. Roper, "Race Relations in America," *The Public Perspective* (July/August 1990).

11. G. Bogatz and S. Ball, *The Second Year of Sesame Street: A Continuing Education* (Princeton, NJ: Educational Testing Service, 1971).
12. G. J. Gorn, M. E. Goldberg, and R. N. Kanungo, "The Role of Educational Television in Changing the Intergroup Attitudes of Children," *Child Development* 47 (1976), pp. 277–280.
13. Ronald Humphrey and Howard Schuman, "The Portrayal of Blacks in Magazine Advertisements: 1950–1982," *Public Opinion Quarterly* 48 (1984), pp. 551–563.
14. John J. O'Connor, "T.V.: Less Separate, More Equal," *The New York Times*, April 29, 1990, sec. 2, pp. 1, 35.
15. Russell H. Weigel, Eleanor L. Kim, and Jill L. Frost, "Race Relations on Prime Time Television Reconsidered: Patterns of Continuity and Change," *Journal of Applied Social Psychology* 25 (1995), pp. 223–236.
16. Joe R. Feagin and Hernan Vera, *White Racism: The Basics* (New York: Routledge, 1995), p. 141.
17. J. A. Parker, "The Largely Unheralded Growth for the Black Middle Class," *The Lincoln Review* (Winter 1988).
18. Thea Lee, "Trapped on a Pedestal," *Dollars and Sense* (March 1990).
19. U.S. Bureau of the Census, Current Population Reports, Series P23-189, *Population Profile of the United States: 1995* (Washington, D.C.: U.S. Government Printing Office, 1995); March 1996 Supplement to CPS.
20. U.S. Bureau of the Census, Current Population Reports, Series P23-189, *Population Profile of the United States: 1995* (Washington, D.C.: U.S. Government Printing Office, 1995).
21. Maggie Jackson, "The Struggle Goes On," Associated Press, reprinted in *The Spokesman-Review*, April 19, 1997, p. A12–A13.
22. Tim Collie, "High Schools Stuck in the 50's," *The Spokesman-Review*, June 4, 1997, pp. A1, A8.
23. Current Population Survey (CPS) March Demographic Files of U.S. Census Bureau (U.S. Government Printing Office, Washington, D.C., 1994).
24. "College Degrees Offer Real Value," *A Special Supplement to the Spokesman-Review*, April 6, 1997, p. 8.
25. Current Population Survey (CPS) March Demographic Files of U.S. Census Bureau, 1994; *Statistical Abstracts of the United States*, 1996 (U.S. Government Printing Office, Washington, D.C.).
26. Current Population Survey (CPS) March Demographic Files of U.S. Census Bureau, (U.S. Government Printing Office, Washington, D.C., 1994).
27. *Statistical Abstracts of the United States*, 1996.

28. Ibid.
29. Ibid.
30. Lee, 1990.
31. U.S. Bureau of the Census, Current Population Reports, Series P23-189, *Population Profile of the United States: 1995* (U.S. Government Printing Office, Washington, D.C., 1995).
32. Parker, 1988.
33. George Gallup, Jr. and Frank Newport, "Blacks and Whites Differ on Civil Rights Progress," *The Gallup Poll Monthly* (August 1991), pp. 54–59.
34. Grant Jerding, "Changes in Race Relations in the USA," *USA Today*, June 11, 1997, p. 9A.
35. Roper, 1990.
36. Philip Perlmutter, "Fallacies of Evolution," *The Lincoln Review*, (Winter 1985).
37. Cited in Edward Alexander, "Racism in Higher Education Is Exaggerated," in William Dudley and Charles Cozic, *Racism in America* (San Diego, CA: Greenhaven Press, 1991), p. 68.
38. Ellis Cose, *Color-Blind: Seeing beyond Race in a Race-Obsessed World* (New York: HarperCollins, 1997), p. 86.
39. Cited in Philip Permutter and Walter E. Williams, "Racism Is No Longer Prevalent," in Bruno Leone, *Racism: Opposing Viewpoints* (San Diego, CA: Greenhaven Press, 1986), p. 148.
40. Robert H. Lauer and Warren H. Handel, *Social Psychology: The Theory and Application of Symbolic Interactionism* (Boston: Houghton Mifflin, 1977), p. 330.

CHAPTER 5

1. Sherman Alexie, *Reservation Blues* (New York: Warner Books, 1995), p. 169.
2. Tom W. Smith, "Ethnic Images," *GSS Topical Report No. 19* (University of Chicago: National Opinion Research Center, 1990).
3. Joe R. Feagin and Hernan Vera, *White Racism: The Basics* (New York: Routledge, 1995), p. 137.
4. Patricia G. Devine, "Stereotypes and Prejudice: Their Automatic and Controlled Components," *Journal of Personality and Social Psychology* 56 (1989), pp. 5–18.
5. Smith, 1990.
6. Michael Parenti, "From Make-Believe Media: 'Make-Believe His-

tory,' " in *On Prejudice: A Global Perspective*, ed. Daniela Gioseffi, (New York: Anchor Books, 1993), pp. 396–397.

7. Russell H. Weigel, Eleanor L. Kim, and Jill L. Frost, "Race Relations on Prime Time Television Reconsidered: Patterns of Continuity and Change," *Journal of Applied Social Psychology* 25 (1995), p. 228.

8. Joseph E. Trimble, "Stereotypical Images, American Indians, and Prejudice," in *Eliminating Racism: Profiles in Controversy*, eds. P. A. Katz and D. A. Taylor (New York: Plenum Press, 1988), p. 190.

9. Alexie, p. 70.

10. Sherman Alexie, "The Warriors," in *Home Field: Nine Writers at Bat*, ed. John Douglas Marshall (Seattle: Sasquatch Books, 1997), p. 12.

11. Julie Sullivan, "Top Thinker on TV's Impact to Speak," *The Spokesman-Review* 6 (April 1997), pp. A1, A14.

12. John J. O'Connor, "Blacks on TV: Scrambled Signals," *The New York Times*, October 27, 1991, p. 36.

13. Weigel et al., p. 223.

14. Ibid., pp. 224–225.

15. Trimble, in *Eliminating Racism*, eds. Katz and Taylor, p. 193.

16. Marilyn Elias, "Comics Entertain at Women's Expense," *USA Today*, August 15, 1995.

17. Jody David Armour, *Negrophobia and Reasonable Racism: The Hidden Costs of Being Black in America* (New York: New York University Press, 1997), p. 40.

18. Ibid, p. 165.

19. Cited in Paul Kivel, *Uprooting Racism: How White People Can Work for Racial Justice* (Gabriola Island, BC: New Society Publishers, 1996), p. 129.

20. Leslie McAneny, "Ethnic Minorities View the Media's View of Them," *The Gallup Poll Monthly* (August 1994), pp. 31–41.

21. Larry Hugick and Leslie McAneny, "White and Black America: Fragile Consensus on Urban Aid," *The Gallup Poll Monthly* (June 1992), pp. 7–15.

22. David Halberstam, "The Stuff Dreams Are Made Of," *Sports Illustrated*, June 29, 1987, p. 43.

23. Jeff Stone, Zachary W. Perry, and John M. Darley, "'White Men Can't Jump' Evidence for the Perceptual Confirmation of Racial Stereotypes Following a Basketball Game," *Basic and Applied Social Psychology*, in press.

24. John Simons, "Special Report: Improbable Dreams," *U.S. News and World Report* 122 (March 24, 1997), pp. 46–52; quote from p. 48.

25. "Opinionline," *USA Today*, April 18 1997, p. 15A.

26. E. M. Swift, "Reach Out and Touch Someone," *Sports Illustrated*, August 5, 1991, p. 58.

27. Michael Wilbon, "Woods' Win Cherished by All Who Went Before," *The Spokesman-Review*, April 16, 1997, pp. C1, C7.

28. Mike Barnicle, "Nonwhite Non-superstar? Good Luck," *The Spokesman-Review*, April 16, 1997, B4.

29. Harvard Sitkoff, *The Struggle for Black Equality: 1954–1992* (New York: Hill and Wang, 1993), p. 230.

30. Jill Nelson, "Black Women Lowest on Happiness Ladder," *USA Today*, April 18, 1997, p. 15A.

31. Larry Hugick, "Blacks See Their Lives Worsening," *The Gallup Poll Monthly* (April 1992), pp. 26–29.

32. U.S. Bureau of the Census, Current Population Reports, Series P23-189, *Population Profile of the United States: 1995* (U.S. Government Printing Office, Washington, D. C., 1995).

33. Trimble, in *Eliminating Racism*, eds. Katz and Taylor, pp. 186–187.

34. Jorge del Pinal, "The Hispanic Population in the United States: March 1993," *Current Population Reports, Series P20-475* (Washington, D. C.: U.S. Census Bureau, 1993), p. 47.

35. U.S. Bureau of the Census, 1995.

36. Bruno Leone, *Racism in America: Opposing Viewpoints* (San Diego, CA: Greenhaven Press, 1991), p. 76.

37. March 1996 Supplement to CPS.

38. Richard Lacayo, "Between Two Worlds," *Time*, March 13, 1989.

39. David H. Swinton, "Economic Progress for Black Americans in the Post-Civil Rights Era," in ed. Gail E. Thomas, *U.S. Race Relations in the 1980s and 1990s* (Bristol, PA: Hemisphere, 1990).

40. Rafeal Valdivieso and Cary Davis, "Racism Causes Hispanic Poverty," in William Dudley and Charles Cozic, *Racism in America* (San Diego, CA: Greenhaven Press, 1991), pp. 108–114.

41. G. Stephanopoulos and C. Edley, Jr., *Affirmative Action Review: Report to the President* (Washington D.C.: Government Printing Office, 1995).

42. Audrey J. Murrell and Ray Jones, "Assessing Affirmative Action: Past, Present, and Future," *Journal of Social Issues 52* (1996), p. 84.

43. Maggie Jackson, "The Struggle Goes On," Associated Press, reprinted in *The Spokesman-Review*, April 19, 1997, pp. A12–A13.

44. Murrell and Jones, 1996, p. 84.

45. James R. Kluegel, "Trends in Whites' Explanations of the Black-White Gap in Socioeconomic Status, 1977–1989," *American Sociological Review 55* (1990), pp. 512–525.

46. Richard Morin and Lynn Duke, "Prejudice Is in the Eye of the Beholder, Poll Indicates," reprinted in *World of Psychology: Readings in Diversity from the Washington Post* (New York: Allyn & Bacon, 1993), p. 23.

47. Feagin and Vera, p. 6.

48. Valdivieso and Davis, 1988.

49. Current Population Survey (CPS) March Demographic Files of U.S. Census Bureau, 1994.

50. Associated Press, "Tribal Colleges Are the Answer, Say Indian Leaders," *The Spokesman-Review*, May 21, 1997, p. B6.

51. U.S. Bureau of the Census, *Statistical Abstract of the United States: 1996* (116th ed.) Washington, D.C.: U.S. Government Printing Office, 1996, Table No. 305.

52. Thea Lee, "Trapped on a Pedestal," *Dollars and Sense* (March 1990).

53. Ibid.

54. U.S. Bureau of the Census, *Statistical Abstract of the United States: 1996* (116th ed.), Washington, D.C., 1996, Table No. 305.

55. "At the Root of Racial Inequity at Colleges," *USA Today*, March 10, 1997.

56. Ibid.

57. Sitkoff, p. 227.

58. U.S. Bureau of the Census, *Statistical Abstract of the United States: 1996* (116th ed.), Washington, D.C., 1996, Table No. 305.

59. James M. Jones, "Racism: A Cultural Analysis of the Problem," in John F. Dovidio and Samuel L. Gaertner, *Prejudice, Discrimination, and Racism* (San Diego, CA: Academic Press, 1986), p. 287.

60. Andrew Hacker, *Two Nations: Black and White, Separate, Hostile, Unequal* (New York: Scribner's, 1992), p. 6.

61. Ethan Bronner, "Reliance of SATs May Resegregate Colleges," reprinted in *The Spokesman-Review,* November 8, 1997, pp. A1, A10.

62. Ellis Cose, *Color-Blind: Seeing beyond Race in a Race-Obsessed World* (New York: Harper-Collins, 1997), pp. 77–96.

63. Arlene Smith McCormack, "The Changing Nature of Racism in College Campuses: Study of Discrimination at the Northeastern Public University," *College Student Journal* 29 (1995), pp. 150–156.

64. Cited in Jon Wiener, "Racism in Higher Education Is a Serious Problem" in William Dudley and Charles Cozic (eds.), *Racism in America* (San Diego, CA: Greenhaven Press, 1991), p. 58.

65. Katherine E. McClelland and Carol J. Auster, "Public Platitudes and Hidden Tensions," *Journal of Higher Education* 61 (1990), pp. 607–642.

66. McCormack, p. 155.
67. S. Hurtado, E. Dey, and J. G. Trevino, "Exclusion or Self-Segregation? Interaction across Racial/Ethnic Groups on College Campuses" (Paper, American Educational Research Association Annual Meeting, Spring 1994).
68. Cose, p. 79.
69. Ibid., p. 83.
70. Ibid., pp. 88, 90.
71. Don Kent, "Spotlight on Research: Is Racism on the Decline in America?," *American Psychological Society Observer* 9 (1996), p. 12.
72. Hugick, April 1992.
73. Hacker, p. 49.
74. Muriel Dobbin, "An Apology, at Last: Nightmare Lives in Minds of African-Americans," Scripps-McClatchy Western Service, *The Spokesman-Review*, April 16, 1997, pp. A1, A6.
75. Sitkoff, p. 230.
76. Hugick and McAneny, June 1992.
77. Leonard Pitts, Jr., "Another Child Dying as Racism Lives," reprinted in *The Spokesman-Review*, March 27, 1997.
78. Leslie McAneny, "The Rodney King Case: White and Black Biases—Some Shared, Some Not—Highlight Difficulties in Choosing Federal Jury," *The Gallup Poll Monthly* (February 1993), pp. 31–36.
79. Feagin and Vera, pp. 5–6.
80. Hugick and McAneny, June 1992.
81. C. Gary Wheeler, "30 Years Beyond 'I Have a Dream'," *The Gallup Poll Monthly* (October 1992), pp. 2–10.
82. David W. Moore and Lydia Saad, "No Immediate Signs That Simpson Trial Intensified Racial Animosity," *The Gallup Poll Monthly* (October 1995), pp. 2–7.
83. McAneny, February 1993.
84. Alvin P. Sanoff, Scott Minerbrook, Jeannye Thornton, and Elizabeth Pezzullo, "Students Talk about Race," *U.S. News and World Report*, April 19, 1993, pp. 57–64.
85. Hugick, April 1992.
86. Hugick and McAneny, 1992.
87. Cose, pp. 182–183.
88. Moore and Saad, October 1995.
89. C. Gary Wheeler, "30 Years Beyond 'I Have a Dream,'" *The Gallup Poll Monthly* (October 1993), pp. 2–10.
90. Lacayo, 1989.

91. Harrison Rainie, "Black and White in America," *U.S. News and World Report* 22 (July 1991), p. 19.
92. Leslie McAneny and Lydia Saad, "America's Public Schools: Still Separate? Still Unequal?," *The Gallup Poll Monthly* (May 1994), pp. 23–29.
93. "Racial Segregation Returning to Schools," *The Spokesman-Review*, April 5, 1997, p. A4.
94. Cose, p. 75.
95. Juan Williams, "Integration Turns 40: The New Segregation," *Modern Maturity* (April/May 1994), p. 28.
96. John Leo, "Separatism Won't Solve Anything," *U.S. News and World Report* 19 (April 1993), p. 65.
97. Jim Carnes, *Us and Them: A History of Intolerance in America* (Montgomery, AL: Southern Poverty Law Center, 1995).
98. "Time for Assault on Hate Crimes," *Los Angeles Times* reprinted in *The Spokesman-Review*, June 8, 1997.
99. Dan Sewell, "Southern Churches Burning Again," *The Spokesman-Review*, May 6, 1996, p. B6.
100. Carnes, p. 128.
101. David Van Biema, "After the Burning," *Time*, July 1, 1996, pp. 52–54.
102. Feagin, p. 564.

CHAPTER 6

1. Joseph Barndt, *Dismantling Racism: The Continuing Challenge to White America* (Minneapolis, MN: Augsburg, 1991), p. 31.
2. Knight–Ridder News Service, "Quiet Acts of Racism Condemned: Clinton Attacks Violence, Subtler Forms of Hatred," *The Spokesman-Review*, March 30, 1997, p. 3A.
3. Karen Boone, "Karen Boone's Response to Hate Mail," reprinted in *The Spokesman-Review*, February 28, 1997.
4. Leonard Pitts, Jr., "Doing Right Thing Still Controversial," *The Spokesman-Review*, June 29, 1997, p. B7.
5. Morris Dees and James Corcoran, *Gathering Storm: America's Militia Threat* (New York: HarperCollins, 1996).
6. Joe R. Feagin and Hernan Vera, *White Racism: The Basics* (New York: Routledge, 1995), p. 161.
7. J. B. McConahay, "Modern Racism, Ambivalence, and the Modern Racism Scale," in Dovidio and Gaertner, 1986, pp. 91–125.

8. Rupert Brown, *Prejudice: Its Social Psychology* (Oxford, UK: Blackwell, 1995), p. 209.

9. H. Schuman, C. Steeh, and L. Bobo, *Racial Attitudes in America: Trends and Interpretation* (Cambridge, MA: Harvard University Press, 1985).

10. George Gallup, Jr. and Dr. Frank Newport, "For First Time, More Americans Approve of Interracial Marriage Than Disapprove," *The Gallup Poll Monthly* (August 1991), pp. 60–62.

11. S. M. Lipset and W. Schneider, "The *Bakke* Case: How Would It Be Decided at the Bar of Public Opinion?" *Public Opinion* 1 (1978), pp. 38–44.

12. Mary R, Jackman, "General and Applied Tolerance: Does Education Increase Commitment to Racial Integration?" *American Journal of Political Science* 22 (1978), p. 302.

13. Harvard Sitkoff, *The Struggle for Black Equality: 1954–1992* (New York: Hill and Wang, 1993), p. 48.

14. Lawrence Bobo, "Group Conflict, Prejudice, and the Paradox of Contemporary Racial Attitudes," in *Eliminating Racism: Profiles in Controversy*, eds. P. A. Katz and D. A. Taylor (New York: Plenum Press, 1988), pp. 85–114.

15. Thomas F. Pettigrew, Racial Change and Social Policy," *Annals of the American Academy of Political and Social Sciences* 441 (1979), pp. 114–131.

16. M. L. King, Jr., *Where Do We Go from Here? Chaos or Community?* (New York: Bantam, 1967), p. 13.

17. S. Vidanage and David O. Sears, as cited by Shelley E. Taylor, Letitia Anne Peplau, and David O. Sears, *Social Psychology* (9th ed.), (Upper Saddle River, NJ: Prentice-Hall, 1997), p. 197.

18. Richard Delgado, "When a Story Is Just a Story: Does Voice Really Matter?" *Virginia Law Review* 76 (February 1990), p. 104.

19. David Myers, *Social Psychology* (4th ed.), (New York: McGraw-Hill, 1993), p. 393.

20. "What We Believe," *Life* (Spring 1998), pp. 69–70.

21. George Yancey, *Beyond Black and White: Reflections on Racial Reconciliation* (Grand Rapids, MI: Baker Books, 1996), p. 40.

22. Mary R. Jackman and Michael J. Muha, "Education and Intergroup Attitudes: Moral Enlightenment, Superficial Democratic Commitment, or Ideological Refinement?" *American Sociological Review* 49 (1984), pp. 751–769.

23. S. Weitz, "Attitude, Voice, and Behavior: A Repressed Affect Model of Interracial Interaction," *Journal of Personality and Social Psychology* 24 (1972), pp. 14–21.

24. M. Hendricks and R. Bootzin, "Race and Sex as Stimuli for Negative

Affect and Physical Avoidance," *Journal of Social Psychology* 98 (1976), pp. 111–120.
25. Brown, p. 214.
26. Samuel L. Gaertner and John F. Dovidio, "The Subtlety of White Racism, Arousal, and Helping Behavior," *Journal of Personality and Social Psychology* 35 (1977), pp. 691–707.
27. E. J. Vanman, B. Y. Paul, D. L. Kaplan, and N. Miller, "Facial Electromyography Differentiates Racial Bias in Imagined Cooperative Settings," *Psychophysiology* 27 (1990), p. 563.
28. John F. Dovidio and Samuel L. Gaertner, "Affirmative Action, Unintentional Racial Biases, and Intergroup Relations," *Journal of Social Issues* 52 (1996), pp. 51–75.
29. McConahay, 1986.
30. C. S. Lewis, *The Screwtape Letters* (New York: Macmillan, 1941), p. 40.

CHAPTER 7

1. Feagin, p. 576.
2. Donald R. Kinder, "The Continuing American Dilemma: White Resistance to Racial Change 40 Years after Myrdal," *Journal of Social Issues* 42 (1986), pp. 151–171.
3. Steven A. Holmes, "New Survey Shows Americans Pessimistic on Race Relations," *The New York Times*, June 1, 1997.
4. David O. Sears, "Symbolic Racism," in *Eliminating Racism: Profiles in Controversy*, eds. P. A. Katz and D. A. Taylor, (New York: Plenum Press, 1988), pp. 53–84.
5. McConahay, in Dovidio and Gaertner, pp. 91–125.
6. Ibid, p. 97.
7. Paul M. Sniderman and Philip E. Tetlock, "Symbolic Racism: Problems of Motive Attribution in Political Analysis," *Journal of Social Issues* 42 (1986a), pp. 129–150.
8. Kinder, p. 161.
9. Sears, 1988.
10. Samuel L. Gaertner and John F. Dovidio, "The Aversive Form of Racism," in *Prejudice, Discrimination, and Racism*, eds. John F. Dovidio and Samuel L. Gaertner (San Diego, CA: Academic Press, 1986), pp. 61–89.
11. Samuel L. Gaertner, "Helping Behavior and Discrimination among Liberals and Conservatives," *Journal of Personality and Social Psychology* 25 (1973), pp. 335–341; S. L. Gaertner and L. Bickman, "Effects of Race on the Elicitation of Helping Behavior: The Wrong

Number Technique," *Journal of Personality and Social Psychology* 20 (1971), pp. 218–222.

12. John F. Dovidio and Samuel L. Gaertner, "Affirmative Action, Unintentional Racial Biases, and Intergroup Relations," *Journal of Social Issues* 52 (1996), pp. 51–75.

13. Thomas F. Pettigrew, "New Black–White Patterns: How Best to Conceptualize Them?," in eds. R. H. Turner and J. F. Short, Jr., *Annual Review of Sociology* 11 (1985), pp. 329–346.

14. Grant Jerding, "Changes in Race Relations in the USA," *USA Today*, June 11, 1997, p. 9A.

15. George Gallup, Jr. and Dr. Frank Newport, "For First Time, More Americans Approve of Interracial Marriage Than Disapprove," *The Gallup Poll Monthly* (August 1991), pp. 60–62.

16. Jerding, p. 9A.

17. David O. Sears and L. Huddy, "The Symbolic Politics of Opposition to Bilingual Education," in *Conflict Between People and Peoples*, eds. J. Simpson and S. Worchel (Chicago: Nelson-Hall, 1993).

18. Faye J. Crosby and Diana I. Cordova, "Words Worth of Wisdom: Toward an Understanding of Affirmative Action," *Journal of Social Issues* 52 (1996), pp. 33–49.

19. Ibid., pp. 34–35.

20. Jerding, p. 9A.

21. Joan Biskupic, "Constitution, Backlash Counter Race Card," *The Spokesman-Review*, June 15, 1997, p. A11.

22. Tim Wise, "Action Words," *The Spokesman-Review*, November 17, 1996, p. B9.

23. *Oakland Tribune*, March 31, 1995, p. A9.

24. *Los Angeles Times*, May 17, 1996, p. 3.

25. The *Playboy* Interview, "Martin Luther King: Candid Conversation," *Playboy* 12, (January 1965), pp. 74, 76.

26. Audrey J. Murrell and Ray Jones, "Assessing Affirmative Action: Past, Present, and Future," *Journal of Social Issues* 52 (1996), pp. 77–92.

27. Scott Plous, "Ten Myths about Affirmative Action," *Journal of Social Issues* 52 (1996), pp. 25–31.

28. Ethan Bronner, "Reliance on SATs May Resegregate Colleges," reprinted in *The Spokesman-Review*, November 8, 1997, pp. A1, A10.

29. Paul Kivel, *Uprooting Racism: How White People Can Work for Racial Justice* (Gabriola Island, BC: New Society Publishers, 1996), p. 72.

30. Kalpana Srinivasan, "Number of Minorities Entering Medical Schools Falls," reprinted in *The Spokesman-Review*, November 2, 1997, p. A11.

31. Statement available from the Association of American Universities,

1200 New York Avenue, NW, Washington, DC 20005; (202) 408-7500.

32. James M. Jones, "Racism in Black and White: A Bicultural Model of Reaction and Evolution," in Phyllis A. Katz and Dalmas A. Taylor (eds.), *Eliminating Racism: Profiles in Controversy* (New York: Plenum Press, 1988), p. 130.

33. Ira Glasser, "Affirmative Action and the Legacy of Racial Injustice," in Phyllis A. Katz and Dalmas A. Taylor (eds.), *Eliminating Racism: Profiles in Controversy* (New York: Plenum Press, 1988), p. 353.

34. Anthony R. Pratkanis and Marlene E. Turner, "The Proactive Removal of Discriminatory Barriers: Affirmative Action as Effective Help," *Journal of Social Issues* 52 (1996), pp. 111–132.

35. Ibid., p. 128.

36. Joe R. Feagin and Melvin P. Sikes, *Living with Racism: The Black Middle Class Experience* (Boston: Beacon Press, 1994), pp. 23–24.

37. Jody David Armour, *Negrophobia and Reasonable Racism: The Hidden Costs of Being Black in America* (New York: New York University Press, 1997), p. 13.

38. Joe R. Feagin, "The Continuing Significance of Race: Anti-black Discrimination in Public Places," *American Sociological Review* (1991), p. 109.

39. Rupert Brown, *Prejudice: Its Social Psychology* (Oxford, UK: Blackwell, 1995), pp. 221–222.

40. Thomas F. Pettigrew and R. W. Meertens, "Subtle and Blatant Prejudice in Western Europe," *European Journal of Social Psychology* 25 (1995), pp. 57–75.

41. J. K. Smith, K. Aikin, W. S. Hall, and B. A. Hunter, "Sexisim and Racism: Old-fashioned and Modern Prejudices," *Journal of Personality and Social Psychology* 68 (1995), pp. 199–214.

42. C. S. Crandall, "Prejudice against Fat People: Ideology and Self-Interest," *Journal of Personality and Social Psychology* 66 (1994), pp. 882–894.

43. Cited in Michael Omi and Howard Winant, "Racism Is Prevalent Today," in Bruno Leone, *Racism: Opposing Viewpoints* (San Diego, CA: Greenhaven Press, 1986), p. 142.

44. Richard Delgado, "When a Story Is Just a Story: Does Voice Really Matter?" *Virginia Law Review* 76 (February 1990), p. 106.

CHAPTER 8

1. Harvard Sitkoff, *The Struggle for Black Equality: 1954–1992* (New York: Hill and Wang, 1993), p. 155.

2. C. H. Cooley, *Human Nature and the Social Order* (New York: Charles Scribner's Sons, 1902).
3. Cited in Ellis Cose, *Color-Blind: Seeing beyond Race in a Race-Obsessed World* (New York: HarperCollins, 1997), p. 41.
4. Claude M. Steele and J. Aronson, "Stereotype Threat and the Intellectual Test Performance of African-Americans," *Journal of Personality and Social Psychology* 69 (1995).
5. Claude Steele, 1992.
6. Marilyn Elias, "Inoculating Minority Students against Prejudice," *USA Today*, August 10, 1995, p. 6D.
7. Martin Luther King, Jr., *Why We Can't Wait* (New York: Mentor, 1963), p. 81.
8. Richard Kluger, *Simple Justice* (New York: Knopf, 1975), p. 318.
9. Sitkoff, p. 22.
10. *New York Times* News Service, "Black Children Still Have Feelings of Inferiority, Doll Studies Show," *Lexington Herald Leader*, August 31, 1987.
11. Jules Tygiel, *Baseball's Great Experiment: Jackie Robinson and His Legacy* (New York: Oxford University Press, 1983), pp. 51–52.
12. Sitkoff, pp. 141–142.
13. Steven Fein and Steven J. Spencer, "Prejudice as Self-Image Maintenance: Affirming the Self through Derogating Others," *Journal of Personality and Social Psychology* 73 (1997), pp. 31–44.
14. Scott Plous, "Ten Myths about Affirmative Action," *Journal of Social Issues* 52 (1996), p. 29.
15. Philip Green, "The New Individualism," *Christianity and Crisis* 41 (1981), p. 79.
16. Feagin, pp. 101–116.
17. Ibid., p. 115.
18. Sherman Alexie, *Reservation Blues* (New York: Warner Books, 1995), p. 217.
19. Audrey J. Murrell and Ray Jones, "Assessing Affirmative Action: Past, Present, and Future," *Journal of Social Issues* 52 (1996), p. 80.
20. David H. Swinton, "Economic Progress for Black Americans in the post–Civil Rights Era," in *U.S. Race Relations in the 1980's and 1990's*, ed. Gail E. Thomas (Bristol, PA: Hemisphere, 1990).
21. Ian Ayres, "Fair Driving: Tests of Gender and Race Discrimination in Retail Car Negotiations," *Harvard Law Review* 104 (1991), pp. 817–822.
22. Walter L. Updegrave, *Money* (December 1989).
23. Melvin Oliver and Tom Shapiro, *Black Wealth, White Wealth* (New York: Routledge, 1995).

24. Penny Loeb, Warren Cohen, and Constance Johnson, "The New Redlining," *U.S. News and World Report*, April 17, 1995, pp. 51–58.
25. Nationline, "Black Farmers' Lawsuit Says USDA Discriminated," *USA Today*, August 29, 1997, p. 3A.
26. Marilyn Elias, "Racism Linked to Blacks' Poor Health," *USA Today*, March 18, 1996, p. D1.
27. Norman B. Anderson, "Racial Differences in Stress-Induced Cardiovascular Reactivity and Hypertension: Current Status and Substantive Issues," *Psychological Bulletin* 105 (1989), pp. 89–105.
28. "Assessing Stress: Getting to the Heart of the Matter," *Odyssey: The Magazine of University of Kentucky Research* 14 (1997), p. 9.
29. Anderson, p. 95.
30. Marilyn Elias, "Routine Discrimination May Be Health Hazard," *USA Today*, March 12, 1997, p. D1.
31. Nancy Krieger and Stephen Sidney, "Racial Discrimination and Blood Pressure: The Cardia Study of Young Black and White Adults," *American Journal of Public Health* 86 (October 1996), pp. 1370–1378.
32. *Time*, November 4, 1996, p. 20.
33. American Cancer Society, *Cancer Facts and Figures—1997* (Atlanta, GA: American Cancer Society, 1997).
34. *Detroit Free Press*, "Alarming Cancer Rise among Blacks, Women," *The Spokesman-Review*, May 25, 1997, p. A3.
35. Julie Titone, "Tribes Face Cigarette Quandary," *The Spokesman-Review* (December 1997), pp. A1, A10.
36. *Washington Press*, "Syphilis Nearly Eradicated," *The Spokesman-Review*, May 25, 1997, p. A3.
37. Sitkoff, p. 227.
38. Sally L. Satel, "Can Racism Make You Sick? The Rise of Critical Medical Theory," *Policy Online*, March 27, 1997.
39. Andrew Hacker, *Two Nations: Black and White, Separate, Hostile, Unequal* (New York: Scribner's, 1992), p. 46.
40. Julie Sullivan, "Maxey Suicide in Line with Trend," *The Spokesman-Review*, July 27, 1997, pp. A1, 17.
41. Elias, p. D1.
42. Larry Hugick, "Blacks See Their Lives Worsening," *The Gallup Poll Monthly* (April 1992), pp. 26–29.
43. Lydia Saad and Leslie McAneny, "Black Americans See Little Justice for Themselves," *The Gallup Poll Monthly* (March 1995), pp. 32–35.
44. Hacker, pp. 180, 182.
45. Dennis Hayes, "Police Brutality: What We Can Do!" *Crisis* (August/September 1993), p. 42.

46. Saad and McAneny, March 1995.
47. Armour, pp. 42–43.
48. Kivel, p. 195.
49. ACLU Newsfeed, electronic transmission, January 30, 1997.
50. Ibid.
51. "Crack Penalties Appear to Hit Minorities Harder," *Oakland Tribune*, May 21, 1995, p. A45.
52. Don Kent, "Is Racism on the Decline in America?," *A.P.S. Observer* (July/August 1996), p. 12.
53. Hayes, p. 42.
54. Hacker, p. 191.
55. Peggy McIntosh, *White Privilege and Male Privilege: A Personal Account of Coming to See Correspondences through Work in Women's Studies* (Working Paper No. 189, Wellesley College, Center for Research on Women, 1988).
56. Thomas Pettigrew, "The Mental Health Impact," in *Impacts of Racism on White Americans*, eds. Benjamin Bowser and Raymond G. Hunt (Beverly Hills, CA: Sage, 1981).
57. George Yancey, *Beyond Black and White: Reflections on Racial Reconciliation* (Grand Rapids, MI: Baker Books, 1996), pp. 152–153.
58. Ronald Takaki, *A Different Mirror: A History of Multicultural America* (Boston: Little, Brown and Company, 1993), p. 88.
59. Quoted in Emily Morrison Beck (ed.), *John Bartlett's Familiar Quotations*, 15th ed. (Boston: Little, Brown and Company, 1980), p. 556.
60. Nelson Mandela, *Long Walk to Freedom* (Boston: Little, Brown and Company, 1994).
61. Hacker, p. 61.
62. J. P. Sartre, "The Anti-Semite," in *Thinking the Unthinkable: Meanings of the Holocaust*, ed. R. S. Gottlieb (Mahway, NJ: Paulist Press), pp. 167–179.
63. Joe R. Feagin and Hernan Vera, *Color-Blind: Seeing beyond Race in a Race-Obsessed World* (New York: Routledge, 1995), p. 169.
64. Ibid.

CHAPTER 9

1. Janet Ward Schofield, "Causes and Consequences of the Colorblind Perspective," in *Prejudice, Discrimination, and Racism*, eds. John F. Dovidio and Samuel L Gaertner, (San Diego, CA: Academic Press, 1986), p. 250.

2. Ellis Cose, *Color-Blind: Seeing beyond Race in a Race-Obsessed World* (New York: HarperCollins, 1997), p. 210.

3. Birt L. Duncan, "Differential Social Perception and Attributes of Intergroup Violence: Testing the Lower Limits of Stereotyping of Blacks," *Journal of Personality and Social Psychology* 34 (1976), pp. 595–597.

4. H. Andrew Sager and Janet Ward Schofield, "Racial and Behavioral Cues in Black and White Children's Perceptions of Ambiguously Aggressive Acts," *Journal of Personality and Social Psychology* 39 (1980), pp. 594–597.

5. R. K. Bothwell, J. C. Brigham, and R. S. Malpass, "Cross-Racial Identification," *Personality and Social Psychology Bulletin* 15 (1989), pp. 19–25.

6. J. Krueger, M. Rothbart, and N. Sriram, "Category Learning and Change: Differences in Sensitivity to Information That Enhances or Reduces Intercategory Distinctions," *Journal of Personality and Social Psychology* 56 (1989), pp. 866–875.

7. L. Huddy and S. Virtanen, "Subgroup Differentiation and Subgroup Bias among Latinos as a Function of Familiarity and Positive Distinctiveness," *Journal of Personality and Social Psychology* 68 (1995), pp. 97–108.

8. Marilynn B. Brewer and Norman Miller, *Intergroup Relations* (Pacific Grove, CA: Brooks/Cole Publishing, 1996), p. 58.

9. R. R. Blake and J. S. Mouton, "Overevaluation of Own Group's Product in Intergroup Competition," *Journal of Abnormal and Social Psychology* 64 (1962), p. 238.

10. H. Tajfel and J. Turner, "An Integrative Theory of Intergroup Conflict," in *The Social Psychology of Intergroup Relations*, eds. W. Austin and S. Worchel (Monterey, CA: Brooks/Cole, 1979), p. 38.

11. "Elements of the Brain Become Less Mysterious," *Seattle Times*, December 8, 1996.

12. C. Perdue, J. Dovidio, M. Gurtman, and R. Tyler, "Us and Them: Social Categorization and the Process of Intergroup Bias," *Journal of Personality and Social Psychology* 59 (1990), pp. 475–486.

13. Patricia G. Devine, "Stereotyping and Prejudice: Their Automatic and Controlled Components," *Journal of Personality and Social Psychology* 56 (1989), pp. 5–18.

14. Somewhat contrary to Devine's work, a recent study by Russell Fazio and his colleagues suggests that considerable variability exists in people's automatic processing of negative stereotypes. See Russell H. Fazio, Joni R. Jackson, Bridget C. Dunton, and Carol J.

Williams, "Variability in Automatic Activation as an Unobtrusive Measure of Racial Attitudes: A Bona Fide Pipeline?" *Journal of Personality and Social Psychology* 69 (1995), pp. 1013–1027.
15. Devine.
16. Melvin J. Lerner, *The Belief in a Just World: A Fundamental Decision* (New York: Plenum Press, 1980).
17. Zick Rubin and Letitia Anne Peplau, "Who Believes in a Just World?" *Journal of Social Issues* 31 (1975), pp. 65–89.
18. R. Janoff-Bulman, C. Timko, and L. L. Carli, "Cognitive Biases in Blaming the Victim," *Journal of Experimental Social Psychology* 21 (1985), pp. 161–177.
19. Linda Carli and J. B. Leonard, "The Effect of Hindsight on Victim Derogation," *Journal of Social and Clinical Psychology* 8 (1989), pp. 331–343.
20. G. Wagstaff, "Attitudes to Rape: The 'Just World' Strikes Again?" *Bulletin of the British Psychological Society* 35 (1982), pp. 277–279.
21. Ronald Takaki, *A Different Mirror: A History of Multicultural America* (Boston: Little, Brown and Company, 1993), p. 128.
22. Mark Winegardner, *The Veracruz Blues* (New York: Penguin, 1997), p. 206.
23. John Duckitt, "Psychology and Prejudice: A Historical Analysis and Integrative Framework," *American Psychologist* 47 (1992), pp. 1182–1193.

CHAPTER 10

1. Paul Kivel, *Uprooting Racism: How White People Can Work for Racial Justice* (New Society Publishers, 1996), p. xii.
2. Henri Tajfel, *Human Groups and Social Categories: Studies in Social Psychology* (Cambridge, UK: Cambridge University Press, 1981), p. 186.
3. Catherine Meeks, "Rage and Reconciliation: Two Sides of the Same Coin," in *America's Original Sin: A Study Guide on White Racism*, eds. Bob Hulteen and Jim Wallis (Washington, DC: Sojourners, 1995), pp. 160–161.
4. "Peace on Earth and Goodwill Towards Men," *The North Columbia Monthly* (December 1995), p. 12; see also Parker J. Palmer, *To Know as We Are Known/A Spirituality of Education* (San Francisco, CA: Harper, 1983).
5. Marilynn B. Brewer and Norman Miller, *Intergroup Relations* (Pacific Grove, CA: Brooks/Cole Publishing, 1996), p. 50.

6. Patricia G. Devine, "Stereotypes and Prejudice: Their Automatic and Controlled Components," *Journal of Personality and Social Psychology* 56 (1989), pp. 5–18.
7. David G. Myers, *Social Psychology* 5th ed. (New York: McGraw-Hill, 1996), p. 396.
8. John F. Dovidio, S. L. Gaertner, A. M. Isen, and R. Lowrance, "Group Representations and Intergroup Bias: Positive Affect, Similarity, and Group Size," *Personality and Social Psychology Bulletin* 21 (1995), pp. 856–865.
9. Oscar Hijuelos, *Mr. Ives' Christmas* (New York: Harper Perennial, 1995), p. 42.
10. Harvard Sitkoff, *The Struggle for Black Equality: 1954–1992* (New York: Hill and Wang, 1993), p. 184.
11. Keith Woods, "Pilgramage against Prejudice," *The Seattle Times,* February 24–25, 1997, p. E3.
12. Kathleen Norris, *Dakota: A Spiritual Geography* (Boston: Houghton Mifflin, 1993), p. 129.
13. Ibid., p. 6.
14. Teresa LaFromboise, Hardin L. K. Coleman, and Jennifer Gerton, "Psychological Impact of Biculturalism: Evidence and Theory," *Psychological Bulletin* 114 (1993), pp. 395–412.
15. Norris, p. 168.
16. Thomas F. Pettigrew, "'Useful' Modes of Thought Contribute to Prejudice," *The New York Times,* May 12, 1987, p. 20.
17. Langston Hughes, "The Negro Artist and the Racial Mountain," *The Nation* 122 (June 23, 1926), pp. 692–694.
18. Virginia de Leon, "Hard Lessons," *The Spokesman-Review,* April 13, 1997, pp. E1, E7.
19. Joe R. Feagin, "The Continuing Significance of Racism: Discrimination against Black Students in White Colleges," *Journal of Black Studies* 22 (1992), p. 552.
20. Manning Marable, "The Rhetoric of Racial Harmony," *Sojourners* (August/September 1990).
21. Clarence Page, "Demonstrate Just How Wrong He Is," *Chicago Tribune* reprinted in *The Spokesman-Review,* September 18, 1997, p. B6.
22. Carol Hampton, "A Heritage Denied: American Indians Struggle for Racial Justice," in *America's Original Sin,* eds. Bob Hulteen and Him Wallis (Washington, DC: Sojourners, 1995), p. 128.
23. For example, R. Brown and L. Wootton-Millward, "Perceptions of Group Homogeneity during Group Formation and Change," *Social Cognition* 11 (1993), pp. 126–149.

24. Kivel, p. 145.
25. James M. Jones, "Racism: A Cultural Analysis of the Problem," in *Prejudice, Discrimination, and Racism*, eds. John F. Dovidio and Samuel L. Gaertner (San Diego, CA: Academic Press, 1986), pp. 279–314.
26. Stuart W. Cook, "Experimenting on Social Issues: The Case of School Desegregation," *American Psychologist* 40 (1985), pp. 452–460.
27. Norris, p. 111.
28. S. L. Gaertner, J. A. Mann, J. F. Dovidio, A. J. Murrell, and M. Pomare, "How Does Cooperation Reduce Intergroup Bias?" *Journal of Personality and Social Psychology* 59 (1990), pp. 692–704.
29. Muzafer Sherif, *In Common Predicament: Social Psychology of Intergroup Conflict and Cooperation* (Boston: Houghton Mifflin, 1966).
30. R. R. Blake and J. S. Mouton, "From Theory to Practice in Interface Problem Solving," in *Psychology of Intergroup Relations*, eds. S. Worchel and W. Austin (Chicago: Nelson-Hall, 1986), pp. 67–82.
31. Gary Fields and Tom Watson, "Decent Folks Don't Accept Arsons, Hatred," *USA Today*, March 19, 1996, pp. 1A, 2A.
32. Rupert Brown, *Prejudice: Its Social Psychology* (Oxford, UK: Blackwell, 1995), p. 245.
33. David van Biema, "After the Burning," *Time*, July 1, 1996, p. 54.
34. Mary R. Jackman and Marie Crane, "'Some of My Best Friends Are Black...': Interracial Friendship and Whites' Racial Attitudes," *Public Opinion Quarterly* 50 (1986), pp. 459–486.
35. David Shenk, *Data Smog: Surviving the Information Glut* (New York: HarperCollins, 1997), p. 201.
36. Mary R. Jackman, "General and Applied Tolerance: Does Education Increase Commitment to Racial Integration?" *American Journal of Political Science* 22 (1978), pp. 302–324.
37. Elliot Aronson and Diane Bridgeman, "Jigsaw Groups and the Desegregated Classroom: In Pursuit of Common Goals," *Personality and Social Psychology Bulletin* 5 (1979), pp. 438–446.
38. Deborah Meier, *The Power of Their Ideas* (New York: Beacon, 1995).
39. Jeff Cohen and Norman Solomon, "Not in Any Town," *The Inlander*, December 13, 1995, p. 4.
40. For a copy, contact Southeast Uplift Neighborhood Program, 3534 SE Main, Portland, OR 97214; (503) 232–0010.
41. For more information, contact Spokane Task Force on Race Relations, 808 West Spokane Falls Boulevard, Spokane, WA 99201-3322; (509) 625–6266.
42. Jerry Buckley, "Mt. Airy," *U.S. News and World Report*, July 22, 1991, p. 23.

43. Wendell Berry, *The Hidden Wound* (San Francisco, CA: North Point Press, 1989).
44. See Brown, 1995, for a complete review.
45. Erin Burnette, "Talking Openly about Race Thwarts Racism in Children," *A.P.A. Monitor* (June 1997), p. 33.
46. A. Davey, *Learning to Be Prejudiced* (London: Edward Arnold, 1983).
47. Henri Tajfel, C. Nemeth, G. Jahoda, J. Campbell, and N. Johnson, "The Development of Children's Preference for Their Own Country: A Cross-National Study," *International Journal of Psychology* 5 (1970), pp. 245–253.
48. See Brown, 1995, for a complete review.
49. Thomas C. Wilson, "Cohort and Prejudice: Whites' Attitudes toward Blacks, Hispanics, Jews, and Asians," *Public Opinion Quarterly* 60 (1996), pp. 253–274.
50. Burnette, p. 33.
51. Joe R. Feagin and Hernan Vera, *White Racism: The Basics* (New York: Routledge, 1995), pp. 175–179.

Bibliography

The following bibliography includes a wide range of books and journal articles for additional reading.

BOOKS

Alexie, Sherman. *Reservation Blues* (New York: Warner Books, 1995).

Allport, Gordon. *The Nature of Prejudice* (Reading, MA: Addison-Wesley, 1954).

Armour, Jody David. *Negrophobia and Reasonable Racism: The Hidden Costs of Being Black in America* (New York: New York University Press, 1997).

Austin, W., and S. Worchel (eds.). *The Social Psychology of Intergroup Relations* (Monterey, CA: Brooks/Cole, 1979).

Barndt, Joseph. *Dismantling Racism: The Continuing Challenge to White America* (Minneapolis, MN: Augsburg, 1991).

Bell, Derrick. *Faces at the Bottom of the Well* (New York: Basic Books, 1992).

Bowser, Benjamin, and Raymond G. Hunt (eds.). *Impacts of Racism on White Americans* (Beverly Hills, CA: Sage, 1981).

Brewer, Marilynn B., and Norman Miller. *Intergroup Relations* (Pacific Grove, CA: Brooks/Cole, 1996).

Brown, Rupert. *Prejudice: Its Social Psychology* (Oxford, UK: Blackwell, 1995).

Carter, Stephen L. *Reflections of an Affirmative Action Baby* (New York: Basic Books, 1991).

Cose, Ellis. *Color-Blind: Seeing beyond Race in a Race-Obsessed World* (New York: HarperCollins, 1997).

Dees, Morris, and James Corcoran. *Gathering Storm: America's Militia Threat* (New York: HarperCollins, 1996).

Dovidio, John F., and Samuel L. Gaertner, eds. *Prejudice, Discrimination, and Racism* (Orlando, FL: Academic Press, 1986).

D'Souza, Dinesh. *The End of Racism* (New York: Free Press, 1995).

Dudley, William, and Charles Cozic, eds. *Racism in America: Opposing Viewpoints* (San Diego, CA: Greenhaven Press, 1991).

Feagin, Joe R., and Hernan Vera. *White Racism: The Basics* (New York: Routledge, 1995).

Feagin, Joe R., and Melvin P. Sikes. *Living with Racism: The Black Middle-Class Experience* (Boston: Beacon Press, 1994).

Gioseffi, Daniela, ed. *On Prejudice: A Global Perspective* (New York: Anchor Books, 1993).

Griffin, John Howard. *Black Like Me* (Boston: Houghton Mifflin, 1960).

Hacker, Andrew. *Two Nations: Black and White, Separate, Hostile, Unequal* (New York: Scribner's, 1992).

Jones, James M. *Prejudice and Racism* (New York: Random House, 1972).

Katz, Phyllis A., and Dalmas A. Taylor, eds. *Eliminating Racism: Profiles in Controversy* (New York: Plenum Press, 1988).

King, Martin Luther, Jr. *Where Do We Go from Here? Chaos or Community?* (New York: Bantam, 1967).

King, Martin Luther, Jr. *Why We Can't Wait* (New York: Mentor, 1963).

Kivel, Paul. *Uprooting Racism: How White People Can Work for Racial Justice* (Gabriola Island, BC: New Society Publishers, 1996).

Lerner, Melvin J. *The Belief in a Just World: A Fundamental Decision* (New York: Plenum Press, 1980).

Oliver, Melvin, and Tom Shapiro. *Black Wealth, White Wealth* (New York: Routledge, 1995).

Report of the National Advisory Commission on Civil Disorders (New York: Bantam, 1968).

Robinson, James L. *Racism or Attitude? The Ongoing Struggle for Black Liberation and Self-Esteem* (New York: Insight Books, 1995).

Rowan, Carl T. *The Coming Race War in America* (New York: Little, Brown and Company, 1996).

Sitkoff, Harvard. *The Struggle for Black Equality: 1954–1992* (New York: Hill and Wang, 1993).

Sleeper, Jim. *Liberal Racism* (New York: Viking, 1997).

Stangor, Charles, and Miles Hewstone, eds. *Stereotypes and Stereotyping* (New York: Guilford Press, 1996).

Steele, Shelby. *The Content of Our Character* (New York: St. Martin's Press, 1990).

Thomas, Gail E., ed. *U.S. Race Relations in the 1980s and 1990s* (Bristol, PA: Hemisphere Publishing Corporation, 1990).

Tygiel, Jules. *Baseball's Great Experiment: Jackie Robinson and His Legacy* (New York: Oxford University Press, 1983).

Washington, James M., ed. *A Testament of Hope: The Essential Writings of Martin Luther King, Jr.* (San Francisco: Harper and Row, 1986).

Winegardner, Mark. *The Veracruz Blues* (New York: Penguin, 1997).

Yancey, George A. *Beyond Black and White: Reflections on Racial Reconciliation* (Grand Rapids, MI: Baker Books, 1996).

JOURNAL ARTICLES

Anderson, Norman B. "Racial Differences in Stress-Induced Cardiovascular Reactivity and Hypertension: Current Status and Substantive Issues." *Psychological Bulletin* 105 (1989):89–105.

Ayres, Ian. "Fair Driving: Tests of Gender and Race Discrimination in Retail Car Negotiations." *Harvard Law Review* 104 (1991):817–822.

Bathwell, R. K., J. C. Brigham, and R. S. Malpass. "Cross-Racial Identification." *Personality and Social Psychology Bulletin* 15 (1989):19–25.

Carli, Linda, and J. B. Leonard. "The Effect of Hindsight on Victim Derogation." *Journal of Social and Clinical Psychology* 8 (1989):331–343.

Crandall, C. S. "Prejudice against Fat People: Ideology and Self-Interest," *Journal of Personality and Social Psychology* 66 (1994):882–894.

Crosby, Faye J., and Diana I. Cordova. "Words Worth of Wisdom: Toward an Understanding of Affirmative Action," *Journal of Social Issues* 52 (1996):33–49.

Delgado, Richard. "When a Story Is Just a Story: Does Voice Really Matter?" *Virginia Law Review* 76 (1990):95–111.

Devine, Patricia G. "Stereotypes and Prejudice: Their Automatic and Controlled Components." *Journal of Personality and Social Psychology* 56 (1989):5–18.

Dovidio, John F., and Samuel L. Gaertner. "Affirmative Action, Unintentional Racial Biases, and Intergroup Relations." *Journal of Social Issues* 52 (1996):51–75.

Duckitt, John. "Psychology and Prejudice: A Historical Analysis and Integrative Framework." *American Psychologist* 47 (1992):1182–1193.

Duncan, Birt L. "Differential Social Perception and Attributes of Intergroup Violence: Testing the Lower Limits of Stereotyping of Blacks." *Journal of Personality and Social Psychology* 39 (1980): 594–597.

Fazio, Russell H., Joni R. Jackson, Bridget C. Dunton, and Carol J. Williams. "Variability in Automatic Activation as an Unobtrusive

Measure of Racial Attitudes: A Bona Fide Pipeline?" *Journal of Personality and Social Psychology* 69 (1995):1013–1027.

Feagin, Joe R. "The Continuing Significance of Race: Antiblack Discrimination in Public Places." *American Sociological Review* 56 (1991): 101–116.

Feagin, Joe R. "The Continuing Significance of Racism: Discrimination against Black Students in White Colleges." *Journal of Black Studies* 22 (1992):546–578.

Fein, Steven, and Steven J. Spencer. "Prejudice as Self-Image Maintenance Affirming the Self through Derogating Others." *Journal of Personality and Social Psychology* 73 (1997):31–44.

Fish, Jefferson M. "Mixed Blood." *Psychology Today* (November/December 1995):55–61, 76–77.

Gaertner, S. L. "Helping Behavior and Discrimination among Liberal and Conservatives." *Journal of Personality and Social Psychology* 25 (1973):335–341.

Gaertner, S. L., and L. Bickman. "Effects of Race on the Elicitation of Helping Behavior: The Wrong Number Technique." *Journal of Personality and Social Psychology* 20 (1971):218–222.

Gaertner, Samuel L., and John F. Dovidio. "The Subtlety of White Racism, Arousal and Helping Behavior." *Journal of Personality and Social Psychology* 35 (1977):691–707.

Gardner, Robert C. "Ethnic Stereotypes: The Traditional Approach, A New Look." *Canadian Psychologist* 14 (1973):133–148.

Haddock, G., M. P. Zanna, and V. M. Esses. "Assessing the Structure of Prejudicial Attitudes: The Case of Attitudes toward Homosexuals." *Journal of Personality and Social Psychology* 65 (1993):1105–1118.

Huddy, L., and S. Virtanen. "Subgroup Differentiation and Subgroup Bias Among Latinos as a Function of Familiarity and Positive Distinctiveness." *Journal of Personality and Social Psychology* 68 (1995):97–108.

Humphrey, Ronald, and Howard Schuman. "The Portrayal of Blacks in Magazine Advertisements: 1950–1982." *Public Opinion Quarterly* 48 (1984):551–563.

Jackman, Mary R., and Michael J. Muha. "Education and Intergroup Attitudes: Moral Enlightenment, Superficial Democratic Commitment, or Ideological Refinement?" *American Sociological Review* 49 (1984):751–769.

Janoff-Bulman, R., C. Timko, and L. L. Carli. "Cognitive Biases in Blaming the Victim." *Journal of Experimental Social Psychology* 21 (1985): 166–177.

Katz, Daniel, and Kenneth Braly. "Racial Stereotypes in One Hundred College Students." *Journal of Abnormal and Social Psychology* 28 (1933):280–290.

Kinder, Donald R. "The Continuing American Dilemma: White Resistance to Racial Change 40 Years after Myrdal." *Journal of Social Issues* 42 (1986):151–171.

Kluegel, James R. "Trends in Whites' Explanations of the Black–White Gap in Socioeconomic Status, 1977–1989." *American Sociological Review* 55 (1990):512–525.

Krieger, Nancy, and Stephen Sidney. "Racial Discrimination and Blood Pressure." *American Journal of Public Health* (October 1996):1370–1378.

Krueger, Joachim, Myron Rothbart, and N. Sriram. "Category Learning and Change: Differences in Sensitivity to Information That Enhances or Reduces Intercategory Distinctions." *Journal of Personality and Social Psychology* 56 (1989)866–875.

Kutner, B., C. Wilkins, and P. R. Yarrow. "Verbal Attitudes and Overt Behavior." *Journal of Abnormal and Social Psychology* 47 (1952):649–652.

LaPiere, R. T. "Attitudes vs. Actions." *Social Forces* 13 (1994):230–237.

Loeb, Penny, Warren Cohen, and Constance Johnson. "The New Redlining." *U.S. News & World Report* (April 17, 1995):51–58.

Martin, Carol Lynn, and Sandra Parker. "Folk Theories about Sex and Race Differences." *Personality and Social Psychology Bulletin* 21 (1995):45–57.

McClelland, Katherine E., and Carol J. Auster. "Public Platitudes and Hidden Tensions." *Journal of Higher Education* 61 (1990):607–642.

McCormack, Arlene Smith. "The Changing Nature of Racism on College Campuses: Study of Discrimination at a Northeastern Public University." *College Student Journal* 29 (1995):150–156.

McIntosh, Peggy. *White Privilege and Male Privilege: A Personal Account of Coming to See Correspondences through Work in Women's Studies.* Working Paper No. 189 (Wellesley, MA: Wellesley College, Center for Research on Women, 1988).

Murrell, Audrey J., and Ray Jones. "Assessing Affirmative Action: Past, Present, and Future." *Journal of Social Issues* 52 (1996):77–92.

Perdue, C., John F. Dovidio, Michael Gurtman, and Richard Tyler. "Us and Them: Social Categorization and the Process of Intergroup Bias." *Journal of Personality and Social Psychology* 59 (1990):475–486.

Pettigrew, Thomas F., and R. W. Meertens. "Subtle and Blatant Prejudice in Western Europe." *European Journal of Social Psychology* 25 (1995): 57–75.

Plous, Scott. "Ten Myths about Affirmative Action." *Journal of Social Issues* 52 (1996):25–31.

Pratkianis, Anthony R., and Marlene E. Turner. "The Proactive Removal of Discriminatory Barriers: Affirmative Action as Effective Help." *Journal of Social Issues* 52 (1996):111–132.

Rainie, Harrison. "Black and White in America." *U.S. News & World Report* (July 22, 1991):18–28.

Rubin, Zick, and Letitia Anne Peplau. "Who Believes in a Just World?" *Journal of Social Issues* 31 (1975):65–89.

Sanoff, Alvin P., Scott Minerbrook, Jeannye Thornton, and Elizabeth Pezzullo. "Students Talk about Race." *U.S. News & World Report* (April 19, 1993):57–64.

Simons, John. "Special Report: Improbable Dreams." *U.S. News & World Report* (March 24, 1997):46–52.

Steele, Claude M. "Race and the Schooling of Black Americans." *The Atlantic Monthly* (April 1992):68–78.

Steele, Claude M., and J. Aronson. "Stereotype Threat and the Intellectual Test Performance of African Americans." *Journal of Personality and Social Psychology* 69 (1995):797–811.

Swim, J. K., K. Aikin, W. S. Hall and B. A. Hunter. "Sexism and Racism: Old-Fashioned and Modern Prejudices." *Journal of Personality and Social Psychology* 68 (1995):199–214.

Vanman, Eric J., Brenda Y. Paul, Tiffany A. Ito, and Norman Miller, "The Modern Face of Prejudice and Structural Features That Moderate the Effect of Cooperation on Affect," *Journal of Personality and Social Psychology* 73 (1997), pp. 941–959.

Wagstaff, G. "Attitudes to Rape: The 'Just World' Strikes Again?" *Bulletin of the British Psychological Society* 35 (1982):277–279.

Weigel, Russell H., Eleanor L. Kim, and Jill L. Frost. "Race Relations on Prime Time Television Reconsidered: Patterns of Continuity and Change." *Journal of Applied Social Psychology* 25 (1995):223–236.

Wilson, Thomas C. "Cohort and Prejudice: Whites' Attitudes toward Blacks, Hispanics, Jews, and Asians." *Public Opinion Quarterly* 60 (1996):253–274.

Index

ABC News surveys, 93, 130
Aboriginal Australians, 138
Abstract principles, 108–109
Accentuation effect, 177
Acquaintance potential, 211
Advanced degrees, 64, 88
Advertisements
  print, 72–73
  television, 73
Affirmative action, 50, 108, 109, 126,
    127–135
  definition of, 127–129
  equal opportunity distinguished
    from, 127, 129
  future of, 134–135
  lawsuits pertaining to, 4, 130,
    133–134
  reasons for vehemence of public
    reaction to, 129–134
  self-esteem and, 149–150
Affirmative Discrimination (Glazer),
    2–3
African-Americans, 13, 14–16, 55; *see
    also* Slavery
  affirmative action and, 129–130,
    133–134
  automatic cognitive processing
    and, 182–183
  business ownership in, 49, 63
  cancer in, 155
  collection of survey data on, 58
  community support for, 213
  crime and, 121

African-Americans (*cont.*)
  cultural racism and, 50
  definitions of race and, 43–45
  discrimination and, 35–36
  economic indicators for, 63, 80, 81,
    82–85
  educational attainment in, 64, 65,
    85, 86, 87–88, 89, 90, 91
  financial costs of racism and,
    152–153
  general social well-being in, 65–66,
    91–92
  generational differences in, 99–100
  historical overview of, 21–22
  hypertension in, 154–155
  immigration restriction favored by,
    110
  indifference toward, 94
  institutional racism and, 48
  justice system and, 158–161
  just-world phenomenon and,
    186–187
  measures of racist stereotypes and
    attitudes toward, 59, 70–71
  media depiction of, 61–62, 72–73,
    75, 76–77
  mistrust and, 93–94
  modern racism and, 135–136
  mortality rates in, 156–157
  national organizations for, 221–222
  neighborhood composition and, 95
  number/percentage of in popula-
    tion, 22

African-Americans (*cont.*)
  old-fashioned racism and, 112, 113,
    114–115
  prejudice against, 33
  prejudice against whites in, 208
  racism in, 52
  rage in, 193–194
  relationship between prejudice
    and discrimination and, 41
  school composition and, 95
  self-esteem damage in, 147–150
  sports and, 15, 78–79
  stereotypes of, 27, 28, 39
  stereotype threat and, 32, 144–146
  syphilis in, 156
  terminology used to describe, 53,
    54
Agassiz, Louis, 33
Agriculture Department, U. S., 153
AIDS, 6, 91, 139, 154, 156
Alaskan Natives, 58, 86, 88
Alexie, Sherman, 74, 151
Allport, Gordon, 29, 30, 35
Almanac of Higher Education, 89
American Civil Liberties Union
    (ACLU), 22, 135, 160, 224
American Council on Education
    (ACE), 88
*American Dilemma, An: The Negro
    Problem and Modern Democ-
    racy* (Myrdal), 55
American Indians: *see* Native Ameri-
    cans
Anderson, Norman, 154
Anti-Defamation League, 71
Antiracism, teaching, 215–219
Antiracism Action Plan, 214
Applied commitment, 108–109
Approximating experiences, 219
Aristotle, 196
Armour, Jody, 76, 135–136, 159
Aronson, Elliot, 212
Aronson, Joshua, 144
Arrest rates, 158–159
Ashe, Arthur, 6
Ashmore, Richard, 28

Asian American Legal Defense and
    Education Fund, 222
Asian-Americans, 14–16
  cancer in, 155
  collection of survey data on, 58
  economic indicators for, 63, 81, 82,
    83
  educational attainment in, 65, 85,
    86–87, 88, 90
  historical perspective on, 22–23
  measures of racist stereotypes and
    attitudes toward, 70–71
  as model minority, 23, 63, 86,
    146–147
  national organizations for, 222
  neighborhood composition and, 95
  number/percentage of in popula-
    tion, 23
  racism in, 52
  stereotypes of, 28
  stereotype threat and, 146–147
  terminology used to describe, 53
Asian Women United, 222
Associate degrees, 64
Association of American Medical
    Colleges, 134
Association of American Universi-
    ties, 134
Association on American Indian Af-
    fairs, Inc, 223
Assumed similarity effect, 176
Attitudes, 25, 33, 35; *see also* Preju-
    dice
  cultural, 35
  measures of, 59–61, 69–71
Augusta National Golf Club, 101
Auster, Carol, 90
Authoritarian personality, 27
Authoritarian Personality, The, 27, 31
Automatic cognitive processing, 174,
    181–183, 196–198
Aversive racism, 124–126
Ayres, Ian, 152

Bachelor's degrees, 64, 88
Baldwin, James, 148–149, 166

Banaji, Mahzarin, 157
Banks, Tyra, 72
Barndt, Joseph, 50–51, 99
Barnicle, Mike, 79
Baywatch (television program), 72
Beckham, Edgar, 67
Behavioral ambiguity, 112–113
Bell, Derrick, 10, 110
Bell Curve, The: The Reshaping of American Life by Differences in Intelligence (Herrnstein & Murray), 46
Bello, Kenya Napper, 157
Bennett, Lerone, Jr., 108–109
Berry, Halle, 73
Berry, Wendell, 215
Bicultural individuals, 201
Billings Gazette, 213
Bill of Rights, 22
Bird, Larry, 78
Black Like Me (Griffin), 7
Blacks: *see* African-Americans
Black Tax, 135–136
Blake, Robert, 178
Blatant racism, 102–105
Bloom, Allan, 4
Boalt Hall law school, 133
Boarding schools, 204
Bobo, Lawrence, 84, 109
Bogus pipeline experiment, 59–60
Boone, Karen, 104
Bootzin, R., 112
Borderland, appreciation of, 203–207
Borrow approximations, 219
Boston Celtics, 78
Boston Globe, 79, 100–101
Boston Red Sox, 89
Bracero program, 23
Bradley, Bill, 211
Bradley, Tom, 111, 119
Braly, Kenneth, 26–27, 31
Brazil, 44
Bressler, Marvin, 79
Brewer, Marilynn, 177
Brinkley, Douglas, 7
Brookes, Warren, 63

Brown, H. Rap, 55
Brown, Rupert, 35, 138
Brown v. Topeka Board of Education, 101, 147–148
Builds-the-Fire, Thomas, 69, 74
Buncan, Birt, 176
Bureau of Labor Statistics, 83
Bush, George, 166
Busing, 126

"Can a Black Be Racist?" (Yancey), 51
Cancer, 154, 155–156
Career Opportunity News, 64
Carli, Linda, 186
Carroll, Lewis, 53
Carter, Deborah, 88
Carter, Stephen, 3
Caucasoid racial group, 43
Census Bureau, U. S., 57–58, 63, 64, 88
Center for Democratic Renewal, 96, 221
Center for the Healing of Racism, 214
Centers for Disease Control, 157
Chicago Tribune, 205
Chicanos: *see* Mexican-Americans
Chinese-Americans, 22, 40–41, 44
Chinese Exclusion Act, 22
Christian Science Monitor, 163
Churches, 96, 210
Civil Rights Act of 1964, 101, 128, 152
Civil Rights Commission, 63
Civil rights movement, 22, 48, 55, 108–109, 200
Clark, Kenneth, 147, 148
Clark, Lenard, 102
Clark, Mamie, 147
Clinton, William, 11, 24, 97, 102
Cocaine, 159
Cognitive processing
automatic, 174, 181–183, 196–198
controlled, 181–183, 196–198
Cognitive schemas, 30–31

Cognitive shortcuts, 32–33, 173
Cohen, Richard, 121
College admissions, 131
College education, 63–64, 65, 85–88, 89–91, 133
Color-Blind: Seeing beyond Race in a Race-Obsessed World (Cose), 10
Color-blind society, 171–190
    affirmative action and, 131–132
    automatic cognitive processing vs.: *see* Automatic cognitive processing
    explanation vs., 174, 183–188
    myth of, 2, 9–11, 17, 18, 71
    social categorization vs.: *see* Social categorization
Comic strips, 76
Coming Race Wars, The?, 110
Commission on Civil Rights, U. S., 49, 225
Commitment to Action for Racial Equality (CARE), 103
Common Destiny Alliance (CODA), 224
Community, 213–215
Congress of National Black Churches, 221
Congress of Racial Equality (CORE), 224
Conservatives, 124, 131–132
    African-American, 3
Conspiracy theories, 91–92
Constitution, U. S., 22, 129
Contact hypothesis, 207–208
Contact situations, 208–213
Controlled cognitive processing, 181–183, 196–198
Conyers, John, 159
Cook, Stuart, 208–209, 212
Cook, Susan Johnson, 11
Cooley, Charles Horton, 142
Corcoran, James, 104
Cordova, Diana, 127–128
Cosby Show, The (television program), 74

Cose, Ellis, 5, 10, 44, 45, 89, 90, 91, 171, 172–173, 189
Crack cocaine, 159, 160
Crandall, C. S., 138–139
Crane, Marie, 211
Crime, 76–77, 121; *see also* Justice system
Crosby, Faye, 127–128
Cuban-Americans, 53, 81, 85–86, 177–178
Cultural attitudes, 35
Cultural Indicators Project, 74–75
Cultural Literacy: What Every American Needs to Know (Hirsch), 49
Cultural racism, 49–50, 55, 97
Cultural stereotypes, 26–27, 31–32, 47
Current Population Survey (CPS), 58

Dakota: A Spiritual Geography (Norris), 201
Darby, Joseph, 211
Davey, A., 216–217
Davis, Cary, 83
Death penalty, 160–161
DeBell, Camille, 76
Decisions, 182
Declaration of Independence, 21
Declining Significance of Race, The (Wilson), 3
Dees, Morris, 104
De facto racism, 3, 22, 49, 60
Deford, Frank, 79
De jure racism, 3, 22, 48, 60
Delany, Martin, 186–187
Del Boca, Frances, 28
DeLeon, Patrick, 12
Delgado, Richard, 10, 139
Demographic data, 57–58
Dershowitz, Alan, 52
Detroit Pistons, 78
Devine, Patricia, 71, 181–183, 196–198, 202
Devlin, Bernie, 46

"Dialogue: Racism" (discussion series), 214
Disagreeing, 192, 194–196
Discrimination, 25, 35–38, 47
  definition of, 36–37
  denial of, 120, 132
  individual, 47
  organizational, 47
  personal, 202–203
  prejudice and, 40–41
  reverse, 63, 66, 130
  stereotypes and, 39, 40
Disraeli, Benjamin, 56
Diversity, 207–213
  Internet sites on, 225
Doctoral degrees, 87, 88
Doctoral universities, 89
Doll experiment, 147–148
Douglass, Frederick, 163
Dovidio, John, 41, 114, 124, 125–126, 160, 198
Drug crimes, 158–159, 160
D'Souza, Dinesh, 5, 66–67, 121
DuBois, W. E. B., 55
Duckitt, John, 188–189
Dukakis, Michael, 166
Duke University, 90–91
DWB (driving while black), 159

Early baselines, 57
Earthquake, India, 210–211
Economic indicators, 62–63, 80–85
Ecumenical Working Group of Asian and Pacific Americans, 222
Educational attainment, 63–65, 85–91; see also Schools
Educational Testing Service, 61
Eisenhower, Dwight D., 101
Elliot, Jane, 178–179
End of Racism, The (D'Souza), 5
Equal opportunity, 127, 129
Equal-status interactions, 208–209
Ethnic stories, 199–202
Executive Order 11246, 128
Explanation, 174, 183–188

Facial muscle physiological recordings, 113–114
Facing History and Ourselves, 224
Farmers, 153
Fat persons, prejudice against, 138–139
Feagin, Joe, 2, 10, 47, 48, 62, 85, 97, 104–105, 135, 150–151, 169, 204
Fear, 94, 164–166
Federal Bureau of Investigation (FBI), 96
Fein, Steven, 31, 149
Financial costs of racism, 151–153
Fire Next Time, The (Baldwin), 148–149, 166
Fish, Jefferson, 45
Footprints of racial inequities, 17, 56, 105
France, 138
Frankfurt Institute for Social Research, 27
Franklin, John Hope, 11, 14
Frederick D. Patterson Research Institute, 87
Friendship Missionary Baptist Church of Columbia, 210
Friendships, 126

Gaertner, Samuel, 114, 124, 125
Gallico, Paul, 18
Gallup Polls, 57, 58, 80, 94
  on affirmative action, 132
  on educational attainment, 91
  on general social well-being, 66, 92
  on interracial friendships, 126
  on interracial marriage, 107
  on media depictions of minorities, 77
  on neighborhood composition, 95
  on perceptions of justice system, 158
  on police racism, 159
  on race relations, 93
Gardner, Robert, 32

Gathering Storm: America's Militia Threat (Dees & Corcoran), 104

Genealogy Internet sites, 225–226

General Social Survey (GSS), 57, 69, 217

General social well-being, 65–66, 91–92

Genetic integrity movements, 44

Gerbner, George, 74–75

Germany, 138

Giants in the Earth (Rolvaag), 202

Gioseffi, Daniela, 18

Glasser, Ira, 135

Glassman, James, 132

Glazer, Nathan, 2–3

Global approximations, 219

Good conscience credits, 103

Gorn, G. J., 61

Gould, Stephen Jay, 12

Graduate Record Examination (GRE), 144

Graglia, Lino, 205

Grant, Madison, 44

Great Britain, 138

Great Depression, 84

Green, Philip, 150

Griffin, John Howard, 6–7

Group interest, 110

Guilt, 166–167

Habitat for Humanity, 209

Habits, 182, 197–198

Hacker, Andrew, 10, 58, 166

Haddock, G., 39

Haizlip, Shirlee Taylor, 43

Haley, Alex, 52

Hall, Gus, 139

Hall, Tony, 104

Hall, Zach, 181

Hamer, Fannie Lou, 141

Hampton, Carol, 205

Handel, Warren, 68

Harlan, John Marshall, 9

Harris, Louis, 1, 3–4

Harris, Marvin, 44–45

Harris Polls, 94

Harvard Graduate School of Education, 95

Harvard Law Review, 152

Harvard University, 65

Hate, 163–164

Hate crimes, 96–97

Hate groups, 96–97, 104, 213–214

Health, 153–157

Hendricks, M., 112

Herrnstein, Richard, 46

High-prejudice people, 197

High-school dropout rates, 64, 65

High-school education, 64, 65, 85, 87

Hijuelos, Oscar, 199, 206

Hindus, 211

Hirsch, E. D., 4, 49

Hispanic-Americans, 14–16
  affirmative action and, 133–134
  collection of survey data on, 58
  economic indicators for, 63, 80, 81, 82, 83, 84–85
  educational attainment in, 64–65, 85–86, 87, 88, 89, 90
  historical perspective on, 23–24
  justice system and, 159, 160
  measures of racist stereotypes and attitudes toward, 60–61, 70–71
  media depiction of, 75
  national organizations for, 222–223
  neighborhood composition and, 95
  number/percentage of in population, 23–24
  relationship between prejudice and discrimination and, 40
  school composition and, 95
  social categorization and, 177–178
  stereotypes of, 28, 29
  terminology used to describe, 53, 54

Hispanic Policy Development Project (HPDP), 222

Hispanic Poverty Development Project, 83

Hmongs, 65

Hoberman, John, 78–79
Hogan, Tiffany, 219
Holocaust, 187, 188, 189
Homosexuals, 39, 121
HONOR, Inc., 223
Horton, Willie, 166
House of Blues Schoolhouse Pro-
    gram, 49–50
Hsia, Jayjia, 86–87
Huddy, L., 177
Hughes, Langston, 204
Hypersegregation, 95
Hypertension, 154–155
Hypodescent, 44–45

"I Have a Dream" speech, 131–132
Immigrants, 109–110, 127, 138; see
    also Nonresident aliens
Immigration Act of 1965, 22
Income, 63, 82, 133
India, 210–211
Indian Law Resource Center, 223
Indian Tribes: A Continuing Quest for
    Survival, 49
Indifference, 94
Individual discrimination, 47
Individual racism, 47–48, 50, 51–52,
    55, 97
Individual stereotypes, 27, 31–32, 47
Infant mortality rates, 156
In-group, 176–181, 198, 216–217
In-group bias effect, 198
In-group favoritism effect, 178, 180,
    216–217
Inouye, Daniel K., 12
Institute for Research on Social Prob-
    lems, 216
Institute of Minority Health, 92
Institutional racism, 48–49, 50,
    52–53, 55, 97
Insurance, 49, 153
Integration, 95, 107, 204
"Intended and Unintended Conse-
    quences: State Racial Dispar-
    ity in Imprisonment"
    (report), 159–160

Internet, 225–226
Internment camps, 22
Interracial friendships, 126
Interracial marriage, 107, 126
Intimate interracial contact, 110

Jackman, Mary, 108, 111, 211
Jackson, James, 153
Jackson, Jesse, 41, 67
Janoff-Bulman, Ronnie, 186
Jans, Nick, 52
Japanese-Americans, 22, 65
Jefferson, Thomas, 109
Jews, 27, 166, 213–214, 218
Jigsaw groups, 212
Johnson, Kenneth, 158
Johnson, Lyndon, 11, 47, 128
Jones, Edward, 59
Jones, James, 47, 50, 51, 134–135, 206
Jones, Ray, 132
Juries, 35–36, 160–161
Justice system, 157–161
Just-world phenomenon, 184–188
Just-World Scale (JWS), 184, 185

Kappelhoff, Mark, 160
Katz, Daniel, 26–27, 31
Katz, Phyllis, 216
Kean, Thomas, 11
Kinder, Donald, 119, 123
King, Martin Luther, Jr., 21, 101,
    108–109, 131–132, 140, 147,
    163, 172, 193, 195, 200
Kivel, Paul, 16, 206
Klanwatch, 96
Kluegel, James, 83–84
Korean-Americans, 13, 52
Krieger, Nancy, 154–155
Ku Klux Klan, 96, 213
Kutner, B., 41

Labor Department, U. S., 132
Lacayo, Richard, 82, 95
LaFromboise, Teresa, 201
Laissez-faire racism, 84
LaPiere, Richard, 40–41

Lauer, Robert, 68
Law of Racial Thermodynamics, 10, 139
Law school admissions, 133–134
Law School Admission Tests (LSATs), 144
Lawsuits
  anti-affirmative action, 4, 130, 133–134
  by farmers, 153
League of United Latin American Citizens (LULAC), 223
Leo, John, 96
Lerner, Melvin, 184
Lester, Julius, 48
Letter from a Birmingham Jail (King), 147
Level playing field ideal, 120, 132
Lewis, C. S., 116
Liberals, 124, 125
Life is good for minorities myth, 2–4, 17
  evidence contradicting, 69–98
  evidence supporting, 55–68
Life surveys, 110
Lincoln, Abraham, 109
Lincoln Institute of Research and Education, 62
Lippmann, Walter, 26
Lipset, S. M., 108
Listening, 192, 193–194
Little Rock, Arkansas, 101
Living with Racism: The Black Middle-Class Experience (Feagin & Sikes), 135
Looking-glass theory, 142
Lorence, Robert, 86
Los Angeles riots, 13, 24, 76–77
Los Angeles Times, 89–90, 131
Los Angeles Times surveys, 76
Losing Isaiah (film), 73
Low-prejudice people, 197
Lung cancer, 155

McClelland, Katherine, 90
McConahay, John, 115, 122, 123

McCormack, Arlene Smith, 90
McNeilly, Maya, 154
Majic Bus, The: An American Odyssey (Brinkley), 7
Malcolm X, 200
Mandela, Nelson, 163
Marable, Manning, 204
Markham, Edwin, 198
Marriage, 107, 126
Martin, Carol Lynn, 46
Martin Luther King Jr. Center for Non-violent Social Change, 221
Massachusetts Institute of Technology (MIT), 65
Master's degrees, 88
Material costs of racism
  for victims, 151–161
  for whites, 167–169
Media, 61–62, 72–79
  news reporting, 76–79
  print advertisements, 72–73
  television advertisements, 73
  television programming, 73–75
Median income, 63, 82, 133
Median net worth, 82–83
Medical College Admission Tests (MCATs), 144
Medical school admissions, 134
Meeks, Catherine, 193
Meertens, R. W., 138
Meier, Deborah, 212
Melting pot theory, 204
Messiah complex, 209
Mexican American Legal Defense and Education Fund (MAL-DEF), 223
Mexican-Americans, 23, 52, 53, 177–178
Mexico, 23
Miami Herald, 93
Microraces, 45
Middle class, 152–153
Miller, Norman, 177
Minimal group experiments, 179–180
Minority racism, 50–53
Mr. Ives' Christmas (Hijuelos), 199, 206

Mistrust, 93–94
Model minority concept, 23, 63, 86, 146–147
Modern racism, 5–6, 17, 105, 119–140, 141–170
    aversive, 124–126
    cognitive burden of coping with, 150–151
    costs to victims, 142–161
        financial, 151–153
        material, 151–161
        psychological, 142–151
    costs to whites, 161–169
        material, 167–169
        psychological, 162–167
    health and, 153–157
    measuring, 121–123
    range of, 138–139
    self-esteem damaged by, 142, 147–150
    symbolic: see Symbolic racism
    tax of, 135–138
    three beliefs underlying, 120
Modern Racism Scale, 121–123, 138
Mongoloid racial group, 43
Mortality rates, 154, 156–157
Mortgage applications, 153
Mt. Zion United Methodist Church, 19
Mouton, Jane, 178
Multiracialism, 45, 58
Murray, Charles, 46
Murrell, Audrey, 132
Muslims, 211
Mutual interdependence, 209–211
Myers, David, 29, 110
Myrdal, Gunnar, 55, 56, 97
Myths: see Color-blind society, myth of; Life is good for minorities myth; Racism decline myth

Nakanishi, Don, 16
National Association for the Advancement of Colored People (NAACP), 222

National Association of Insurance Commissioners, 153
National Basketball Association (NBA), 15
National Center for Health Statistics, 80, 156
National Civil Rights Museum, 195–196
National Coalition Building Institute (NCBI), 224
National Congress of American Indians, 223
National Council of La Raza, 223
National Education Association, 89
National Institute Against Prejudice and Violence (NIAPV), 224
National Opinion Research Center (NORC), 57, 58, 60; see also General Social Survey
National organizations, 221–223
National Research Council Committee on the Status of Black Americans, 60
National Urban League, 222
Native American Rights Fund, 223
Native Americans, 14–16, 201
    boarding schools for, 204
    cancer in, 155
    collection of survey data on, 58
    community support for, 213
    cultural racism and, 49
    economic indicators for, 80–82
    educational attainment in, 65, 85, 86, 88
    historical perspective on, 24–25
    media depiction of, 73–74, 76
    national organizations for, 223
    number/percentage of in population, 24
    stereotypes of, 28
    terminology used to describe, 53–54
Naturalization Act of 1790, 24
Nazi Germany, 44, 46
Negroid racial group, 43
Neighborhood composition, 95

Nelson, Jill, 80
Neo-Nazi groups, 96
Neosexism, 138
Netherlands, 138
Net worth, 82–83
Netzer, Julie, 219
News reporting, 76–79
Newsweek, 79
Newsweek surveys, 80, 94
New York Mets, 89
New York Times, 62
New York Times Magazine, 15
New York University Law Review, 133
Nonresident aliens, 86, 88; *see also*
    Immigrants
Nonverbal behavior measures, 112
Norris, Kathleen, 201, 202, 209
Not in Our Town (documentary), 214

Oakland Tribune, 160
O'Connor, John J., 62, 75
Office of Federal Contract Compli-
    ance Programs, 133
Office of Management and Budget,
    U. S., 58
Oh, Angela, 11
Old-fashioned racism, 5–6, 17,
        105–117, 119, 121, 123, 124
    behavioral ambiguity and, 112–113
    decline in as genuine, 108
    decline in as genuine but limited,
        108–110
    decline in as not genuine, 110–111
    facial muscle recordings and,
        113–114
    measuring, 106–107
    mutation of, 115–116
    nonverbal behavior measures of,
        112
    priming and response-latency
        measures of, 114–115
    self-esteem damaged by, 147
    symbolic racism and, 127
    tax of, 136
    three sets of beliefs underlying,
        106

Old-Fashioned Racism Scale,
        106–107, 111, 115, 121, 122
Oliver, Melvin, 152
Orfield, Gary, 95
Organizational discrimination, 47
Othello (Shakespeare), 53
Out-group, 176–181, 198, 213, 217
Out-group homogeneity effect,
        176–177
Overlapping approximations,
        219

Pacific Asian American Center for
        Theology and Strategies,
        222
Pacific Islanders, 58, 86, 88
Page, Clarence, 205
Page, Lisa, 44
Palmer, Parker, 196
Pannell, William, 110
Parenti, Michael, 72
Parker, J. A., 62–63
Parker, Sandra, 46
Parks, Rosa, 101
Passing of the Great Race, The (Grant),
        44
Peplau, Letitia Anne, 184
Perlmutter, Philip, 66
Personal beliefs, 197
Personal discrimination, 202–203
Personal prejudice, 202–203
Personal stereotypes, 202–203
Pettigrew, Thomas, 109, 126, 138,
        162, 203
Pires, Alexander, Jr., 153
Pitts, Leonard, Jr., 93, 103–104
Playboy, 132
Plessy v. Ferguson, 9, 48
Plous, Scott, 132–133
Police, 159
Political cartoons, 76
Poverty, 63, 80–84
Power, 50–53
Power of Their Ideas, The, 212
Pratkanis, Anthony, 135
Pregnancy, 154, 156

Prejudice, 25, 32–35, 36, 37–38, 47
  of African-Americans against
    whites, 208
  with compunction, 197
  contact situations fostering,
    212–213
  definition of, 33–35
  discrimination and, 40–41
  generational differences in,
    217–218
  kernel of truth in, 35
  personal, 202–203
  social categorization distinguished
    from, 175
  stereotypes and, 38–39
Prenatal care, 156
Presidential task force on race rela-
    tions, 11, 14
Price, Hugh, 97
Prime Time Live (television program),
    152
Priming, 114–115, 182–183
Princeton University, 78
Print advertisements, 72–73
Prison population, 88, 159–160
Problem fatigue, 19, 213
Prostate cancer, 155
Psychological costs of racism
  for victims, 142–151
  for whites, 162–167
Puerto Ricans, 53, 81, 177–178
Puerto Rico, 172–173
Pure merit objection to affirmative
    action, 131

Quality-of-life indicators, 62–66,
    80–92; see also Economic in-
    dicators; Educational attain-
    ment; General social
    well-being
Quiet acts of racism, 104, 105
Quinn, Diane, 143
Quotas, 128

Race, definition of, 43–45
Race card, 3

Race relations, status of, 66–67,
    92–97
Racial reconciliation, 191–220
  appreciation of borderland in,
    203–207
  disagreeing in, 192, 194–196
  listening in, 192, 193–194
  personal interactions with diver-
    sity in, 207–213
  self-awareness in, 199–203
Racial stories, 199–202
Racism decline myth, 2, 4–6, 17
Racism definitions, 45–53
Racism-free zones, 214
Rage, 193–194
Ramirez, Albert, 16
Ramirez, Luis, 206
Rape, 88, 186, 187
REACH Center, 224
Reagan, Ronald, 66
Real racism, 100–102
Redlining, 153
Relationships, sacrifice of, 167–168
Religious stories, 199–202
Report of the National Advisory
    Commission on Civil Disor-
    ders, 46–47
Resegregation, 95–96, 208
Reservation Blues (Alexie), 74, 151
Response-latency measures, 114–
    115
Reverse discrimination, 63, 66, 130
Rickey, Branch, 148
Robber's Cave study, 210
Robinson, Jackie, 79, 100–101
Robinson, James L., 3
Rodman, Dennis, 78
Roosevelt, Franklin, 128
Roper, Burns W., 66
Roper Organization, Inc., 66
Roper surveys, 65
Ross, John, 163
Rothenberg, Paula, 51
Rowan, Carl T., 10
Rubin, Zick, 184
Ryan, Bob, 100–101

Sartre, Jean-Paul, 166
Schneider, David, 28
Schneider, W., 108
Schoenfeld, Bruce, 15
Schofield, Janet Ward, 171–172
Scholastic Aptitude Test (SAT), 89
Schools, 95–96, 208; see also Educa-
     tional attainment
Screwtape Letters, The (Lewis), 116
Sears, David, 119, 120, 123
Self-awareness, 199–203
Self-esteem, 142, 147–150, 180
Self-hatred, 148–149
Self-image, 31
Self-interest, 109
Seniority laws, 49
Sentencing, 159–161
Sentencing Project, 159
Separate but equal doctrine, 9
Sesame Street (television program),
     61
Sexism, 138; see also Women
Shakespeare, William, 53
Shapiro, Tom, 152
Sheatsley, Paul, 60
Sherif, Muzafer, 210
Sidney, Stephen, 154–155
Sigall, Harold, 59
Sikes, Melvin, 135
Sincere fictions, 2
Sitkoff, Harvard, 92
Skinheads, 96, 213
Slaughter, John Brooks, 89–90
Slavery, 21–22, 103–104, 109
Sleeper, Jim, 4
Smith, Jacqueline, 195–196
Smith, Jerry, 4
Smith, Tom W., 60, 69–70, 71
Smoking, 155
Sniderman, Paul, 123
Social categorization, 173–181, 218
     consequences of, 176–181
     origins of, 216–217
     supercategories and, 198
Social cognition, 27–28
Social identity theory, 180

Socialization, 187
Social norms, 211–212
Societal benefits, sacrifice of,
     168–169
Sojourners Resource Center, 224
Southeast Uplift Neighborhood Pro-
     gram, 214
Southern Poverty Law Center, 96
Spencer, Steven, 31, 143, 149
Spokane Task Force on Race Rela-
     tions, 103
Sports, 15, 18, 78–79
Sports Illustrated, 72
Sports journalists, 78
Statistical Policy Directive Number
     15, 58
Steele, Claude, 32, 143–145
Steele, Shelby, 3
Stereotypes, 25–33, 36, 37–38, 42, 173
     automatic cognitive processing
          and, 182–183, 196–198
     coining of word, 26
     cultural, 26–27, 31–32, 47
     definition of, 28–31
     disconfirmation of, 209
     discrimination and, 39, 40
     history of research in, 26–28
     individual, 27, 31–32, 47
     kernel of truth in, 29, 35
     measures of, 59–61, 69–71
     personal, 202–203
     prejudice and, 38–39
     social categorization and, 175–177
Stereotype threat, 32, 143–147
Stewart, Donald, 89
Stone, Jeff, 78
Student Nonviolent Coordinating
     Committee (SNCC), 48
Study tours, 7–9, 164–166, 206–207,
     209
Sudden infant death syndrome
     (SIDS), 154
Suicide, 157
Supercategories, 198
Superordinate groups, 198, 202, 210
Supreme Court, U. S., 9, 48, 95, 208

Survey data, 57
Swinton, David H., 83
Symbolic racism, 124, 126–135
    affirmative action and, 127–135
Syphilis, 154, 156

Tajfel, Henri, 179, 180, 192, 217
Tarfon, Rabbi, 191
Tatum, Beverly, 219
Taylor, Dalmas, 50
Teenage pregnancy, 154
Television advertisements, 73
Television programming, 73–75
Tetlock, Philip, 123
Thernstrom, Abigail, 3
Thernstrom, Stephan, 3
Thirteenth Amendment, 22
Thomas, Charlie, 148
Thomas, Isiah, 78
Thomas, Lewis, 12
Thomas, Robert, 11
Thompson, Linda Chavez, 11
Through the Looking Glass (Carroll),
    53
Tigrett, Isaac, 50
Till, Emmett, 99
Time, 82, 155
Title VII of the Civil Rights Act, 128
Toynbee, Arnold, 21
Traffic Stops Statistics Act, 159
Trimble, Joseph, 16, 74, 76
TRIOS model, 206
True Colors (television program), 152
Truman, Harry, 101
Tubman, Harriet, 19
Turner, Marlene, 135
Tuskegee experiments, 92
21st Century Program, 145–146

Underemployment, 85
Unemployment, 84–85, 133
United Nations, 36, 43
University of California at Berkeley,
    27, 65
University of California at Los An-
    geles, 131

University of California Boalt Hall
    law school, 133
University of Chicago, 95; see also
    National Opinion Research
    Center
University of Massachusetts at Am-
    herst, 89
University of Michigan, 145, 153
University of Texas School of Law, 4,
    133–134
Updegrave, Walter, 152, 153
U.S. News & World Report, 79, 94, 153

Valdivieso, Rafael, 83
Vanman, E. J., 113–114
Vera, Hernan, 2, 10, 48, 62, 85,
    104–105, 169
Veracruz Blues, The (Winegardner),
    188
Victim blaming, 84, 186–188
Virtanen, S., 177
Voting, 113, 115, 119–120, 160

Wallace, George, 101
Waller, Brennan Martin, 56
Warren, Earl, 147–148
Washington Post, 79, 132
Washington Post surveys, 130
Washington Times, 67
Wasiolek, Susan, 90–91
Weigel, Russell, 62, 75
Weitz, S., 112
Wexler, 171–172
Whisnits, 26
White racism, 48
Whites
    affirmative action and, 129–130
    African-American prejudice
        against, 208
    cancer in, 155
    collection of survey data on, 58
    cost of modern racism to, 161–169
    economic indicators for, 63, 80, 81,
        82–85
    educational attainment in, 64, 85,
        86, 87, 88, 89

Whites (cont.)
  encouraging understanding in, 6–9
  general social well-being in, 66,
    91–92
  indifference in, 94
  mistrust and, 93–94
  mortality rates in, 156
  neighborhood composition and, 95
  power and, 50–53
  social categorization and, 177
  syphilis in, 156
Whites-only racism theory, 51
Wilbon, Michael, 79
Wilder, Douglas, 111
Williams, David, 157
Williams, Walter, 67, 121
Wilson, Thomas, 217–218
Wilson, William J., 3
Winegardner, Mark, 188
Winter, William, 11
Wise, Tim, 130

Women, 138
  affirmative action and, 129,
    132–133, 149–150
  African-American, 80, 83
  cancer in, 155
  as heads-of-household, 81–82
  Hispanic, 83
  media depictions of, 76
  stereotype threat and, 143–144
Woods, Eldrick ("Tiger"), 37, 39, 42,
    79, 100–101
Woods, Keith, 200
World Series, 89
World War II, 22
Wounded Knee, 76
Wrong number experiment, 125–126

Yancey, George, 51, 163
Yorty, Sam, 119

Zoeller, Fuzzy, 37–38, 42